**Methodology in Finance—
Investments**

Methodology in Finance— Investments

James L. Bicksler
Rutgers University
Editor

Lexington Books
D.C. Heath and Company
Lexington, Massachusetts
Toronto   London

Library of Congress Cataloging in Publication Data

Bicksler, James L
Methodology in finance-investments.

"Outgrowth of a Symposium on Methodology in
Finance-Investments held at Rutgers University on
May 13-14, 1971."
1. Investments– addresses, essays, lectures.
I. Symposium on Methodology in Finance-investments,
Rutgers University, 1971.
II. Title.
HG4539.B43   332.6'7   72-167980
ISBN 0-669-75762-4

Published simultaneously in Canada.

Printed in the United States of America.

International Standard Book Number: 0-669-75762-4

Library of Congress Catalog Card Number: 72-167980

There will be stars in heaven for unnamed and unknown kindnesses on earth.

Contents

List of Tables

List of Figures

Preface

This volume is an outgrowth of a Symposium on Methodology in Finance-Investments held at Rutgers University on May 13-14, 1971. The spirit of the Symposium reflected in the readings in this volume are, in large part, a result of the editor's conviction that (1) investments-finance share common methodological foundations with other fields of scientific inquiry as to "how we know, what we know," (2) the theoretical underpinnings of finance-investments are the postulates of normative behavior and that limitations in the latter are likewise limitations in the former, and (3) there has been and, quite likely, will continue to be forthcoming a veritable explosion of knowledge about the structure of the finance world. Stated slightly differently, (1) argues that the foundations and, many times even the tools, of probabilistic inductive inference are the same for all disciplines and that increments to empirical knowledge of finance-investments will be a result only of the application of these tools of inductive inference to "meaningful" hypotheses, (2) indicates that frameworks for "rational" or optimal investor behavior are contingent upon, among other things, the nuances of normative choice axioms, and (3) practitioners and, likely to an even greater degree, academics will increasingly have to keep current with the rapidly expanding state of finance knowledge emanating from (1) and (2). It is hoped that this book adds, illustrates, and transfers a modicum of knowledge, awareness, or understanding to each of these three arenas.

Acknowledgments

My thanks for ideas and encouragement regarding the Symposium are due to Dean Horace J. DePodwin, Richard Behnke, Carl Hempel, Abraham Kaplan, Ernest Nagel, Sidney Nemetz, and Paul A. Samuelson. A note of appreciation of financial support is also in order to Robert Behnke of Systems Corporation, the Esso Education Foundation, and the Alfred P. Sloan Foundation. Fred W. Bolman and Arthur L. Singer were the individuals facilitating the grants at these respective institutions. Gratitude for longer term inspiration in the field of finance is accorded to Arnold W. Sametz, my graduate finance advisor, along with Robert Lindsay and Eugene Lerner. Mrs. Janet Davis ably assisted on the coordination aspects of the Symposium and Giles Mellon lent his assistance in numerous ways. Murray Mohl, K. Sasaki, and Nachum Finger also gave moral sustenance during the planning stage.

Introduction

It is natural in looking at and in analyzing the papers presented at the Symposium to view them in the context of "present knowledge" and in terms of their contribution and relevance to major issues and queries in finance-investments. The comments herein are, hopefully, organized on this basis.

The essays in this volume fall into five broad categories. These are (1) methodological foundations (Borch and Levi), (2) stock prices (Samuelson, and Friend and Blume), (3) information, expectations, and investment decision (Morgenstern, Winkler, Treynor, and Philippatos), (4) lifetime utility strategies (Hakansson), and (5) testing portfolio strategies and investment timing rules (Jen and Bicksler).

The first part of the book contains two papers on foundations and methodology. The foundations of the normative theory of economic choice rests upon propositions about the structure of preferences. The propositions, called axioms, form the topic of the Borch paper. It views the decision problem as deriving a preference ordering over a set of intertemporal stochastic processes of risk-return parameters. Further, empirical knowledge of the utility function and operational assistance in deriving this function is deemed to be of more importance, Borch argues, than academic debate over the minimum axiomatic base, or other more appropriate standard, needed to derive the Bernoulli maxim. An interesting implication is alluded to for determination of the appropriate discount rate for selecting capital investment projects. Specifically, it is shown there is no a priori rationale for deciding between constant or variable discount rates apart from utility theory and that the estimates of these cost of capital surrogates are simply an exercise in preference orderings applied to the market mechanism. An Allais genre example is also offered to Tobin mean-variance enthusiasts to shake their faith in that portfolio selection rule. Providing arguments for the demise of the M-V framework is, of course, a favorite activity and pastime of Borch and further illustrates the important role utility plays in any investment decision under uncertainty framework. A number of quite provocative comments on the historical development of key strands of economic theory (Arrow's Impossibility Theorem, the Nash Solution, and the Shapley Value) and its feedback influence on a later emerging underlying axiomatic formulation are also provided.

Levi's paper focuses on the conceptual foundations of measures of the degree of confirmation of hypotheses. Further, Levi surveys the elements of a theory of inductive inference. He argues that one does not merely assign probabilities (betting quotients) to hypotheses on evidence but, extends or contracts "truth" statements to our body of knowledge. This, of course, is recognition of the corrigibility of human knowledge.

An interesting section details the aims of scientific inquiry and its raison d'être handmaiden of practices, but as a partner; it contributes advice to decision makers while pursuing its own objectives." A sketch of the viewpoints of Keynes, Carnap, Popper, Neyman, Wald, and the Bayesians on many of these methodological issues is also presented.

The second part of the volume focuses on, among other things, securities and an empirical understanding of their speculative movements and the market mechanism determining component returns. The dynamics of speculative price has a mythical appeal to laymen and has increasingly become the focus of rigorous mathematical investigation by economists. Samuelson sets forth an insightful and wide-ranging examination of various dynamic models of price behavior. These include such frameworks as shadow pricing, stochastic cobweb cycles, and the Einstein-Wiener-Brownian motion process. A variant of the latter, discussed via Bachelier's theory, has many ramifications for investors such as the efficient markets hypothesis a la martingales, the theory of stochastic prices, the form (Pareto-Levy) of the limiting distribution of stock price changes, rational pricing of warrants, and the integration of the limited liability feature into the valuation equation, etc.

A superb section on welfare economics, Pareto optimality, and the inter-temporal equilibrium price conditions of speculative behavior is also offered along with jibes at the Latané-Kelley geometric mean portfolio selection rule. Since this was a survey essay, the above brief synopsis only gives a flavor of the range of topics covered.

A general equilibrium theory of stock prices is based on the assumption that investors are Tobin maximizers in their portfolio behavior. A number of other assumptions are usually postulated in developing such a framework. These typically include homogeneous expectations, a single period framework, and equality of borrowing and lending rates. While the capital asset pricing model (hereafter called the CAP model) has undeniable appeal vis á vis most of its competitors, two broad categories of reservations have been expressed. First, there have been voiced a number of theoretical objections to the CAP model's conceptual foundations (mean-variance assumption, etc.). While the repartee has been in the spirit of positive economics, the Black-Jensen-Scholes' findings (that high [low] beta portfolios earn a lower [higher] return than predicted by the model) raise substantive objections of an empirical nature.

Another recent important paper investigating the robustness of the CAP model has been the Friend and Blume paper ("Measurement of Portfolio Performance Under Uncertainty," *American Economic Review*, September 1970) wherein the empirical estimates of the one-parameter measures of performance were shown to be biased. The primary causative factor, according to Friend and Blume, appears to be unequal borrowing and lending rates.

The present Friend and Blume paper addresses itself to the above issues. Specifically, it examines the theoretical and empirical reasons for the CAP model's inability to explain differential returns on selected capital market along with the relationship of science to other goal directed activity such as investment decision making. Levi views the relationship of science "not as a instruments. Friend and Blume conclude that the evidence seems to indicate that the CAP model has major deficiencies in explaining real world yield phenomena and, further, that there exists a segmentation phenomenon between NYSE stocks and the bond market. This finding has a number of highly relevant implications for corporate financial officers, investment and portfolio managers, and financial economists regarding optimal financial structure, cost of capital, and portfolio performance measurement.

The four papers in the third section of this volume deal with variations on the theme of expectations. Morgenstern's "Information Flow and Stock Market Price Changes" is a probing of queries having a goodly number of ramifications and implications for investors. Morgenstern views the market participants as actors in the price making scenario where (1) expectations are interdependent, (2) there is misinformation (how is this measured?) as well as incomplete or irrelevant information, (3) investors have heterogeneous expectations, and (4) temporal aspects a la the speed of adjustment mechanism of equilibrium yields and prices are a highly important determinant of ex post portfolio performance. The resultant mesh of these characteristics is a market mechanism whose properties are consistent with the weak and semi-strong form of the efficient markets hypothesis.

Morgenstern offers, further, some engaging remarks regarding the uselessness of standard demand theory for explaining stock market price changes. The reasoning involves the role of the specialist in the auction market and the apparent difficulty of casting this player in the framework of standard demand-supply or buyer-seller analysis.

The grand conclusion of the Morgenstern paper is that "investing is an art." The logic is namely that the formation of expectations is an ingenious task devoid of mechanical rules or application. Since the sine qua non of science is systematic, organized, and verified knowledge capable of being replicated, the view that investing is an art seems notably sensible.

The topic Winkler addresses is the derivation of probabilistic inputs for the normative portfolio management decision process under uncertainty. The problem in a broad context is a subset of inference under incomplete information with the task of the assessor being the quantification of human judgment or, equivalently, the assignment of subjective probabilities. Winkler surveys several interrogation methods (successive fractiles and relative densities) for deriving probabilistic distribution functions along with an evaluation of their pluses and minuses. Empirical relevance of these methods in assessing portfolio inputs is given via review of the Bartos and Staël von Holstein studies. Since the investment decision process is postulated to be adaptive in nature, considerable attention is given to the Bayesian framework of learning about and revising probabilities. A Bayesian model for predicting these portfolio parameters is presented.

There have been a multitude of studies (Jensen, Sharpe, Treynor-Mazuy,

Friend, et al.) documenting the fact that the ex post performance of professional investors, usually mutual funds, has not been substantially better, after adjusting for risk, than random selection and, indeed, in many cases, has been "worse." There are a multitude of reasons accounting for this phenomenon.

Treynor's paper, viewed within this context, could be labeled as some advice to portfolio managers to improve performance. His suggestions aim at the vortex of the role of information in the investment decision process. The paper views the conditional forecasts of conventional security analysis built upon a chain-of-logic preceeding from macroeconomic analysis to industry forecast, company projections, and on through to buy-sell recommendations as conceptually unappealing.

Instead, Treynor suggests that a far more appealing alternative is the separation of these tasks, referred to above, in assessing state probabilities. A simple regression model indicating the spirit of his analysis is formulated. Further, Treynor implies that the reconstituting of informational assessing and processing is "The Coming Revolution in Investment Management." Thus, exit portfolio management as gymnastics concerned with administrative logrolling and adjudicating and enter an information decision process having a far more compelling logic.

Philippatos delineates a veritable compendium and taxonomy of issues, paradoxes, and countervailing points of view of the expectations literature with particular focus on that which is pertinent to micro-finance. It ranges from causal and teleological theories of expectations to Shackle's surprise coefficient and psychological search procedures.

The fourth section consists of the Hakansson paper and deals with the lifetime utility maximization problem under uncertainty. Since the 1962 Phelps model, ("The Accumulation of Risky Capital: A Sequential Utility Analysis," *Econometrica*, October 1962) there has been a continuing stream of analytic refinements for dealing with the multi-period investment-consumption problem under uncertainty. The Hakansson paper is of this genre and his specific contribution is the integration of lexicographic preferences into the above framework. Arguments delineating the economic and behavioral rationale and superiority of a lexicographic preference structure vis a vis ordinary utility theory are provided. Insightful examples and scenarios illustrating the robustness of this particular investment-consumption model's properties to "real world" problems are given.

The fifth part of the volume is comprised of two papers testing the usefulness and examining the economic rationale of various portfolio strategies or timing rules. The optimal solution to the multi-period portfolio selection problem is conceptually of interest from the standpoint of analytic technique and pragmatically relevant from the viewpoint of utility maximization. Jen's paper deals with aspects of both of the above issues with emphasis on measuring the ex post performance of alternative multi-period strategies. Specifically, the probability distribution of wealth for the strategies of (1) buy an index and hold, and (2) portfolio rebalancing are examined for (1) the lognormal and (2) positively skewed distributions. The mean and variances of the simulated distributions are calculated and compared. Though significance tests are utilized for inference, the small size of the sample and the absence of an integrated risk-return parameter makes substantive conclusions about ex post performance hazardous.

An aspect of this paper akin to the Chen-Jen-Zionts exposition ("The Optimal Portfolio Revision Policy," *Journal of Business* , January 1971) is an analytic derivation, within a dynamic programing context, of the conditions required for rebalancing to be optimal, non-optimal and maybe even inferior to a buy and hold strategy. For example, given stationary returns, the number of investor horizons, and no transactions costs, Jen shows that the expected utility of wealth is maximized under a rebalancing strategy. Likewise, given adaptive expectations, then both buy and hold and rebalancing may be non-optimal. A review of the current literature regarding the empirical dominance (non-dominance) of particular multi-period investment strategies is also presented.

Economists, in examining economic behavior and relationships many times analyze time series data. Historically, many of the techniques of econometrics and the achievements of the founding fathers in that discipline have dealt with attempts to analyze economic time series. Thus, the Shuster periodogram, Fourier analysis, spectral analysis and the studies of (the founder of statistical economics) Henry L. Moore, Sir William Beveridge, R.A. Fisher, and W.L. Crum come readily to mind.

Compared to traditional methods for examining business cycle predictors, such as the National Bureau indicators, spectral analysis offers numerous conceptual advantages for empirical investigation. Indeed, Morgenstern feels that spectral analysis is the most powerful technique available to investigate the behavior of time series.

A current fashionable predictive device based on National Bureau empiricism is the Sprinkel stock market forecasting framework. Its a priori economic rationale, according to Sprinkel, is that of monetarism, which is the causal link in the determination of the level of stock prices.

According to Bicksler, the theory before empiricism of the Sprinkel hypothesis rests on rather tenuous grounds as it denies the well-known Samuelson property that "properly anticipated prices fluctuate randomly" and likewise is inconsistent with the semi-strong form of Fama's efficient markets hypothesis. A number of other substantive theoretical and empirical reasons also reaffirm the suspicion that Sprinkel's conclusions are, at best, rather dubious.

Empirical results a la cross-spectral analysis are then presented and shown to be consistent with the Granger-Morgenstern finding that there are virtually no stock market cycles. Suggestions as to the research design of future investigations of lead-lag relationships in stock prices are also presented.

To conclude, the Symposium papers have contributed to our understanding of finance-investments in at least three important ways. First, they have reinforced the importance of both (1) the foundations of choice under uncertainty and (2) the methods of empirical inquiry. Second, they have extended our empirical and theoretical understanding of the price of risk, stock market price movements, and the uselessness of selected portfolio strategies and timing rules. Third, there are a number of normative suggestions regarding assessing portfolio parameters and the role and nature of information in decision theoretic frameworks. It appears that each of the three categories having a number of implications for investment decision making in the real world.

There are, of course, many unresolved problems and challenges remaining in finance. Quite likely, their solutions will involve ramifications of the material discussed in this volume. Surely, there is no absence of problems and challenges within the profession.

Part I:
Methodological Foundations

1

Axioms of Rational Choice under Uncertainty

Karl Borch

1. Introduction

1.1. The title of this paper may appear dull, and possibly a little out of date. The axiomatics of decision theory does not seem to be such a hot topic today as it was twenty years ago. I hope, however, that this observation will not be interpreted to mean that I attach little importance to my assigned subject. Axioms will always be interesting, and sometimes important.

In economic theory we have to be very precise when we specify our assumptions, and this virtually means that we must formulate them as axioms. From these assumptions—essentially assumptions about the economic behavior of people—we try to derive "meaningful theorems." Naturally we want few assumptions, and we do not want to make them stronger than necessary, but relatively few economists seem interested in maximizing output at this point. To prove the most general theorem from the weakest possible set of axioms is, I think rightly, considered a problem for specialists. Such problems can be fascinating, but I must refer those who share my views in this respect, to the recent book by Fishburn [6]. In the following I shall have little to say on the subject.

1.2. In retrospect it is easy to see that it was game theory which gave axiomatics a fairly prominent place in economics. In the original book [10] von Neumann and Morgenstern proved some results which were far from obvious, but which with logical necessity followed from simple and innocent looking axioms. The Minimix Theorem and The Expected Utility Theorem are the best examples. In the literature which followed—on game theory, or on related subjects—we can find some other striking examples. The "Impossibility Theorem" of Arrow [3], the Nash Solution to the Bargaining Problem [9], and the Shapley Value [11] are strong results derived from very weak axioms. These results are "surprising" in the sense that they may be rejected on intuitive reasons by people who are quite willing to accept the axioms. The mathematical argument leads from "obvious" axioms to unexpected conclusions.

I think this situation, created by game theory, is exceptional. Axioms do not come first in the development of a theory. On the contrary, the axiomatic formulation is usually the last step, proving the internal consistency of theorems we feel or believe must be true. It seems that we need at least an outline of theory, before axiomatic treatment can serve any useful purpose. In the

3

following I hope to show that some important decision problems still are so diffuse that it appears premature to seek an axiomatic formulation.

2. A Hierarchy of Decision Problems

2.1. In this section I shall give a brief survey of different classes of decision problems, and I shall try to show that they can be arranged in a natural order of increasing complexity.

In general a decision problem consists in selecting an action a from a given set A of available actions. The choice of a particular action a_i will lead to an outcome x_i in a set X of possible outcomes. If two different actions lead to the same outcome, we can consider them as one single action, and assume that there is a one-to-one correspondence between the elements in the sets A and X.

In this paper I shall have little to say about the set A. It is, however, worth noting that this set may consist of very complex elements in many familiar decision problems, for instance when we have to choose between different production schedules or different sales campaigns. In an allocation problem, the elements of A will typically be n-dimensional vectors. In the simplest possible case A will have just two elements, for instance to accept or reject a particular offer.

2.2. Let us now focus our attention on the set X. In the simplest decision problem the elements of X will be scalar numbers. Without much loss of generality, we can interpret these numbers as amounts of money. In such problems the difficulty lies in "sorting out" the alternatives and computing the x_i, which corresponds to each a_i. This may, as we have indicated, be very difficult, but once the job is done, the decision itself is trivial. We can take it as an axiom that any rational decision maker, whether rich or poor, whether a person or a firm, will prefer a larger amount of money to a smaller. With this simple and natural *preference ordering* over the set of outcomes, the problem is reduced to determine the action a_i, which maximizes the payoff x_i.

2.3. In the next problem in the order of increasing complexity, the elements of the elements of X are finite vectors $\{x_0, x_1, \ldots, x_n\}$. The classical economic interpretation of this model is the consumer's choice among "market baskets" or "commodity bundles." In this problem there is no natural preference ordering, and we must assume that one exists, if we want to make any progress. We can do this with one single axiom, to the effect that the consumer has a complete preference ordering over the positive orthant of the vector space X. An additional axiom is required to ensure that this preference can be represented by the familiar utility function $u(x_1 \ldots x_n)$. The purpose of this axiom is to rule out the lexicographic ordering and similar pathological cases. The axiom must include an "Archemedian principle" in some form.

The utility function $u(x_1 \ldots x_n)$ is usually taken to represent the personal taste of the consumer. Normally one does not make any assumptions about the shape of the function, except that it is a non-decreasing function of all its arguments. This can, of course, be taken as an axiom, but it can hardly be considered as an important or interesting one.

Once the existence of a utility function is established, the problem is reduced to the simpler problem considered in the preceding paragraph. The solution is the action a_i which maximizes the utility function.

2.4. As our next step it is natural to consider the case in which the element of X are infinite vectors $\left\{ x_0, x_1, \ldots, x_t, \ldots \right\}$. By stretching our imagination we can consider such vectors as commodity bundles. It is, however, more convenient to interpret them as "cash flows," and take x_t to be an amount of money payable at the time t, or at the end of period t. It is then natural to interpret A as a set of possible investments in plant and equipment.

The traditional way of handling this problem is to convert the vectors to scalar numbers, by computing the discounted sum of the elements, or the "present value" of the cash flow:

$$V = \sum_{t=0}^{\infty} v^t x_t,$$

where v is a discount factor ($0 \leqslant v \leqslant 1$). This procedure reduces the problem to the simpler one, discussed in par. 2.2. The decision maker will select the action which gives the cash flow with the greatest present value.

There is little doubt that this traditional method has its origin in assumptions about perfect capital markets, with a constant or normal rate of interest. With such assumptions the problem becomes quite trivial, since payments can be shifted backwards and forwards at will, at the market rate of interest.

Without any assumptions about a market, the discount factor can be interpreted as a measure of the decision maker's "impatience," or the strength of his preference for an early payment over a later one. This preference will obviously be "personal" or "subjective," and will correspond to the "taste" which in the preceding paragraph was represented by the utility function.

It seems very arbitrary to express impatience by discounting at a constant rate. Any decreasing, convergent sequence $c_0, c_1, \ldots$ may serve the same purpose, and there is no reason why the traditional "present value" should not be replaced by the more general expression

$$U = \sum_{t=0}^{\infty} c_t x_t.$$

Preference orderings based on such linear functions of a cash flow, leave no room for the "desire for stability," which seems important to many decision makers. A cash flow   2,1,2,2,1,1   will be preferred to   1,1,1,1,2,2   by discounting at any rate—constant or variable. It is easy to think of interpretations in which the preference ordering may be reversed:

(i) If the flows represent possible dividend records of a company, top management may well prefer the latter to the former, because it will create an impression on steady growth and sound management.
(ii) If the flows are interpreted as national income available for private consumption under alternative development plans, a government may have to choose the latter flow if it wants to survive politically.

These examples show that an element of inter-temporal dependence may be desirable in preference orderings over sets of cash flows. We may need rules for tradeoff between higher level of payments and greater stability in the payment sequence. At present it seems difficult even to indicate what the contents of such rules should be, and it may, therefore, be premature to try to formulate the rules in axiomatic form.

Several authors, i.a., Williams and Nassar [13], have derived the principle of discounting at a constant rate from axioms which do not appear particularly strong, apart from the assumption of complete intertemporal independence. Koopmans [7] has presented axioms which are considerably weaker, but still contain some independence of this nature.

2.5. As our next problem, let us take the elements of the set X to be stochastic variables represented by probability distributions $F_1(x) \ldots F_i(x) \ldots$. We lose little by formulating the problem in terms of money, so that $F_i(x)$ is the probability that the decision maker at most gets the amount x if he chooses the action a_i.

The first problem for the decision maker is then to lay down some rule as to when a distribution $F_i(x)$ shall be considered as better than a distribution $F_j(x)$. If this rule can be described by a preference ordering over the set of all probability distributions, and if this ordering is consistent in the sense of von Neumann and Morgenstern [10], it can be represented by a utility function $u(x)$, so that $F_i(x)$ is preferred to $F_j(x)$, if and only if

$$\int_{-\infty}^{+\infty} u(x)dF_i(x) > \int_{-\infty}^{+\infty} u(x)dF_j(x).$$

This operation transforms the stochastic variables into scalar numbers— "expected utilities"—and the decision problem again is reduced to the simple problem, discussed in par. 2.2. In principles the problem is solved, but in practice a decision maker may find it difficult to describe his utility function. This function expresses the decision maker's personal "attitude to risk," and $u(x)$ can be interpreted as the "utility of money." A priori any function is acceptable, although there are good economic reasons for assuming that $u(x)$ is differentiable, and that $u'(x) \geqslant 0$, and further $u''(x) \leqslant 0$, at least for large values of x.

I shall discuss expected utility in some detail in section 3 below. Before doing this, it is natural to study the last level in our hierarchy.

2.6 Let the elements of the set X be stochastic processes $\{x_0, x_1 \ldots, x_t, \ldots\}$, or equivalently joint probability distributions $F(x_0, \ldots, x_t, \ldots)$. This model contains as special cases the models considered in the two preceding paragraphs.

The return from an investment in real life will usually be an uncertain cash flow, which in mathematical terms must be described by a stochastic process. The problem of selecting the best investment in a given set will then consist in selecting the most preferred among the available stochastic processes. Our first problem should then be to describe reasonable preference orderings over sets of stochastic processes. This problem has hardly been discussed in literature, although it appears fundamental in a rational theory of investment. The obvious reason for this neglect is that the problem seems to be very difficult. In current theory there are two standard ways of simplifying the problem:

(i) Assume away the uncertainty, for instance by considering only expected values of the payments, and taking these as certain, i.e., reduce the problem to the one discussed in par. 2.4.
(ii) Ignore the time element, for instance by taking the sum or the average of the payments. This means that the stochastic process is contracted into a single stochastic variable, and that the problem is reduced to the one considered in par. 2.5.

Both these procedures are clearly unsatisfactory, but it is not easy to suggest useful generalizations. One possibility would be to consider the stochastic variable

$$z = \sum_{t=0}^{\infty} v^t x_t,$$

and use the approach outlined in par. 2.5. As an illustration we shall study the auto-regressive process

$$x_{t+1} = ax_t + \epsilon_{t+1}$$

where $|a| < 1$ and $\epsilon_1, \epsilon_2, \ldots, \epsilon_t, \ldots$ are independent, identically distributed stochastic variables.

Multiplying by v^{t+1} and summing over t from 0 to ∞, we obtain

$$(1 - av) \sum_{t=o}^{\infty} v^t x_t = x_o + \sum_{t=1}^{\infty} v^t \epsilon_t .$$

If the characteristic function of ϵ is $\varphi(s) = E\left\{e^{is\epsilon}\right\}$, the characteristic function of z is

$$\varphi_z(s) = \exp\left\{\frac{isx_o}{1-av}\right\} \prod_{t=1}^{\infty} \varphi\left(\frac{isv^t}{1-av}\right) .$$

From this expression we can find the distribution function of z, and we can also find all moments of the distribution. It is easy to verify that we have

$$E(z) = \frac{1}{1-av} \left\{x_o + \frac{vE(\epsilon)}{1-v}\right\}$$

$$Var(z) = \frac{1}{(1-av)^2} \frac{v^2 Var(\epsilon)}{1-v^2}$$

Hence it appears possible to analyse the time-and-uncertainty-elements simultaneously with pedestrian mean-variance methods. I shall, however, not explore these possibilities in the present paper.

3. Expected Utility

3.1. I shall now return to the problem discussed in par. 2.5. Most undergraduates today know that the "Expected Utility Theorem" can be proved from some very simple axioms. They also know that the proof can be very lengthy if one wants to make the axioms as simple or "basic" as possible. I do not think it is particularly interesting to go deeply into this question. What we really want, is a rule for assigning a real number—a utility—to an arbitrary probability distribution. Further we want this rule to give a preference ordering over a set of—possibly all—probability distributions.

Many economists seem quite willing to accept a single strong axiom to the effect that a rational decision maker has a complete preference ordering over the set of all probability distributions. There is much to be said for taking this pragmatic view, even if many rational persons may find it very difficult to describe their preference ordering, but it is also worth while trying to derive the strong axiom as a theorem from simpler axioms. The usual approach is then to assume:

(i) The decision maker is able to choose from pairs, i.e., he has a rule which enables him to decide if $F_1 (x)$ is better, worse, or just as good as $F_2 (x)$.

(ii) The rule for choices from pairs is transitive, i.e., $F_1 (x)$ better than $F_2 (x)$ and $F_2 (x)$ better than $F_3 (x)$ imply that $F_1 (x)$ is better than $F_3 (x)$.

The transitivity assumption has been contested by some authors. There is ample evidence that people in experimental situations make choices which violate the assumption. I do not, however, attach much importance to this evidence. People undoubtedly make mistakes, but a person who consistently applies a circular rule of choice, cannot survive for long in a competitive environment. It would indeed be nice, and profitable, to meet a person who always would choose F_1 from the pair (F_1, F_2), F_2 from (F_2, F_3) and F_3 from (F_1, F_3). If this person owns F_1, he should be willing to pay me something if I give him F_3 instead of F_1. He should then be willing to pay an additional amount if I give him F_2 in exchange for F_3, and he should be willing to pay again to exchange F_2 for F_1.

There may exist people who can be pulled through such circular processes several times, but I do not think they play an important part in our economy. Hence I am not particularly interested in generalizing the theory of economic behavior, so that it can include such people.

3.2. To prove the Expected Utility Theorem we need an axiom with a content which can be illustrated by the following table:

	E	$\overline{E}$
a_1	A_1	Z
a_2	A_2	Z

If we choose action a_i, the outcome is A_i if the event E occurs. If the event does not occur, the outcome will be Z. The axiom states that if a person in this situation prefers A_1 to A_2, he will choose a_1 over a_2 – for any E and any Z.

To me this is so obvious that I find it virtually impossible to understand people who refuse to accept the rule as an axiom of rational behavior. Such people do still seem to exist, however, and my discussions with them have been frustrating.

If a person states that he definitely prefers A_1 to A_2, and then chooses a_2, I can think of only two explanations:

(i) He made a mistake.

(ii) He believed that $\Pr(E) = 0$, so that the choice was trivial.

If we can rule out the second possibility, our problem should be to study the circumstances under which people make mistakes. In psychology this is a worthwhile problem, but in economics we have—rightly or wrongly—paid little attention to errors in calculations.

It is not very tolerant to classify other people's views as mistakes, so I shall try to outline one argument which has tempted some people to reject the axiom. Let us take $\Pr(E) = 0.11$, and $A_1 = \$1$ million. Let further A_2 be the lottery

0	with probability	1/11
\$5 mill	with probability	10/11

The two acts will then give the following lotteries:

a_1:	\$1 mill	with probability	0.11
	Z	with probability	0.89
a_2:	0	with probability	0.01
	\$5 mill	with probability	0.10
	Z	with probability	0.89

Allais [1] and [2] has constructed several examples of this kind. He found that many or most people preferred a_2 for $Z = 0$, and a_1 for $Z = \$1$ million. This is a clear violation of the axiom. Such violations have been observed in many experiments, i.a., by MacCrimmon [8], who also found that subjects who made "mistakes" were ready to defend their choices by lengthy arguments.

3.3. The axiom we have discussed is really stronger than necessary. We have assumed that the entries in the table A_1, A_2 and Z could be anything from sacks of potatoes to stock in a gambling casino. In the problem under consideration these entries must be probability distributions, and it is convenient to rewrite the table as follows:

	E	$\bar{E}$
a_1	$F_1(x)$	$G(x)$
a_2	$F_2(x)$	$G(x)$

If $\Pr(E) = \alpha$, the choice of a_i will give the probability distribution

$$H_1(x) = \alpha F_1(x) + (1 - \alpha) G(x).$$

The axiom now simply says that $F_1(x)$ preferred to $F_2(x)$ implies that $H_1(x)$ is preferred to $H_2(x)$ for any $G(x)$, and for any a such that $0 < a \leqslant 1$.

Our problem is to assign a number $U(F)$ to an arbitrary probability distribution $F(x)$. It is clear that the axiom will be satisfied if the operator U satisfies the condition

$$U(\alpha F + (1-\alpha)G) = \alpha U(F) + (1-\alpha)U(G).$$

By repeated application of this formula we can obtain an expression of the form

$$U(F) = \int_{-\infty}^{+\infty} u(x)dF(x)$$

and this gives the ordering indicated in par. 2.5.

For discrete (or arithmetic) distributions the result is almost trivial. To illustrate this, let us introduce the degenerate distribution

$$\epsilon_i(x) \quad = \quad 0 \quad \text{for} \quad x < i$$
$$1 \quad \text{for} \quad x \geqslant i$$

and the distribution defined by

$$\Pr(x=i) \quad = \quad f_i.$$

For the cumulative distribution we then have

$$F(x) \quad = \sum_{i \leqslant x} f_i \quad = \sum_{i \leqslant x} f_i \epsilon_i(x)$$

and hence

$$U(F) \quad = \sum_i f_i U(\epsilon_i).$$

Here $U(\epsilon_i)$ must obviously be interpreted as the utility $u(i)$ assigned to the amount of money i, payable with certainty. By simply writing $u(x)$ for $U(\epsilon_i)$ and $dF(x)$ for f_i, we obtain the expected utility formula in the familiar form.

It is not difficult to prove that the result holds for an arbitrary distribution, although some care is required. The function $u(x)$ represents a preference ordering over the set of all probability distributions. If two utility functions

$u(x)$ and $v(x)$ represent the same preference ordering, it is easy to prove that there must exist a linear relation of the form

$$u(x) = av(x) + b,$$

where a and b are constants, and $a > 0$. This means that the utility function is determined up to a positive linear transformation.

3.4. In the preceding paragraphs I may have treated axiomatics in a high-handed manner. I have done so because I believe it is less interesting, and less important, to quibble over axioms, than to seek knowledge about the shape of the utility functions which represent the preference ordering of different classes of decision makers in real life. If some economists still are reluctant about using "expected utility," it is hardly because they find some of the axioms unacceptable. The reason is more likely to be that they feel that too little is known about the utility function.

At this stage it is useful to go back and look at the oldest of all decision rules, a rule which it is natural to associate with Pascal, the founder of probability theory. Pascal argued that a rational person should always choose the lottery which gave the greatest expected gain. In our notation this means

$$U(F) = \int x \, dF(x).$$

Mathematicians seem to have felt uneasy about the general validity of this rule almost from the beginning. The decisive counter-example is the so-called "St. Petersburg Paradox" of Daniel Bernoulli [4]. Bernoulli suggested that the rule should be:

$$U(F) = \int u(c + x) \, dF(x),$$

where c can be interpreted as the "initial wealth" of the decision maker. This suggestion was taken up by several mathematicians, and with particular enthusiasm by Laplace, who gave the name "moral expectation" to the integral, to distinguish it from the usual mathematical expectation. Bernoulli's suggestion has been strangely ignored by economists for more than 200 years. It is mentioned in two notes in the Mathematical Appendix to Marshall's *Principles*, but he seems to be virtually the only economist in the nineteenth century who could see the connection between marginal utility and Bernoulli's idea.

The reason for this neglect is probably that Bernoulli argued that the utility function must be of the form $u(x) = \log(c + x)$. This assumption is very arbitrary, and much too strong. It seems, however, that Bernoulli was prepared to accept Cramer's suggestion $u(x) = \sqrt{c + x}$, or that utility might be represented by any other function of similar shape.

3.5. There is another generalization of Pascal's rule, which is almost as old as Bernoulli's, and which I find naturally can be associated with the name of Tetens [12]. Pascal's rule implies that the ordering is established by the expected value, i.e., by the first moment of the distributions. Tetens observed that this could only be a first approximation, and that other properties of the distributions also must be taken into consideration. To statisticians of the nineteenth century it was then natural to look at the moments of the distributions.

This approach will lead to decision rules independent of the decision maker's "initial wealth," which in a sense means that the main point of Bernoulli is lost. Bernoulli starts his discussion with stressing that a rich man and a beggar should not, and would not gamble in the same manner. If a decision rule, which is independent of initial wealth, shall satisfy the axioms of expected utility, the functions $u(x+c)$ and $u(x)$ must represent the same preference ordering. This means that we must have

$$u(x+c) = au(x) + b,$$

where a and b are independent of x. Differentiating this equation with respect to x and to c, and eliminating $u'(x+c)$, we obtain the differential equation

$$a'u(x) - au'(x) + b' = 0,$$

where a' and b' are derivatives with respect to c. For $a' = 0$ the equation has a solution of the form

$$u(x) = Ax + B,$$

which gives Pascal's rule.

For $a' \neq 0$ the solution will be of the form

$$u(x) = \kappa e^{\alpha x}.$$

The conditions $u'(x) > 0$ and $u''(x) < 0$ are satisfied if we take $u(x) = -e^{\alpha x}$, where $a > 0$. The utility assigned to the distribution $F(x)$ will then be

$$U(F) = - \int_{0}^{\infty} e^{-\alpha x} dF(x) = -\varphi(\alpha).$$

The right-hand side is the moment-generating function of the distribution, or the characteristic function if we take $a = -it$.

Hence, if moments exist, we have

$$U(F) = -1 + \alpha m_1 - \frac{1}{2}\alpha^2 m_2 \dots$$

We get the same ordering if we take

$$U(F) \;=\; -\frac{1}{\alpha}\log\phi(t)$$

and

$$U(F) \;=\; \kappa_1 - \frac{1}{2}\alpha\kappa_2 + \frac{1}{3!}\alpha^2\kappa_3 \ldots$$

Where $\kappa_1\kappa_2\ldots$ are the cumulants of the distribution. We have κ_1 = mean, κ_2 = variance, and $\kappa_3\kappa_2{}^{-\frac{3}{2}}$ = the conventional measure of skewness.

3.6 The expansions above will converge if moments of all orders exist. If this is the case, the expansions will give an ordering over the set of all distributions with finite moments, in fact the only ordering which is independent of initial wealth, and which satisfies the axioms of expected utility. A generalization to forms such as

$$U(F) \;=\; a_1\kappa_1 + a_2\kappa_2 + a_3\kappa_3 + \ldots$$

or

$$U(F) \;=\; U(\kappa_1,\kappa_2,\ldots)$$

should then be of limited interest. Expressions of this kind must either lead to inconsistencies, or they must be recalculated for every change in initial wealth.

It is worth noting that the expansion in the preceding paragraph contain only one parameter, a, which can be interpreted as "risk aversion" of the decision maker.

If the expansion converges, it is by no means assured that the first few terms will give a useful approximation. In fact, cutting the expansion after a finite number of terms will in general lead to a nonsense result. If a preference ordering based on a finite number of moments is consistent, the underlying utility function $u(x)$ must be a polynomial. This means that $u'(x)$ and $u''(x)$ both have the same sign for large values of x. If this sign is negative, we get decreasing utility of money, which makes little economic sense. If the sign is positive, marginal utility will be increasing. This is not outright nonsense, but it is an implication which is undesirable in investment analysis.

If the distribution $F(x)$ is normal, all cumulants except the two first vanish, so that one can safely write

$$U(F) \;=\; \kappa_1 - \frac{1}{2}\alpha\kappa_2$$

There is no other distribution with a finite number of non-zero cumulants. The family of normal distributions is closed under the convolution operation— i.e., a "portfolio" of normally distributed assets will be normally distributed. This property of the normal distribution is the justification of the mean-variance method of portfolio analysis. It seems important to stress that this method can lead to meaningless results unless all distributions involved are normal.

3.7. I have been on the warpath against the mean-variance approach to investment analysis for some time, and I want to present my favorite counter example [5]:

Let E and S^2 be respectively mean and variance of a distribution. Assume that a person states that he considers the two distributions represented by the pairs (E_1, S_1) and (E_2, S_2) as equally desirable. We can then always construct two gambles:

c	with probability	p
x	with probability	$1-p$

with mean E_1 and variance $S_1{}^2$, and

c	with probability	p
y	with probability	$1-p$

with mean E_2 and variance $S_2{}^2$.

The unknowns p, c, x and y are uniquely determined by E_1, S_1, E_2, and S_2 as follows:

$$c = \frac{S_1 E_2 - S_2 E_1}{S_1 - S_2}$$

$$x = \frac{S_1(S_1 - S_2)}{E_1 - E_2}$$

$$y = \frac{S_2(S_1 - S_2)}{E_1 - E_2}$$

$$p = \frac{(S_1 - S_2)^2}{(E_1 - E_2)^2 + (S_1 - S_2)^2}$$

It is obvious that no rational person will consider the two gambles as equivalent if $x \neq y$. To me this means that mean and variance analysis is highly suspect—also as an approximation.

To drive the point home, let us consider the two gambles

$$0 \quad \text{with probability} \quad \frac{1}{2}$$

$$2 \quad \text{with probability} \quad \frac{1}{2}$$

and

$$-2 \quad \text{with probability} \quad \frac{1}{5}$$

$$3 \quad \text{with probability} \quad \frac{4}{5}$$

There is no reason to question the rationality of a person who considers these two gambles as equivalent. If, however, he states that the gambles are equivalent *because* the mean-variance pairs (1,1) and (2,4) are equivalent, we can present him with the gamble

$$0 \quad \text{with probability} \quad \frac{1}{2}$$

$$4 \quad \text{with probability} \quad \frac{1}{2}$$

This gamble has mean = 2 and variance = 4, and should then be equivalent with the two original gambles. This last gamble is, however, clearly preferable to the former of the two original ones.

I have presented examples of this kind to some of my friends, and I believe I have been able to shake their faith in mean-variance analysis. If they feel too unhappy about it, I have asked them to imagine that they have found their optimal portfolio of investments, characterized by a mean E and variance S^2. I have asked them if they were willing to exchange this portfolio for the gamble:

$$0 \quad \text{with probability} \quad \frac{S^2 - c}{S^2 + E^2 - c}$$

$$\frac{S^2 + E^2 - c}{E} \quad \text{with probability} \quad \frac{E^2}{S^2 + E^2 - c}$$

This gamble has a mean = E and a variance = $S^2 - c$, and should thus be preferable to the portfolio if $c > 0$.

My friends have then usually arrived at the correct conclusion that there is more to investment than mean-variance analysis.

3.8. The approach I have associated with the name of Tetens has been developed mainly by actuaries and practical men who worked with empirical probability distributions—estimated with some inaccuracy. They seem to have felt that they did not know enough about the distributions to calculate an expectation of the form

$$\int u(x)\,dF(x),$$

but that they could make reasonable estimates of the first few moments. Such feelings seem to be the historical origin of the idea that the utility assigned to a probability distribution can be expressed in terms of the first moments.

Tetens' approach misses the main point of Bernoulli, that a realistic decision rule must depend on the initial wealth of the decision maker. This point is obviously important, and I can see no justification for ignoring initial wealth, except when it is necessary to delegate authority.

A large corporation may have objectives which can be represented by a utility function. If this function is such that the optimal decision depends strongly on the "initial" or "actual wealth" of the corporation, a representative cannot make a decision on behalf of the corporation without complete information at hand. In practice this may be impossible. The London representative of an insurance company will usually accept a reinsurance treaty after having considered its inherent merits, without calling back to obtain the most up to date information on the state of his own company.

4. Concluding Remarks

4.1. The definition of a decision problem given in par. 2.1 is so general that it should give an adequate representation of most situations in the real world. It may, however, not always be convenient or natural to formulate practical problems as such decision problems. In real life an investment decision does not often consist in selecting a stochastic process, once and for all, and then to sit and watch the development of the process. There may be possibilities of correcting or changing the decision at a later date, and it may be possible to influence the development of the process, if it should run in an undesirable way. In such cases the real problem is to steer or control the process so that it develops in the most favorable manner. In principle there is nothing new in this sequential view.

The problem consists in deciding on a "strategy" for controlling the process, i.e., it can in principle be reduced to a decision problem, with a very complex set of possible actions. The real difficulty may then be to state how we want the process to develop, i.e., to describe a preference ordering over a set of stochastic processes.

4.2. In general we can think of $S_t = S^1_t, S^2_t, \ldots, S^n_t$ as a vector which describes the "state" of our "portfolio" or of a firm at the end of period t. As a concrete interpretation we can think of the elements of S_t as the entries in the firm's balance sheet at the end of period t. The balance sheet at the end of the next operating period, S_{t+1}, can be assumed to depend on S_t, and a stochastic vector $x_t = \quad x^1 \dots x^m$ with the joint probability distribution $F_t(x^1 \dots x^m)$. The dependence can be expressed by a relation of the form

$$S_{t+1} = G(S_t, x_t).$$

This relation, which will represent the "law of motion," describes the development of the firm as a multidimensional stochastic process. In order to give management a function, we must assume that management can influence or steer the development of the process. To formalize this, we can write

$$S_{t+1} = G(S_t, x_t, z),$$

where z is a set of control variables, which can be chosen by the management. The task of management is then to select the control variables z so that the S-processes—i.e., the sequence of balance sheets—develop in the most favorable manner.

This formulation of the decision problem is not very useful unless the decision maker knows how he would like to see the S-process develop, i.e., unless he has a well-defined preference ordering over a set of attainable stochastic vector processes. It may as we have seen, be very difficult to describe this preference ordering, and this may be the most serious difficulty connected with decision problems in real life.

At the present stage I think that some general exploration of this problem is of more interest than a rigorous axiomatic formulation of decision rules for more special or simpler decision problems.

2

Confirmation, Information, and Induction

Isaac Levi

I

When Rudolf Carnap set out in the 1940s to provide an "explication" of the concept of confirmation, he had a twofold ambition. He hoped, in the first place, to define a measure of degrees of confirmation of hypotheses relative to evidence which would mirror in a precise and systematic fashion those factors which scientific practice indicate to be relevant in using data to support or undermine scientific hypotheses.[1] Following Keynes[2] and Jeffreys,[3] his probabilistic measures of confirmation were intended to be sensitive to the role which the variety and number of confirming instances for general, law-like statements play. Thus, the more varied the instances and the greater their number, the higher the degree of confirmation was supposed to be.

Carnap's measures of confirmation were also intended to contribute to our understanding of the manner in which support for hypotheses is used to guide our practical conduct. The degree of confirmation accorded a hypothesis h on evidence e was supposed to determine a fair betting quotient for gambles on the truth of h—i.e., for risky policies whose outcomes depend upon the truth value of h.[4]

These two ambitions did not always sit easily together. According to Carnap's account, when h is a universal generalization or, for that matter, when h is a simple statistical hypothesis asserting that the chance of some event occurring on a random trial is a definite real value, in an infinitely or indefinitely large universe, the degree of confirmation is 0 no matter how much supporting data one has.[5] Indeed, even when the universe of discourse is finite, but large, the degree of confirmation for such hypotheses will be quite low—at least in the usual case. Such results seem to conflict with Carnap's ambition to account for how positive instances confirm generalizations.

The technical details of Carnap's resolution of this difficulty need not detain us here.[6] The important point for present purposes concerns the vision of the aims of the scientific enterprise underlying his response. According to Carnap, we seek positive confirming instances for laws not to provide them with high degrees of confirmation, but to obtain high degrees of confirmation for future

Research for this paper was partially supported by the National Science Foundation Grant Number NSF GS 28992.

instances of these laws. The engineer who relies on the laws of mechanics cares very little whether these laws apply in all regions of space and time. What matters is whether he can rely on them in designing the bridge he is contracted to build.

In offering this resolution of the problem of confirming general hypotheses, Carnap claimed, in effect, that the sole purpose of efforts to confirm or disconfirm hypotheses in scientific inquiry is to provide fair betting quotients useful to decision makers engaged in moral, political, economic, technological, or other practical deliberation. Pure research is the handmaiden of practice. It has no autonomous purposes of its own.

Thus, appearances to the contrary notwithstanding, Carnap's efforts to explicate the concept of confirmation are not concerned exclusively with clarifying the meanings of words. Behind his explications lurk controversial views of the aims of scientific inquiry. His position is congenial with what L.J. Savage has called the "behavioralist" approach to statistical inference.[7] According to the otherwise different views of Neyman and Pearson, of Wald and of the Bayesians, statistical inference is a form of decision making. In Neyman's words, inductive inference is nothing but inductive behavior.[8]

Karl Popper has objected to Carnap's explications of the concept of confirmation and has proposed nonprobabilistic explications of "corroboration" in their stead.[9] His own proposals are explicitly tied to a rival vision of the aims of inquiry in opposition to the behavioralist point of view.

Popper holds that measures of confirmation ought to indicate what may be called the "testworthiness" of hypotheses and has insisted that testworthiness does not automatically increase with probability. On his view, scientific inquiry is concerned with devising very strong hypotheses about the world, testing them, casting off rejects, and retaining the survivors for further scrutiny in the hopes that in the long run we might obtain better approximations to a correct understanding of the world.[10] The function of scientific inquiry in providing counsel to practical decision makers is at best a secondary concern to which Popper himself has paid little systematic attention.

The debate which raged a few years ago between students of Popper and of Carnap concerning the relative merits of their rival explications of confirmation sometimes had the appearance of mere logomachy.[11] In this case, however, appearances are deceiving. The fundamental issue has been and continues to be what are or ought to be the aims of scientific inquiry and how do these aims determine the legitimacy of scientific inferences and the extent to which hypotheses are supported by evidence.

I am inclined to agree with Popper or those statisticians, like R.A. Fisher, who object to the idea that the sole purpose of scientific inquiry is to provide guidance to practical decision makers.[12] On the other hand, if one is to insist that scientists in pure research have aims distinct from economic, political, or other moral concerns, it is fair to demand that some systematic characterization of these aims be offered, that an account of rational decision making applicable both to practical decision problems and to these cognitive decision problems be developed, and that the resulting decision theory be used together with the characterization of the aims of "pure research" to derive criteria for legitimate inference. Until recent years, none of the critics of the behavioralist point of view have attempted seriously to meet these demands. In the absence of such efforts, their healthy skepticism with respect to the various forms of behavioralism infecting so much thinking about statistical and inductive inference has been rendered impotent. Few people will take objections to well-developed theories seriously unless the objections are accompanied by well-developed alternatives. In this paper, I shall indicate in outline form some elements of an approach to inductive inference which recognizes that scientific inquiry has aims more or less independent of practical concerns.[13]

II

A coin is about to be tossed. X is offered a bet on the outcome. Two possible outcomes are normally distinguished: landing heads and landing tails. Sometimes provision is made for the coin's landing on its edge (although few take this prospect seriously when a smooth surface is available). However, many other logical possibilities are ruled out. As far as logic goes, the coin might, even when tossed in a normal fashion, move straight up in the direction of Alpha Centauri. Some mysterious process might result in the heads side becoming tails and the tails side becoming heads in the process of tossing. The coin might melt. Such eventualities are totally and utterly discounted. Pious Bayesians might tell us that we do not really rule them out, that we do assign extremely small probabilities to such eventualities, that we rule them out in practice but not in principle.[14] But we *do* rule them out in practice and what we do in practice guides our decisions and the future conduct of our inquiries.

Thus, in designing a statistical experiment the specification of a sample space not only determines what is to count as a possible outcome of an experiment, but what is ruled out as impossible. The same goes for specification of an "action space" identifying options open to an investigator, to a "consequence space" determining possible consequences of the various options. Such determinations of possibilities and impossibilities are not based exclusively on considerations of logic and mathematics, but presuppose a background of theory, laws, statistical assumptions, and observation. Hence, even in situations where our concern is with deliberation aimed at realizing moral, political, economic, or other practical objectives, we rely not only on probabilities which determine fair betting quotients, but on other factual and theoretical knowledge. We need this knowledge to distinguish the possible from the impossible. Moreover, this knowledge or "evidence" should be regarded as both necessary and certain in the senses of central importance for practical deliberation and scientific inquiry. If not–*h* is impossible (i.e., inconsistent with what we know),*h* must be necessary (i.e., entailed by what we know). *h* must be certain in the sense that it bears probability 1. Thus, in accepting a gamble on the outcome of a toss of a coin, we normally set the risk of error involved in the coin's failing to land heads up or tails up at 0. We are "practically certain" that the coin will land heads up or tails up and this is the only certainty of relevance to a realistic theory of knowledge.

These words undoubtedly ring harshly in the ears of men brought up on the view that human knowledge is fallible. According to conventional wisdom, fallible knowledge bears probability less than 1 and is possibly false. In opposition to this view, I submit that all knowledge is certain and necessary and, hence, infallible.

Remember, however, that probabilities and possibilities are determined by the assumptions being used. Consequently, the fallibility of a sentence *h* is relative to the same assumptions. If *h* is a member of a set of assumptions *A* or is deducible from *A*, it is, relative to *A*, necessary, certain, and infallible.

Our concern has not been with any set of assumptions one might use to define possibility and probability, but with the corpus of knowledge *K* relative to which probabilities and possibilities relevant to inquiry and deliberation are determined. Of course, some members of *K* will be fallible relative to sets of assumptions different from *K*—e.g., the laws of logic. But as long as the laws of logic do not exhaust the resources we use in inquiry and deliberation, fallibility relative to logic seems to bear but minor epistemological significance.

Jones contemplates a holiday in Europe and is trying to decide how he shall travel. Should he fly or take a liner? Anyone who took him to task for neglecting the option of swimming would be silly[15]—even though it is logically possible for Jones to swim across the Atlantic. Is Jones negligent in failing to consider sailing on a raft? This option is physically possible as well as logically possible. Again the answer is (at least for the average Jones who does not keep company with Thor Heyerdahl) obvious. Relative to what he knows, both options are unfeasible and there is no reason why he should take them into account in his deliberations. The modalities that matter are relative to what one knows. The probabilities that matter are relative to what one knows. The fallibility that matters is relative to what one knows; and relative to what one knows, what one knows is necessary, certain, and infallible.

Yet, fallibilism is not to be dismissed lightly. Its central thesis may be confused; but the chief corollaries which this thesis is used to support are of considerable importance. Fallibilists have insisted correctly that when we attempt to expand our knowledge our efforts are fraught with risk of error. They have asserted, also correctly, that human knowledge is corrigible. Underlying both claims is the important observation that knowledge is subject to change and improvement.

Sometimes we engage in inquiry in order to obtain new information. Such information is often of service in practical deliberation; but should the information be unreliable, its serviceability is diminished. Consequently, in expanding our knowledge, we look for more than new information. We seek new error free information. However, no matter what strategy we use to expand our knowledge, relative to what we already know any new items not entailed by that knowledge is added only at the risk of error. Such risk is generated by the fact that, relative to what we know, increments in knowledge are possibly false and bear positive probability of being false. Fallibilists insist that we risk error in extending our knowledge, and, on this score, they are undoubtedly right. To be sure, they overreach themselves when they insist that what we already know is also fallible, contingent, and merely probable. Relative to what we know, what we know is certain, necessary, and infallible; but what we contemplate adding to what we know is, again relative to what we know, genuinely fallible.

Of course, once one has decided that the risk of error involved in expansion is worthwhile and has added new information to one's body of knowledge, possibilities and probabilities are to be determined relative to the enlarged corpus. Relative to the expanded corpus, all the new information is necessary, certain, and infallible. The new information is fallible *ex ante* but not *ex post*.

The second important insight we owe to fallibilists is their insistence on the thoroughgoing corrigibility of knowledge. The inverse operation of expansion is contraction. Sentences can be removed from as well as added to a body of knowledge. Deletion or contraction involves shifting the status of deleted sentences from that of necessary, certain, and infallible assumptions to that of possibly false, less than certain, and fallible hypotheses subject to critical review. Advocacy of corrigibilism involves recognition of the legitimacy under suitable conditions of subjecting erstwhile items of knowledge to critical scrutiny in this way.

Fallibilists take for granted that their doctrine is a necessary presupposition of corrigibilism. To show that they are mistaken would take us too far afield. My major concern in this essay is with questions pertaining to inductive and statistical inference and the confirmation of hypotheses. These matters are discussed most naturally in the context of an examination of the conduct of inquiries aimed at expanding a body of knowledge. Yet, it is important to keep in mind the need for an account of contraction to supplement an account of expansion and to recognize the corrigibility of human knowledge which the need for an account of contraction presupposes.

III

Even if knowledge is considered only in the context of its applications to practical deliberation, it requires improvement; and one way in which its value is enhanced is through the addition of new error free information. Of course, we use our knowledge in contexts other than those where we aim to realize moral, political, economic, and other practical goals. For example, we use it to systematize and explain various subject matters. But even if we ignore such theoretical or cognitive purposes and restrict our attention to demands for new information occasioned by practical needs, the *proximate* goal of any attempt to answer a question expressing such a demand is the provision of new error free information. Such proximate goals direct the conduct of inquiries aimed at expansion both by determining what is to count as a potential answer to the question raised and by contributing to the identification of that potential answer which is to be selected as best on the evidence available. Whether one wants to call these goals "practical" or not is a verbal matter. It is, however, important to notice that they are different from typical moral, political, and economic goals. To that extent they are "cognitive" rather than "practical."

On this view, problems of statistical estimation, inductive generalization or choosing between theories are decision problems. They are goal oriented and the conduct of inquiries aimed at realizing these goals resembles in many respects the conduct of deliberations aimed at realizing goals more clearly identifiable as practical. Consequently, statisticians of the behavioralist persuasion are right in insisting that an adequate account of inference be based on an account of general principles of rational decision making applicable both to efforts to realize practical and to realize cognitive objectives.[16] Their error resides in their insistence upon reducing cognitive objectives to practical ones or denying the propriety of such objectives altogether.

We do not engage in inquiry to acquire any information that comes along. Inquiry is directed toward the acquisition of information of some specific kind—namely, of the kind demanded by the question or problem being raised. In many situations, clarification of the problem and the demands for information it occasions is an important and difficult task involving much ingenuity. Moreover, such clarification often does not take place until one is already well on the way to an answer. However, my concern is not with the details of the temporal and psychological processes involved in inquiry, but with criteria for evaluating the propriety, the rationality, or adequacy of the manner in which various tasks subject to critical scrutiny in inquiry are handled.

Thus, clarifying the demand for information embedded in a given problem or question involves two closely related tasks: (a) the identification of potential answers to the question under consideration, and (b) the appraisal of the informational value of the potential answers.

In some situations, the identification of potential answers is automatically suggested by the way in which the question is posed. When predicting the frequency with which a coin will land heads in n tosses or how many round seeds will be found in an F_2 generation of peas, the potential answers consist of various possible estimates of relative frequency in the samples. If the question is to estimate the chance p of a coin's landing heads on a single toss on the basis of an observed sample, the potential answers will be all point and interval estimates of p where p may take values between 0 and 1.

On the other hand, where the problem is to devise a theory to systematize some subject matter, the construction of suitable potential answers often involves considerable genius. Yet, once a theory has been proposed, even in such cases, whether it is eligible to be a potential answer to the question raised (i.e., whether it does provide a potential systematization of the subject matter) is subject to critical evaluation. To this extent there is a "logic" of discovery or, as Peirce put it, a logic of abduction.[17]

I shall not discuss abduction and its logic here except to suggest a standardized format for representing all the potential answers to a given question. Such a format will be useful in discussing criteria for choosing between potential answers.

Let K consist of those sentences known to be true by an investigator at a given time. Idealizing somewhat and ignoring certain controversies, we may regard K as a deductively closed set. K contains any sentence deductively implied by any subset of K. Hence, when an investigator expands a corpus by adding new items, he may be viewed as shifting from the deductively closed set K to another deductively closet set K' such that K' contains all members of K.

Looked at in this manner, a potential answer is a set K' containing K; for a potential answer is a possible expansion of K. However, in typical cases (the only sort to be considered here), any such potential answer can be represented by a single sentence h; for the new corpus K' can be regarded as consisting of the deductive consequences of the old corpus K and the sentence h. h is a strongest sentence to be accepted via induction from K. (There may be more than one such sentence yielding the same expansion K'. If K deductively implies the equivalence of h and g, accepting h as strongest breeds the same K' as accepting g as strongest.) In ordinary discourse, potential answers to questions are usually expressed by single statements. There is no harm and much advantage in doing so as long as it is kept in mind that the answer, strictly speaking, consists of the deductive consequences of K and the sentence h accepted as strongest via induction.

Consider a case where one potential answer is formed by adding h to K and taking the deductive closure and a distinct potential answer is obtained by adding g to K and taking the deductive closure. Both answers differ from adding $h \vee g$ to K and forming the closure. The latter operation yields a deductively closed set which is a proper subset of each of the two other potential answers and, hence, is distinct as a potential answer from either of them. In ordinary language, to accept $h \vee g$ as strongest is to suspend judgment between h and g which is clearly a distinct answer from endorsing h or from endorsing g. In the subsequent discussion, $D(h,K)$ shall represent the deductive closure of the addition of h to K.

Thus, suppose the task is to predict the relative frequency with which a coin will land heads on n tosses. The potential answers include all $n+1$ predictions of the form: The coin will land heads r times. ($0 \leqslant r \geqslant n$)

There are, however, far more potential answers than these. One can predict that the coin will land heads once or twice, but suspend judgment as to exactly which. This is tantamount to accepting as strongest "the coin will land heads one or two times." One can predict that the coin will land heads an even number of times. Suspension of judgment can be carried to still further extremes. One can suspend judgment between all $n+1$ frequencies. This is tantamount to refusing to add anything to K. At the other extreme, one can contradict oneself.

Predictions of the form "Exactly r out of the n tosses will land heads" bear a special status among the potential answers. The only potential answer stronger than any of these (i.e., which entails one of these but is not entailed by any of them) is the self-contradictory answer. Each of these $n+1$ potential answers is a strongest consistent potential answer.

Someone might object that stronger answers can be imagined. Any prediction which specifies not only relative frequence, but the order in which heads and tails follow one another is both consistent and stronger than the prediction that the coin will land heads r out of n times. But so is the prediction that the coin will land heads r out of n times and it will snow on May 16 in Hobart, Tasmania. We are concerned here with potential answers to the question under investigation. If that question is concerned with predicting relative frequencies, then permutations are not distinguishable as potential answers. The additional information they convey is ignored precisely because it is not demanded by the question.

Of course, some other question might demand the extra information. The order in which heads follow tails might matter. If so, the set of strongest consistent potential answers will be different and so will the total set of potential answers. Thus, what constitutes a strongest consistent potential answer and what constitutes a potential answer both depend upon the question raised and on the demand for information it makes.

The relativity of strongest consistent potential answers to questions raised does not imply that a given question uniquely determines the set of such potential answers. Because the devising of potential answers is not always a routine affair, but often requires inventiveness, allowance must be made for cases where someone has devised a set of strongest consistent potential answers which itself may be revised during the course of inquiry. Consider a person seeking a theory to systematize some body of information. He may devise a theory T_1 which potentially gratifies the demand for information occasioned by the problem. Yet, he should consider as a potential answer the "residual hypothesis" R_1 which asserts that T_1 is false. At that stage in inquiry, R_1 is (for our investigator) a strongest consistent potential answer because no consistent potential answer stronger than R_1 is devisable or desirable given the demands of the questions. Obviously, R_1 is not a theory and satisfies the demands of the question very poorly. It is a strongest consistent answer by default. The investigator is not able or has not had the opportunity to partition R_1 into theories.

Of course, the investigator (or some colleague) might subsequently devise a new theory T_2 which is a satisfactory potential answer to the question under consideration. The set of strongest consistent potential answers will then consist of two theories: T_1, T_2, and a new residual hypothesis R asserting that both of the theories are false. In inquiries looking for theories, one rarely if ever reaches a situation where, relative to the corpus of knowledge already available, all strongest consistent potential answers are theories. In general, a residual hypothesis will remain as a strongest consistent potential answer.

By way of contrast, when the problem is to predict relative frequencies or estimate values of parameters, the list of strongest consistent potential answers is routinely and completely determined without resort to a residual hypothesis.

By an "ultimate partition" U, I shall mean the set of sentences representing strongest consistent potential answers recognized by an agent to a given question at a given time. Each element of U is consistent with the corpus of knowledge K already available and K implies that at least and at most one element of U is true.

Let U consist of a finite number of sentences $h_1, h_2, \ldots, h_n$. Let M represent the set of potential answers. If $h_{i1} v h_{i2} v \ldots {}^{v} h_{i_k}$ is a disjunction of k ($k \leqslant n$) members of U, $D(h_{i1} v h_{i2} v \ldots v h_{i_k}, K)$ is in M. When $k = 0$, the potential answer is the contradictory one.

Thus, when the problem is to predict the relative frequency r/n of tosses landing heads in n tosses of a coin, U contains $n+1$ members and M contains 2^{n+1} potential answers. Where U consists of the theories T_1, T_2, and the residual hypothesis R, M contains 8 distinguishable potential answers: complete suspension of judgment (accepting $T_1 v T_2 v R$ as strongest), three cases of suspending judgment between two members of U, three cases of accepting single members of U as strongest and, finally, self-contradiction.

Potential answers may also be represented usefully as cases of rejecting subsets of members of U and taking the deductive consequences. Total suspension of judgment then becomes rejection of no members of U and contradiction involves rejecting all of them.

When U consists of all point estimates of some parameter taking real values in some interval (finite or infinite), U is infinite and, hence, cannot be characterized in the manner just indicated. Yet, there is a natural way to extend that method: each potential answer in M may be regarded as a case of accepting as strongest a sentence asserting that the true value of the parameter is a member of a Borel subset A of the set of points in the real interval over which the parameter ranges. Alternatively (and equivalently), a potential answer may be regarded as consisting of the deductive consequences of rejecting all point values in the Borel set A (the complement of A). Thus, in estimating the value of the chance p of a coin landing heads, each point and interval estimate of p is a potential answer as well as all possible ways in which one might suspend judgment between any of these answers.

IV

Closely related to the abductive task of identifying potential answers is the problem of evaluating the information afforded by the various members of K. One noncontroversial assumption can be made at the outset:

(1) Let $D(h,K)$ and $D(g,K)$ be in M. $D(h,K)$ is more informative than $D(g,K)$ if $D(g,K)$ is a proper subset of $D(h,K)$.

Thus, if h and K deductively imply g, accepting h as strongest is more informative than accepting g as strongest. Alternatively, rejecting a set of members of U containing another such set is to embrace a more informative answer than the one corresponding to the second set.

All of these equivalent formulations yield a partial ordering of members of M with respect to informational value. Indeed, they generate a lattice structure in which the least informative member of M is total suspension of judgment where no member of U is rejected and no modification of K is made and the most informative potential answer is the contradictory option where every member of U is rejected.

Can we improve on this partial ordering? In particular, can we obtain a quantitative measure of the informational value or utility of potential answers?

Elsewhere I have proposed a set of conditions plausibly imposed on measures of informational value.[18] The main implication of these conditions may be stated as follows:

(2) If U is finite and Cont(h/K) is a measure of informational value defined over all Boolean combinations of members of U subject to the condition that two sentences bear equal cont-values if they are equivalent given the truth of all members of K, then there is a probability measure $M(h/K)$ defined on the same set of sentences such that

$$\text{Cont}(h/K) = 1 - M(h/K)$$

If U consists of all point estimates of a parameter p whose range is a *finite* interval of the real line, such measurability is assured if there is a probability density $m(p/K)$ defined over the interval such that for any potential answer asserting that p falls in some Borel subset A of the points in the interval $M(p\epsilon A/K) = {}_{A}m(p/K)$ and Cont $(p\epsilon A/K) = 1 - M(p\epsilon A/K)$.

Most writers on measures of informational value of sentences (misleadingly called "semantic information") acknowledge that the measure Cont(h/K) = 1−M (h/K) is one candidate meriting serious consideration as determining informational value. They recognize others as well. For example, 1/M (h/K) and −log$M$ (h/K) both receive serious attention. I have argued elsewhere that none of these alternatives are satisfactory for the purpose of representing informational value or utility.[19]

The position advocated here differs from received doctrines in still other respects. Writers on semantic information from Popper[20] to Carnap and Bar Hillel,[21] Hempel,[22] and Hintikka[23] all take for granted that the probability measure used to define Cont(h/K) is either the measure P (h/K) which represents the degree to which the current knowledge or evidence "confirms" h and determines a fair betting quotient for gambles on h or the measure P (h) which represents the prior probability or degree of confirmation of h relative only to knowledge of logical truth. In my opinion, both variants of orthodoxy are untenable and I have argued to this effect elsewhere.[24]

The positive position I advocate is that the measure M (h/K) represents the demand for information reflected in the question under consideration. Such a demand may bear little relation to the degree of confirmation either prior or relative to the available evidence.

Consider the fair coin about to be tossed n times. Usually the measure of probability that determines fair betting quotients assigns the value ($\binom{n}{v}$) $.5^n$ to the coin's landing heads r times in the n tosses. This probability is greatest for values of r/n near .5 and smallest for values near 0 and 1. However, if one is concerned to predict the relative frequency r/n, each of the $n+1$ members of U specifying a definite value of r will be regarded as informative as any other. Consequently, the probability measure used to determine informational value will assign equal probability of $1/(n+1)$ to all such predictions. Clearly, the fair betting quotient determining probability P ((r/n)/K) is quite different from the information determining probability M ((r/n)/K). So is, in general, the prior P (r/n).

Thus, not only do the demands for information control what is to count as a potential answer to a given question, including what is to count as a strongest consistent potential answer, but they determine the informational value of potential answers once devised. It should be not at all surprising, therefore, that the probability measure representing informational value will, in general, differ from the probabilities determining fair betting quotients. The latter control odds one should take on the knowledge already available. The former determine whether the demands of the question warrant risking the error involved by endorsing a particular potential answer.

A caveat should be entered at this point. In cases where the demands for information clearly require that all members of U be regarded as equally informative, condition (2) breeds a definite measure M (h/K) and informational measure Cont(h/K). It would be fanciful, however, to suppose that such sharp quantitative measures can be devised for every situation. Consider, for example, the case where U consists of the theories T_1 and T_2 along with the residual hypothesis R. Given the demand for a theory to systematize a given domain, both T_1 and T_2 are to be regarded as more informative than R and, indeed, even substantially so. Hence, the two theories ought to bear greater C-values (and, hence, lower M-values) than R.[25] Whether the two theories are to be regarded as equally informative or not may depend on other factors. Thus, let T_1 be classical thermodynamics and T_2 the kinetic theory. T_2 may explain all the phenomena that T_1 does and more and this consideration may argue in favor of rating T_2 as informationally more valuable than T_1. However, if a scientist is committed to a program of explanation which eschews appeals to atomistic hypotheses, he might regard T_1 as more informative than T_2. No matter how one decides the matter, however, it seems fairly clear that no precise numerical values could be assigned to the M-function or the Cont-function.

Account will eventually have to be taken of the vagueness of the M-measure in such contexts. Yet, there are plausible cases in statistics where uniform assignments of M-values to members of U do seem appropriate and where we can legitimately and realistically deal with numbers. For the present we shall focus on these.

Complications arise if U is infinite. Consider again the case where U consists of all point estimates of the chance p of a coin's landing heads on a single toss. Informally, it seems clear that all such point estimates are equally informative. This implies that all such estimates bear 0 M-value and Cont-value of 1. Such assignments are compatible, however, with a wide variety of different assignments of M-values to interval estimates of p.

In regarding all point estimates of p as equally informative, we mean, as I understand it, to consider all interval estimates of equal "length" as equally informative as well. This implies, however, that the M-function is to be generated by means of a uniform density function $m(p/K)$.[26]

If we are estimating the value of a parameter taking real values in some finite interval of length a, the uniform density function that is appropriate takes $1/a$ as its value. When a is infinite, new complications arise. I intend to consider them in another paper.

V

Any linear transformation of the function $C(h/K)$ could be used to represent the objective of an effort to expand a body of knowledge K were the goal of such an effort solely to obtain new information of the sort demanded by a given question regardless of the truth value of that information. To suppose, however, that in scientific inquiry such goals are judged legitimately is clearly false; for the best strategy to follow in expanding K, when information regardless of truth value is the goal, is to contradict oneself. Contradictory answers are the most informative.

The trouble is not to be found in the Cont-function. Contradictions do bear maximal informational value or utility. They logically imply more than other potential answers. They rule out more logical possibilities. If men were concerned only with obtaining more information *regardless of whether such information* led them into error or not, self-contradiction would be the best strategy. That self-contradiction is almost universally considered objectionable is a manifestation of a widespread respect for truth.[27] In expanding our knowledge we seek not merely new information, but new error free information. Thus, although the Cont-function represents the goal of acquiring more information where truth value is of no interest, it does not represent the goals of scientific inquiry; for in science truth does matter.

We may approach substantially the same result from a different vantage point. Just as the Cont-function represents the utility of potential answers when the goal is to obtain new information regardless of truth value, we can introduce a new function $T(h,x)$ defined over members of the set M of potential answers when avoidance of error regardless of informational value is the goal. Let $D(h,K)$ and $D(g,K)$ be two members of M. $T(h,t) = T(g,t) = 1$ is the utility of $D(h,K)$ [or $D(g,K)$] when endorsing that answer breeds no error. $T(h,f) = T(g,f) = 0$ is the utility when error results.[28]

Relative to the goal represented by the T-function, the optimal policy would be never to expand beyond K, but to suspend judgment between members of U completely; for in this way no risk of error is incurred. When our exclusive concern is to avoid error, there is nothing to induce us to take any risk.[29] The fact that we sometimes think it worthwhile to risk error in enlarging our knowledge suggests that information is a desideratum.

Thus, the quest for error free information must be represented by a third utility function $V(h,x)$ (where x takes the value t or f). The V-function is plausibly regarded as a function of the Cont-function and the T-function. It is rather more controversial to assume that the V-function is a weighted sum of the T-function and the Cont-function. Yet, as I have suggested elsewhere,[30] some case can be made for this view. In the following discussion, I shall adopt the assumption.

(3)
$$V(h,x) = \alpha T(h,x) + (1-\alpha)\,\mathrm{Cont}\,(h,K)$$
$$= \alpha T(h,x) + (1-\alpha)(1 - M(h,K))$$
$$V(h,t) = \alpha + (1-\alpha)\,\mathrm{Cont}\,(h,K)$$
$$V(h,f) = (1-\alpha)\,\mathrm{Cont}\,(h,K)$$
$$\tfrac{1}{2} < \; = \alpha < 1$$

In (3), the condition that a be greater than or equal to ½ is equivalent to the requirement that no erroneous potential answer ever be preferred to any error free potential answer.

Sometimes it is more convenient to use the following linear transformation of the V-function:

$$(4) \qquad F(h,x) \;=\; T(h,x) - q\,(1 - \text{Cont}\,(h,K))$$

$$=\; T(h,x) - qM(h,K)$$

$$q \qquad =\; (1 - \alpha)/\alpha$$

q is greater than 0 and less than or equal to 1. As q increases, the greater the "weight" attached to the Cont-function and the less to the T-function. We shall consider the q-parameter again. Assuming, however, that a value for q has been set, the expected utility of a potential answer relative to the fair betting quotient determining probability function (or confirmation function) $P(h,K)$ is as follows:

$$(5) \qquad EV(h,K) \;=\; P(h,K)\,V(h,t) + (1 - P(h,K))\,V(h,f)$$

$$=\; \alpha P(h,K) + (1 - \alpha)\,\text{Cont}\,(h,K)$$

$$EF(h,K) \;=\; P(h,K) - qM(h,K)$$

When U is finite, an optimal potential answer (i.e., one bearing maximum expected utility) will be any $D(g,K)$ in M meeting the following condition:

(6) g is equivalent given K to a disjunction of members of U such that
   (i) All members of U bearing positive EF-values are disjuncts.
   (ii) Members of U bearing 0 EF-values may or may not be disjuncts.
   (iii) Members of U bearing negative EF-values are not disjuncts.

Maximizing expected utility will not breed a unique optimal answer in every case. However, for reasons that shall not be reviewed here, ties for optimality can plausibly be broken by picking the weakest optimal answer (there is always a unique such optimal potential answer). The weakest optimal answer g meets the following condition:

(7) g is equivalent given K to a disjunction of members of U in which all members of U bearing non-negative EF-values are disjuncts and all members of U bearing negative EF-values are not.

The answer recommended by (7) can be characterized as follows:

Rule (A): Reject all members h_i of U such that

$$P(h_i,K) < qM(h_i,K).$$

Accept all the deductive consequences of these rejections.

As it stands, rule (A) applies only to situations where U is finite. In the case where U consists of the point estimates of a parameter ranging over some interval of the real numbers and where information determining and fair betting quotient determining densities $m(p,K)$ and $p(p,K)$ are available, a plausible modification of the argument given above leads to the following rule:

Rule (A'): Reject all hypotheses asserting that the true value of the parameter bears the value p such that

$$p(p,K) < qm(p,K)$$

Before examining applications of these rules, the role of the q-index deserves some further discussion.

As q increases from zero to 1, rule (A) tends to reject more elements of U and, on the same evidence, a stronger conclusion tends to be recommended. When q is near 1, the investigator is prepared to take a very great risk of error for the sake of information. When q is near zero, he is prepared to risk very little. The tradeoff between information and risk of error is more favorable to information when q is high. A high value of q registers the exercise of a low "degree of caution" or, as R. Jeffrey has put it, a high "degree of boldness."[31]

I have no definite proposal to make for the choice of a degree of caution or boldness. However, when the information is to be added to a body of scientific knowledge to be used subsequently by a wide variety of different individuals in inquiries into diverse subjects and for diverse purposes, the q-index used should be one which all such individuals but those who regard virtually no risk of error as worthwhile would endorse. q should be quite low. Undoubtedly it should be less than .5 and perhaps as low as .1.

VI

To apply rules (A) and (A'), definite numerical measures of M-values and P values are required. Such conditions are sometimes met in real life—in particular, in cases of so-called "direct inference" where the distribution of some random variable is known and the task is to predict the outcome of sampling. Our example of coin tossing will serve to illustrate.

$P(r,K)$, the probability of obtaining r heads in n tosses is equal to $\binom{n}{r}.5^n$. Moreover, the information determining probability $M(r,K)$ is also known. Since each prediction of exact relative frequency is as informative as any other, $M(r,K) = 1/(n+1)$. Rule (A) recommends rejecting every prediction of a relative frequency r/n such that $\binom{n}{r} .5^n < q/(n+1)$. In the more general case where the chance of landing heads is known to be p (where p need not equal .5), the condition of rejection is $\binom{n}{r} p^r (1-p)^{n-r} < q/(n+1)$.

Qualitatively speaking, the predictions recommended by rule (A) assert that the relative frequency r/n will fall in an interval around p. As n increases, for fixed q, the interval around p becomes smaller approaching 0 length in the limit.

To illustrate, let $p = .5$. When $n = 20$, the interval estimate of r/n is $(.35, .65)$ when $q = 1$, $(.3, .7)$, when $q = .5$ and $(.2, .8)$ when $q = .1$. When $n = 100$, the interval estimates are $(.39, .61)$, $(.38, .62)$, and $(.35, .65)$ for the q values 1, .5 and .1 respectively. When $n = 400$, the intervals are (approximately) $(.44, .56)$, $(.43, .57)$, and $(.42, .58)$. When $n = 10,000$, the intervals are (approximately) $(.4852, .5148)$, $(.4841, .5159)$, and $(.4818, .5182)$.

Consider now the inverse problem of estimating the unknown chance p of the coin landing heads on a given toss on the basis of background knowledge K and data indicating the frequency r with which the coin has already landed heads in n tosses. As before, we may assume that we know the probability $P(r/n, K\&p) = \binom{n}{r} p^r (1-p)^{n-r}$. This is the probability that would be assigned the assertion that the coin lands heads r/n times were his total knowledge K together with value p of the chance of the coin's landing heads on a single toss. The fair betting quotient determining probability we need, however, is $P(p, K\& (r/n))$ representing the probability density for the chance p given the total knowledge K and that the coin has landed heads r out of n times. If we knew the "prior" density $P(p, K)$, we could compute $P(p, K\& (r/n))$. In many situations, however, we may not be able to do so. Thus, rule (A′) is not applicable to such cases as it stands. However, to appreciate what would happen if we did know how to determine $P(p, K\& (r/n))$ precisely, suppose that $P(p, K) = 1$ for all values of p in the interval from 0 and 1. The posterior density $P(p, K\& (r/n))$ is then the beta density $\dfrac{(n+1)!}{r!(n-r)!} p^r (1-p)^{n-r}$.

We are assuming that the informational density $m(p, K\&(r/n))$ is uniform bearing the value 1. Rule (A′) then requires that values of p be rejected if and only if the following holds:

$$\frac{(n+1)!}{r!(n-r)!} p^r (n-r)^{n-r} < q .$$

Notice, however, that this rejection condition is met if and only if the following holds:

$$\binom{n}{r} p^r (1-p)^{n-r} < q/(n+1)$$

Thus, when the prior distribution of the parameter p of a binomial distribution is uniform, the rejection rules allow us to rely solely on the "likelihoods." When the likelihood of a specific value of p on given data r/n is low enough the hypothesis that the true value is that one is to be rejected. Thus, we should reject the hypothesis that a coin is fair ($p = .5$) when $q = .1$ when the data shows that in 20 tosses the coin has landed heads only 1 time or as many as 19 times. If it has landed heads twice, or 18 times we should fail to reject it.

These results obtain when we can assign a uniform density to p relative to K prior to its augmentation by the data that r heads resulted from the n tosses. Suppose, however, that our prior judgments are not so definite as this. We may, nonetheless, be able to use rules (A) and (A$'$).

Suppose, for example, that we do judge that the prior density p (p,K) falls in an interval between $1-e$ and $1+d$. (Both e and d are positive.) The posterior density then falls in an interval between $(n+1)!/r!\,(n-r)!\; p^r\,(1-p)^{n-r}$ $(1-e)/(1+d)$ and $(n+1)!/r!\,(n-r)!\; p^r\,(1-p)^{n-r}\,(1+d)/(1-e)$.

Consider now all densities for p compatible with this condition. We are entitled to reject all values of p (for a given q-index) such that these values would be rejected no matter which of these densities is used. Clearly, all those values of p which would be rejected when the upper bounds for their density values are used meet this condition. Hence, a sufficient condition for rejecting a value of p will be the following:

$$\binom{n}{r} p^r (1-p)^{n-r} < \frac{q(1-e)}{(n+1)(1+d)}$$

Since e and d are both positive, $(1-e)/(1+d)$ is less than 1. Hence, the virtual effect of vagueness in judgment of the prior distribution in cases of the sort under consideration is to increase the degree of caution exercised.

The ideas outlined here can be extended in at least a qualitative way to apply to situations where there is vagueness not only in betting quotient determining probability, but in information determining probability as well. Thus, when choosing between two theories T_1 and T_2 and the residual hypothesis R, we may perhaps make no other judgment than that R is decidedly less informative than either of the two theories. This suffices, however, to warrant the following recommendations: (a) R is to be rejected even when its probability is considered quite high, and (b) rejecting either of the remaining alternatives T_1 or T_2 requires that their probabilities be extremely low.

In some situations, it may be possible to be somewhat more specific. Thus, where one theory is more effective in systematizing the phenomena than the other, we would require its probability to be extremely low before rejection. It would be farfetched, however, to suppose that we can play with numbers when choosing between theories in quite the same way we can in problems of statistical estimation.

Nonetheless, the structure of arguments involved in choosing between theories is, according to the view advocated here, strikingly similar to that involved in statistical inference. In both types of situation, a body of knowledge is to be expanded in order to obtain new error free information. Both kinds of inquiries are, therefore, goal directed endeavors. In this respect, they resemble practical deliberations aimed at realizing ethical, political, and economic objectives. Yet the goals involved are of a special kind distinct from such practical purpose. Inductive inference is, in some respects, like inductive behavior; but it is not reducible to it.

In the context of inductive inference, probabilities determining fair betting quotients in a manner similar to that envisaged by Carnap were supposed to play an important role. They still do according to the position advanced here. They determine risks of error. However, high probabilities do not always indicate that a hypothesis is well confirmed if by that it is meant that the hypothesis is well established. As we have seen, in choosing between theories, residual hypotheses are often rejected even when their probabilities are very high. They are well confirmed in Carnap's sense, but they are not established firmly enough to be added to the body of knowledge.

These last remarks echo views long advocated by Popper. Popper's position, however, is not beyond reproach. Recall that for Popper testworthiness is the feature of hypotheses that is to be prized. This is not surprising; for Popper's concern is with the devising of hypotheses for purposes of testing and criticism. This activity is part of what we have called abduction, whereas we have been concerned with induction here. Popper's focus is different than ours.

Unfortunately, Popper not only ignores, but seems to deny the problem of choosing between testworthy hypotheses to be admitted into a body of knowledge to be used as an assumption in subsequent inquiry. Yet, without this inductive step, there would be no point in engaging in the formulation of hypotheses and testing them. We do not devise hypotheses in order to test them. We test the hypotheses we devise in order to provide ourselves with a basis for choosing which of them to add to our knowledge.

This difference between Popper's view and the position taken here is mirrored in differing conceptions of testworthiness. Popper maintains that a hypothesis is testworthy if it is highly vulnerable to falsification. This position makes sense given Popper's vision of the scientific enterprise as being primarily concerned with testing and criticism. To the extent, however, that we reject Popper's view of the aims of science and take seriously the view that scientists do seek to expand our knowledge, falsifiability is seen to be not a benefit, but a liability; for falsifiability, as Popper construes it, increases with probability of error. Anyone who manifests his respect for truth by attempting to avoid error will regard probability of error and falsifiability as evils.

I have argued, in contrast to Popper, that testworthiness depends upon how well a potential answer answers the question under consideration. If it gratifies the demand for information well, it is highly worthy. If it is irrelevant to the question or answers it in a weak manner, its testworthiness relative to that question is relatively small.

Testworthiness as measured by informational value is a decreasing function of probability. However, the probability function is the information determining function $M(h,K)$ which is to be distinguished from the confirmational or fair betting quotient determining probability $P(h,K)$ or its "prior" $P(h)$. There is some more or less imperfect correlation between testworthiness and falsifiability; and this fact has lent some plausibility to Popper's doctrine. Nonetheless, the plausibility is specious. We prize hypotheses which gratify our demands for information. It is a tragic fact of life and logic that highly informative hypotheses tend to be highly informative as well. We are not, therefore, committed to prizing falsifiability. That is to make a virtue out of necessity. We put up with falsifiability because of the information it brings.

Indeed, avoidance of error and information are the twin desiderata which impel our efforts to expand our knowledge. These desiderata are in tension. This tension is reflected in our need to tradeoff risk of error against informational benefit in deciding how to expand our knowledge. An adequate understanding of this tradeoff is, in my opinion, a crucial element in any effort to develop a comprehensive and adequate account of statistical and inductive inference in the context of scientific inquiry.

Notes

1. R. Carnap (5), 1-2.
2. J.M. Keynes (14).
3. H. Jeffreys (13).
4. R. Carnap (5), 165-67.
5. R. Carnap (5), 570-71.
6. R. Carnap (5), 571-75.
7. L.J. Savage (28), 159-62.
8. J. Neyman (18).
9. K.J. Popper (20), ch.X and new appendix ix.
10. K.J. Popper (21), 215-50.
11. Bar Hillel (2) and (3), R. Carnap (6), K.R. Popper (22), (23), (24), (25), and (26).
12. R.A. Fisher (7), 1-7.
13. The ideas presented in outline here are extensions and modifications of views developed in I. Levi (16) and (17).
14. R.C. Jeffrey (11), 156.
15. Of course, if the critic is engaged in undermining those assumptions relative to which swimming is unfeasible, his endeavor may not be at all silly.
16. Nonbehavioralists often fail to appreciate this point even when they recognize the goal-oriented character of scientific inquiry. See I. Levi (15) for a critique of Popper on this score.
17. C.S. Peirce, (19), 11.

18. I. Levi (17).

19. I. Levi (17).

20. Popper (20), 116-21, ch. X, appendices *vii, *viii, *ix.

21. Bar Hillel and Carnap (4).

22. C.G. Hempel (8).

23. J. Hintikka and J. Pietarinen, (10).

24. I. Levi (17).

25. Popper would agree but insist on a different explanation. On his view, T_1 and T_2 are more informative because they are more falsifiable than R.

26. Thus, assigning equal density to all values of p^2 is not to regard each point estimate of p as equally informative as every other. Rather it is to consider each point estimate of p^2 as informative as every other.

27. See A. Tarski (27), 76-77.

28. Remember that these cardinal utility functions are unique up only to linear transformations.

29. For further comment see Levi (16) and (17).

30. I. Levi (17).

31. R.C. Jeffrey (12).

Bibliography

1. Y. Bar Hillel. "An Examination of Information Theory." *Philosophy of Science* 22 (1955), 86-105.
2. _____ . "Comments on 'Degree of Confirmation' by Professor K.R. Popper. *Br. Jour. for Philosophy of Science* 6 (1955-56), 155-57.
3. _____ . "Further Comments on Probability and Confirmation." *Br. Jour. for Philosophy of Science* 7 (1956-57), 245-48.
4. _____ , and R. Carnap. "Semantic Information." *Br. Jour. for Philosophy of Science* 4 (1953), 145-157.
5. R. Carnap. *Logical Foundations of Probability.* 2nd ed., Chicago: U. of Chicago Press, 1962.
6. _____ , . "Remarks on Popper's Note on Content and Degree of Confirmation." *Br. Jour. for Philosophy of Science* 7 (1956-57), 243-44.
7. R.A. Fisher. *Statistical Methods and Scientific Inference.* 2nd ed. New York: Hafner, 1959.
8. C.G. Hempel. "Inductive Inconsistencies." *Synthese* 12 (1960), 439-69.
9. _____ . "Deductive Nomological vs. Statistical Explanation." In H. Feigl and G. Maxwell, *Minn. Studies in Philosophy of Science* III. Minneapolis: U. of Minnesota Press, 1962, 98-169.
10. J. Hintikka and J. Pietarinen. "Semantic Information and Inductive Logic." In Hintikka and Suppes, *Aspects of Inductive Logic.* Amsterdam: North Holland (1966), 96-112.
11. R.C. Jeffrey. *Logic of Decision.* New York: McGraw-Hill, 1965.
12. _____ . Review of (16). *J. Phil.* 65 (1968), 313-23.
13. H. Jeffreys. *Scientific Inference.* 2nd ed. Cambridge: Cambridge University Press, 1957.
14. J.M. Keynes. *A Treatise on Probability.* London: Macmillan, 1921.
15. I. Levi. "Corroboration and Rules of Acceptance." *Br. Jour. for Philosophy of Science* 13 (1962-63), 307-313.
16. _____ . *Gambling with Truth.* New York: Knopf, 1967.
17. _____ . "Information and Inference." *Synthese* 17, 17 (1967), 369-91.
18. J. Neyman. *Lectures and Conferences on Mathematical Statistics.* Washington, U.S. Department of Agriculture, 1937.
19. C.S. Peirce. "Fixation of Belief." In J. Buchler (ed.), *The Philosophy of Peirce.* New York: Harcourt Brace, 1950, 5-22.
20. K.R. Popper. *The Logic of Scientific Discovery.* London: Hutchison, 1959.
21. _____ . *Conjectures and Refutations.* New York: Basic Books, 1962.
22. _____ . "Degree of Confirmation." *Br. Jour. for Philosophy of Science* 5 (1954-55), 143-49.
23. _____ . " 'Content' and 'Degree of Confirmation': A reply to Dr. Bar Hillel." *Br. Jour. for Philosophy of Science* 6 (1955-56), 157-63.

24. _____ . "Adequacy and Consistency: A Second Reply to Dr. Bar Hillel." *Br. Jour. for Philosophy of Science* 7 (1956-57), 149-256.

25. _____ . "A Second Note on Degree of Confirmation." *Br. Jour. for Philosophy of Science* 7 (1956-57), 350-53.

26. _____ . "Reply to Professor Carnap." *Br. Jour. for Philosophy of Science* 7 (1956-57), 244-45.

27. A. Tarski. "The Semantic Conception of Truth." In Feigl and Sellars, *Readings in Philosophical Analysis*. New York: Appleton, Century, Crofts, 1949, 52-84.

28. L.J. Savage. *Foundations of Statistics*. New York: Wiley, 1954.

Part II:
Stock Prices

3 Mathematics of Speculative Price

Paul A. Samuelson

1. Introduction. Great mathematicians have often been important contributors to applied science. One has only to think of the names of Newton, Gauss, Euler, and Poincaré. Now that the social and managerial sciences have emerged as professional disciplines, spinoffs from pure mathematics play an increasing role in their development. John von Neumann made two immortal contributions to economics. Best known to the outside world is his theory of games; no less seminal for modern economic analysis was his 1931 input-output model of dynamic general equilibrium.

The subjects that I shall survey were not, as far as I can remember, within the direct range of von Neumann's research interests. But the methods and techniques he stressed infiltrate every branch of modern economics.

2. Shadow prices. Is there any other kind of price than "speculative" price? Uncertainty pervades real life and future prices are never knowable with precision. An investor is a speculator who has been successful; a speculator is merely an investor who has lost his money.

In the Santa Claus examples of textbooks, however, there are theoretical prices that play a role in organizing the resource allocation of a competitive society. The simplest example I can give that still has some richness of texture is the following ideal case of "homothetic general equilibrium," as sketched in Samuelson [93].

There are n goods and services, $(q_1, \ldots, q_n)$, each producible out of r factors of production $(V_1, \ldots, V_r)$ by concave, homogeneous-first-degree production functions. The sum of the amounts of each factor used in the respective n industries is an assigned positive constant. Finally, the owners of the incomes from the factors all spend their incomes in the same common proportions at all income levels, so as to maximize an ordinal utility function:

Delivered as the twelfth John von Neumann Lecture at the 1971 SIAM Fall Meeting on October 11, 1971, in Madison, Wisconsin. Reprinted with permission from *SIAM Review* (1972). Copyright 1972 by Society for Industrial and Applied Mathematics.

The writing of this paper was supported in part by a grant from the National Science Foundation. I owe thanks to Professor Robert C. Merton of MIT for the valuable Appendix on continuous-time analysis, and for other stimulus; also thanks to Jill Pappas and K. Iwai for editorial aids. This paper is dedicated to a great mind, L.J. Savage of Yale, who died after this lecture was given.

one admissible cardinal indicator of the utility to be maximized is seen to be concave, homogeneous-first-degree in its consumption arguments.

Certain regularity conditions being assumed—such as existence of repeated partial derivative, non-satiability, strong concavity, and others familiar in the economics literature—the system is defined by

$$q_j = Q^j(V_{1j}, \ldots, V_{rj}) \qquad , \qquad (j = 1, \ldots, n) \qquad (2.1)$$

$$\sum_{j=1}^{n} V_{ij} = V_i \qquad , \qquad (i = 1, \ldots, r)$$

$$p_j \partial Q^j / \partial V_{ij} = w_i \qquad , \qquad (j = 1, \ldots, n; i = 1, \ldots, r)$$

$$u = u[q_1, \ldots, q_n]$$

$$p_j = \partial u / \partial q_j \qquad , \qquad (j = 1, \ldots, n)$$

Here (p_j) is the vector of prices of the goods (q_j), expressed in "real GNP" units; (w_i) is the vector of real prices of the factors (V_i); V_{ij} is the non-negative amount of the ith factor allocated to the jth industry; u is the real GNP, invariant to redistributions of incomes among individuals because of our strong assumption of uniform, homothetic tastes.

The $n + r + nr + 1 + n$ "independent" relations of (2.1) do suffice to determine the $n + nr + n + r + 1$ unknown variables: (q_j), (V_{ij}), (p_j, w_i), u, as can be proved by the non-algebraic consideration that (2.1) can be shown to be equivalent to an interior maximum solution to

$$U(V_1, \ldots, V_n) = \text{Max } u[Q^1(V_{11}, \ldots, V_{r1}), \ldots, Q^n(V_{1n}, \ldots, V_{rn})]$$

$$\text{s.t.} \sum_{j=1}^{n} V_{ij} = V_i \qquad (2.2)$$

Even if we weaken the assumed regularity conditions, the equality-inequality version of (2.1) can be shown to have a solution by the Kuhn-Tucker version of (2.2).

Now the (p_j, w_i) prices are prices never seen on land or sea outside of economics libraries. But they do serve the role of Lagrangian multipliers or shadow prices that, in the absence of competitive markets, might be employed by a central planning agency in computing ideal socialist pricing, as Pareto [77], Barone [6], Taylor [107], Lerner [58], Lange [53], and other economists have argued. (A socialist might redistribute ownership in the V_i and their income-fruits.)

A question, for theoretical and empirical research and not ideological polemics, is whether real life markets—the Chicago Board of Trade with its grain futures, the London Cocoa market, the New York Stock Exchange, and the less-formally organized markets (as for staple cotton goods), to say nothing of the large Galbraithian corporations possessed of some measure of unilateral economic power—do or do not achieve some degree of dynamic approximation to the idealized "scarcity" or shadow prices. In a well-known passage, Keynes [49] has regarded speculative markets as mere casinos for transferring wealth between the lucky and unlucky, the quick and the slow. On the other hand, Holbrook Working [115-118] has produced evidence over a lifetime that futures prices do vibrate randomly around paths that a technocrat might prescribe as optimal. (Thus, years of good crop were followed by heavier carryover than were years of bad, and this before government intervened in agricultural pricing.)

3. Stochastic cobweb cycles. Let me describe a process famous in economics for more than forty years.[1] A crop, call it potatoes, is auctioned off for what it will fetch according to the *dd* demand relation. But the amount supplied in the next period is a function of today's price, as shown by *ss*. The demand and supply relations are respectively

$$p_t = D[q_t] \quad , \quad D' < 0 \tag{3.1}$$

$$q_t = S(p_{t-1}) \quad , \quad S' > 0$$

$$p_t = D[S(p_{t-1})] = P(p_{t-1}) \quad , \quad P' < 0$$

These non-linear difference equations, subject to initial conditions q_0 or p_0, generate a determinate solution

$$q_t = Q(t; q_0) \quad , \quad p_t = P(t; p_0) \quad , t > 0$$

A stationary solution to the dynamic equations is defined by the intersection of the curves

$$p^* = P(p^*) \tag{3.2}$$

$$p^* = D[q^*] \quad , \quad q^* = s(p^*)$$

This is locally unstable, as shown, if

$$|P'(p^*)| = |D'[s(p^*)] s'(p)| < 1 \tag{3.3}$$

with every-other-period oscillations exploding away from (p^*, q^*).

If, as is shown in the diagram, there exists a motion of period 2, we shall have repeating terms (. . . $f_0, f_1, f_0, f_1, \ldots ; \ldots g_0, g_1, g_0, g_1, \ldots$)

$$p_t = f_t \equiv f_{t \pm 2} > f_{t+1} \tag{3.4}$$

$$q_t = g_t \equiv g_{t \pm 2} < g_{t+1}$$

with

$$f_0 = P(f_1) \quad , \quad f_1 = P(f_0) \tag{3.5}$$

$$f_1 = D[g_1] \quad , \quad f_0 = D[g_0]$$

$$g_1 = S(f_0) \quad , \quad g_0 = S(f_1)$$

As Leontief [56] showed, it will suffice for local stability of the periodic motion that $p_{t+2} = P(P(p_t)) = P_2(p_t)$ be a stable difference equation, with

$$P'(f_0)P'(f_1) = |D'(g_1)S'(f_0)D'(g_0)S'(f_1)| < 1 \tag{3.6}$$

All this is intuitively obvious, but can be verified by a theory of difference equations with periodic coefficients that parallels the familiar Floquet theory of differential equations with periodic coefficients. (See Samuelson [97] for discussion parallel to Coddington and Levinson [15].)

The system (3.1) has a certain vogue in agricultural economics as being related to a supposed corn-hog cycle. It has the great merits that it solves with a stroke of the pen how to get, from one set of (p_t, q_t) data, *both* an identified demand function *and* an identified supply function. As readers of Haavelmo [35] and F. Fisher [33] know, the specified lag structure permitted older writers such as H.L. Moore and his pupil Henry Schultz to crack the identification puzzle.

But surely the cobweb cycle is an oversimplification of reality. If prices varied year after year in a predictable fashion, why shouldn't farmers and and the agricultural information services recognize this, or at least why wouldn't commodity speculators or the board of trade do so? Such recognition would lead to an alternation of the postulated $q_t = S(p_{t-1})$ relation, perhaps replacing it by

$$q_t = S \text{ (price expected at period } t) \tag{3.7}$$

$$= S(\pi_t)$$

Thus, in the absence of chance variations in harvests or in tastes, experience with (3.1) might lead after a time to the self-warranting inference

$$\pi_t \quad \equiv \quad \pi_{t+1} \quad \equiv \quad p^* \tag{3.8}$$
$$q_t \quad \equiv \quad q^* \quad = \quad S(p^*)$$

Real life can hardly be so simple since there are, at the least, chance variations in supply harvested. To illustrate one might replace (3.8) by

$$q_t \quad = \quad S(\pi_t) + X_t \tag{3.9}$$

where X_t is an independent random variable

$$\text{Prob} \left\{ X_t \leqq x \right\} = F(x) \quad \text{for all } t$$

Intuitively, depending upon whether the chance draw of X_t has its outcome knowable late or early in the intention-to-plant stage, one would expect (3.8)'s stationary equilibrium to be replaced by kind of a Brownian-motion vibration around equilibrium: when adverse X_t is drawn, p_t tends to be low. Depending upon how much one can infer about the unknown probability distribution $F(x)$, farmers will form different decision rules on how to guess Π_t, and hence how to decide what amounts to plant of each crop.

The next sections will pursue this issue of stochastic variation.

4. Bachelier's absolute-Brownian motion. It is not easy to get rich in Las Vegas, at Churchill Downs, or at the local Merrill Lynch office. That price changes of common stocks and commodity futures fluctuate somewhat randomly, something like the digits in a table of random numbers or with algebraic sign-patterns like that of heads and tails in tosses of a coin, has commonly been recognized. Just as men try to develop systems and hunches to outguess random devices, so speculators purport to be able to infer from charts certain "technical" patterns that enable profitable prediction of future price changes.

As against the chartist-technicians, who are in as low repute as ESP investigators because they usually have holes in their shoes and no favorable records of reproducible worth, there are the "fundamentalists" and economists who think that the future algebraic rise in the price of wheat will have something to do with possibly discernible patterns of what is going to happen to the weather in the plains states, the price of nitrogen fertilizer, the plantings of corn, and the fad for reducing diets. It came as something of a surprise to these fundamentalists that Alfred Cowles [17 through 20] and M.G. Kendall [48], along with occasional earlier writers, found that their computers could hardly tell the difference between random number series and historical price differences. As Kendall put it, in discussing over 2,000 weekly price changes in Chicago spot wheat, recorded for years between 1883 and 1914: "The series looks like a 'wandering' one, almost as if once a week the Demon of Chance drew a random number from a symmetrical population of fixed dispersion and added it to the current price to determine next week's price." (p. 87 of [16]).

As measured by the absence of significant absolute magnitude, 18 English common-stock-price series were found also to look much like random walks. The only cases of systematic serial correlation or dependence Kendall found were in such monthly series as New York spot cotton; but Working [119] and S.S. Alexander soon independently showed that these weak effects were precisely what one should expect from random-difference series averaged in the monthly fashion of Kendall's series.

In 1900 a French mathematician, Louis Bachelier, wrote a Sorbonne thesis, Bachelier [5], on the *Theory of Speculation*. This was largely lost in the literature, even though Bachelier does receive occasional citation in standard works on probability. Twenty years ago a circular letter by L.J. Savage (now, sadly, lost to us), asking whether economists had any knowledge or interest in a 1914 popular exposition by Bachelier, led to his being rediscovered. Since the 1900 work deserves an honored place in the physics of Brownian motion as well as in the pioneering of stochastic processes, let me say a few words about the Bachelier theory.[2]

After some incomplete observations about the difference between objectivist-frequency notions of probability and subjectivist-personal notions of probability as entertained by (a) the buyer of a stock, (b) its seller, (c) the necessarily-matched resultant of buyers' and sellers' pressures to form, so to speak, the probability in the "mass-mind of the market" (my phrase, not Bachelier's), he in effect posits

$$\text{Prob} \quad X_{t+T} \leqq x_T \mid X_0 = x_0 \quad = F(x_t - x_0; T) \quad (4.1)$$

Here x_0 is the known price of, say General Motors stock, now at $t = 0$. GM's price T periods from now is a random variable, X_T following the indicated probability distribution. Although Bachelier does not linger sufficiently long over the fact, evidently t and T are not to be restricted to integral values corresponding to discrete time periods, but are to be real numbers. Today we would call this a Wiener Brownian-motion process involving infinitely-divisible independent *increments*.

Bachelier gives three or four proofs, or purported proofs, that the resulting distribution for F must have the normal de Moivre-Laplace-Gauss form. Since we can go from here to there in two intermediate jumps, he anticipates a form of the Chapman-Komolgorov relation and, in effect,[3] writes

$$F(x; T_1 + T_2) = \int_{-\infty}^{\infty} F(x - u; T_1) F(du; T_2) \quad (4.2)$$

He purports to deduce that (4.2) implies

$$F(x;t) \equiv F\left(\frac{x - \mu t}{\sigma\sqrt{t}}; 1\right) \equiv N\left[\frac{x - \mu t}{\sigma\sqrt{t}}\right] \qquad (4.3)$$

where the well-known Gaussian integral is defined by

$$N[y] = \frac{1}{\sqrt{2\pi}} \int_{-\infty}^{y} e^{-\frac{1}{2}u^2} du \qquad (4.4)$$

Since any member of the Lévy-Pareto stable-addive class satisfies (4.2), and since all the members of this class that lack finite second moments are non-Gaussian, such a demonstration is invalid. The recent works of Mandelbrot [61 through 64] and Fama [25 through 31] suggest that the non-Gaussian Lévy distributions, with so-called kurtosis a between the 2 of the Gaussian distribution and the 1 of the Cauchy distribution, must be taken seriously in evaluating empirical time series. Thus, when we supply Bachelier with the regularity conditions, such as finite second moment, to make his deduction valid, we must do so as a temporary loan and with some reservations.

Bachelier goes from (4.2) to (4.3) by varied arguments. He verifies (p.30) the sufficiency of (4.3) for (4.2) by direct substitution, still leaving open the problem of necessity. Later (pp. 32-34) he uses the familiar demonstration, by Stirling's approximation, of the central limit law for the binomial process. Still later he gives two arguments, one (p. 39) involving random movements in discrete time on a discrete lattice of points, and the other (p. 40) reminiscent of Einstein's approximation involving zero probabilities outside an infinitesimal range in short-enough time intervals, to deduce the Bachelier-Einstein fourier equation

$$c^2 \frac{\partial F(x;t)}{\partial t} - \frac{\partial^2 F(x;t)}{\partial x^2} = 0 \qquad (4.5)$$

with well-posed boundary conditions at $t = 0$.

Bachelier applies his theory to observations in the Paris market of 1894-98, with what he considers impressive corroboration and which we must regard as not-interesting. To illustrate his typical researches, let me sketch his rational theory of warrant or call pricing.

Axiom: The expected value of a common stock's price change $X_{t+k} - X_t$, is always zero, as in a fair game or "martingale." An option enabling you to buy it at an exercise (or "striking") price of a dollars exactly T periods from now is to be given a market price today, W, such that it also faces you with a fair-game process.

I shall not spell out in detail the arguments. But notice that if X_T ends up below the exericse price a, you will not want to exercise and will lose what you paid for the warrant; and for every dollar X_T exceeds a, you make a dollar of gross profit by exercising. Hence, the value of the warrant that makes your net profit zero must be the following function of the time left for the warrant to run T, and the current price of the common stock, x

$$W(x; T,a) = \int_a^\infty (u - a)F[d(u - x); T]\tag{4.6}$$

Assuming that F does satisfy Bachelier's Gaussian form of (4.3), it is easy to derive

$$W(a; T,a) = k\,\sigma\sqrt{T}\tag{4.7}$$

where k is a simple normalizing constant and σ is a parameter measuring the "volatility" of the stock's unbiassed random walk per unit time period.

Thus, such a warrant or "call" with 2 years to run will be worth only about 40 percent more than one with 1 year to run (since $\sqrt{2} \cong 1.4$). To be double the worth of a 1-year warrant, we must pick a 4-year warrant. One morning, I checked the newspaper ads for puts and calls and verified that this square-root-of-T law does hold approximately for call quotations over 30-day, 60-day, and 180-day periods.

As another empirically good approximation when price changes can be represented by a probability density that is symmetrically distributed around zero—as Bachelier deduces and Kendall's observations loosely confirm over short time intervals—we can differentiate (4.6) to get, as I did some 20 years ago,

$$\frac{\partial W(x; T,a)}{\partial x} = +\frac{1}{2}\text{ at } x = a\tag{4.8}$$

This confirms the market rule of thumb: for each dollar rise or fall in market price above or below the exercise price, a warrant and call is marked up or down by approximately $\$\frac{1}{2}$. Perhaps this common rule was developed from the cruder argument that the chances are $1/2$ that the option will be worth exercising and that you will collect that dollar above the exercise price.

Note that the Bachelier model has only one parameter in it to be estimated, namely σ. When that is known, all kinds of random variables that depend on x—such as $W(x; T,a)$, such as the probability of making a positive profit on a warrant—take on a determinable probability distribution whose parameters can be compared with observed statistics of performance. Bachelier makes several such tests, with results he considers highly satisfactory.

Moreover, here art has improved on nature. Many modern researchers on warrant pricing, such as Shelton [105] and Kassouf [45, 46], have come out with regressions that sometimes deny the significance of a stock's volatility. This result I consider incredible—imagine paying as much for a warrant on sluggish A.T.&T as on jumpy Ling-Temco, price and durations being similar. Bachelier's formulas show that volatility is the name of the game. Indeed, if stock A has twice the σ volatility of stock B, then as much will happen to A in one year as to B in 4 years and A's 1-year warrant will have the same value as B's 4-year warrant. Specifically, for F Gaussian with zero mean, we can write

$$W(x; T, a, \sigma) \equiv aW(x/a, \sigma^2 T, 1, 1) \qquad (4.9)$$

where

$$W(x; \tau, 1, 1) = \frac{1}{\sqrt{2\pi\tau}} \int_1^\infty (u-1) \exp\left\{-\frac{1}{2}(u-x)^2/\tau\right\} du \qquad (4.10)$$

a definite integral easy to tabulate.

5. Absurdity of unlimited liability. Seminal as the Bachelier model is, it leads to ridiculous results. Thus, as the running period of a warrant increases, its value grows indefinitely, exceeding any bound (including all the money that there is in the universe)! A perpetual warrant, of which Tricontinental or Alleghany are only two out of numerous examples, should sell for an *infinite* price; but why would anyone in his right mind ever pay more than the value of the common stock itself for a perpetual call on it—since owning it is such a perpetual call, and at zero price?

I have skipped the details of how Bachelier allows for accruing interest (or dividends) since it is the discussion of these tedious details at the very beginning of his book that has served to lose him many readers. It suffices to say that the absurdities of the model do not trace to this feature of the problem.

Before I had become aware of Bachelier's work, my own experiments with random walks and those of Richard Kruizenga [51, 52], who was writing his put-and-call thesis[4] under my direction, had shown the untenability of an absolute random-walk model except as a short-run approximation. An ordinary random walk of price, even if it is unbiased, will result in price becoming negative with a probability that goes to 1/2 as $T \to \infty$. This contradicts the limited liability feature of modern stocks and bonds. The General Motors stock I buy for $100 today can at most drop in value to zero, at which point I tear up my certificate and never look back.

The absurdities to which the negative prices of the absolute random walk leads[5] are a result of its supposition that independent absolute increments,

$$(X_{t+1} - X_t) + (X_{t+2} - X_{t+1}) + \ldots\ldots$$

can lead to $X_T - X_0$ losses indefinitely greater than the original X_0 principal. Since the warrant buyer avoids these alleged indefinite losses, if he is to experience a fair game he must pay an indefinitely high price for the warrant.

There is a hidden subtlety that must be unearthed here. Bachelier, a European, always has in mind what I have called in [90] a "European" rather than an "American n" warrant. In America a warrant with T time to run can be exercised at any time in the interval from now to then, i.e., at an t' in the interval

$$t_0 \leq t' \leq t_0 + t$$

Moreover, the American warrant holder has paid for it in advance and can throw the warrant away whenever he wishes to. By contrast, a European warrant is exercisable only at the end of the period, at $t_0 + T$, and final settlement involving the premium originally agreed upon for the warrant must be made then. The warrant holder cannot simply walk away from his obligation in the interim.

Now it is a theorem that the European warrant and the American warrant have the same value, and that an American warrant will *never* rationally be exercised prior to its termination date—*provided* the common stock and the warrant are postulated to earn the same mean percentage return per unit of time (in Bachelier's fair-game case, a common zero expected return) with all accruing dividends or interest being ignorable. See Samuelson and Merton [95] and Appendix footnote A4.

Let us now "Europeanize," so to speak, the holding of the common stock and suppose that at the end of some stipulated time period T, say at the time when it is known that I will die, I must settle my stock holding, receiving positive dollars if $X_T > 0$ and having to pay negative dollars if $X_T < 0$. I am not sure that I, as a prudent concave-utility maximizer, would ever dare hold a common stock that involves such *unlimited* European liability. Certainly I would not hold it in preference to cash at Bachelier's postulated zero mean return!

To summarize: the absolute-Brownian motion or absolute random walk model must be abandoned as absurd. My own solution was to fasten upon Gertrude Stein's Lemma: "A dollar is a dollar is a dollar." This leads naturally to the geometric-Brownian motion of the next section.

6. The economic geometric Brownian motion. The simplest hypothesis to circumvent difficulties is the postulate that every dollar's worth of a common stock's value is subject to the same probability distribution. I.e.,

$$\text{Prob} \left\{ X_{t+T} \leq x_T \mid X_0 = x_0 \right\} = P \left[x_T / x_0 ; T \right] \quad (6.1)$$

with $x_T \geq 0$.

Since

$$x_{T_1+T_2}/x_0 = (x_{T_1+T_2}/x_{T_1})(x_{T_1}/x_0)$$

we can write

$$P(x_{T_1+T_2}/x_0; T_1 + T_2) = \int_0^\infty P(x_{T_1+T_2}/x_{T_1}; T_2) P[d(x_{T_1}/x_0); T_1] \quad (6.2)$$

where x_0 is a given constant.

Warning: This explicitly assumes "independence" of the various ratios ($X_{T_1+T_2}/X_{T_1}, X_{T_1}/X_0$). In terms of more general conditional probabilities, one would have to write

$$F(x_{T_1+T_2} \mid x_{T_1}, x_0) \not\equiv F(x_{T_1+T_2} \mid x_{T_1})$$

When writers speak of the "random walk theory of speculative prices," there are actually many ambiguous possibilities being implicitly contemplated. Sometimes price changes, or changes in such a function of prices as $\log X_t$, are assumed to be subject to probability distributions independent of all previous prices. But sometimes no more is meant than that the expected value of such a price change is uniformly zero (or some other prescribed drift parameter) regardless of past known prices. Almost every random-walk theorist assumes, at a minimum, the Markov property that conditional probabilities of future prices depend at most on present prices, in the sense that knowledge of X_{0-k} does not add anything about X_{0+T} once X_0 itself is specified. When this is denied, theoretical formulas of warrant prices $W(x; T)$ have to be written as $W(x,y; T)$, where y is some vector of past common-stock prices.

Equation (6.2) obviously is the multiplicative counterpart of (3.1)'s additive process. Were it not for the complication that there may be a positive probability of ruin, i.e., $P(0, T) > 0$, we could work with the logarithms

$$y_t = \log x_t, y_t - y_0 = \log(x_t/x_0) \quad (6.3)$$

and employ analogous integrals to those in the Bachelier absolute Brownian motion. At Bachelier's level of rigor, which ignores infinite-moments of Lévy-Pareto additive distributions and infinitely divisible distributions involving discrete probabilities of the Poisson type, we could state that the only solution to (6.2) for T_i non-negative real numbers would be the log-normal distribution

$$P(x; T) = L(x; \mu T, \sigma\sqrt{T}) \quad (6.4)$$

where

$$L(x; \mu T, \sigma\sqrt{T}) = N\left(\frac{\log x - \mu T}{\sigma\sqrt{T}}\right)$$

N being the normal distribution of (4.4), and where

$$\mu = E\left\{\log X_1/X_0\right\} = \int_0^\infty \log X \, L\,(dx;\,\mu,\,\sigma) \qquad (6.5)$$

$$= \frac{1}{\sqrt{2\pi}\sigma}\int_\infty^\infty y \exp\left[-\frac{1}{2}(y-\mu)^2/\sigma^2\right] dy$$

$$\sigma^2 = \mathrm{Var}\left\{\log X_1/X_0\right\} = \frac{1}{\sqrt{2\pi}\sigma}\int_0^\infty (y-\mu)^2 \exp\left[-\frac{1}{2}(y-\mu)^2/\sigma^2\right] dy$$

$$e^\alpha = \left\{E \ \ X_1/X_0\right\} = \int_0^\infty xL\,(dx;\,\mu,\sigma)$$

$$= \frac{1}{\sqrt{2\pi}\sigma}\int_0^\infty e^y \exp \ -\frac{1}{2}(y-\mu)^2/\sigma^2 \quad dy$$

$$= e^{\mu \ + \ \frac{1}{2}\sigma^2}$$

Even if (6.2) holds only for integral values of T and T_i, the central limit theorem will ensure in a large variety of cases—e.g., where specified moments are finite and $P\,(0;1) = 0$—that $P\,(x;\,T\,)$ is "approximated" by $L\,(x;\,\mu T,\,\sigma\sqrt{T}\,)$ as T becomes large. This means that certain normalized variates, such as

$$[\log\,(X_T/X_0) \ - \ TE\left\{\log\,(X_1/X_0)\right\}]\,[T^2\,\mathrm{Var}\left\{\log\,(X_1/X_0)\right\}]^{-\frac{1}{2}} \ (6.9)$$

have a distribution that is well approximated by $N\,[\,\cdot\,]$. This fact does not mean that necessarily we get a tolerable approximation of the following form

$$E\left\{X_T/X_0\right\}\,[\exp T(\mu + \frac{1}{2}\sigma^2)\,]^{-1} \ = \ 1 \ \text{ as } T \to \infty \quad (6.10)$$

as uncritical combination of (6.5) and (6.9) might suggest.

Actually, if $P(x;\,1)$ is not itself log normal, we shall have

$$E\left\{X_1/X_0\right\} \ = \ \exp\,(\mu + \frac{1}{2}\,\sigma^2 + b) \qquad (6.11)$$

where b is not zero save for singular coincidence. In that case the left-hand side of (6.10) becomes e^{bT} which departs ever farther from unity as $T \to \infty$! This will come as no real surpise to student of limits.

Having altered Bachelier's assumption of an absolute to a relative random walk, I might as well generalize his assumption that the random walk is an unbiased profitless-in-the-mean fair game.

Instead I assume that the mean or expected outcome grows like compound interest at the rate $\alpha \geqq 0$. I.e.,

$$E\left\{X_T/X_0\right\} \quad = \int_0^\infty xP\,(dx;\,T) \tag{6.12}$$

$$= e^{\alpha T} = \left\{\int_0^\infty xP(dx;\,1)\right\}^T$$

Bachelier's special case is that where $\alpha = 0$.

The value of a warrant can be directly calculated by quadrature if we stipulate that holding it is also to produce a mean return per unit time, β, and with β to be exactly equal to a.

As shown in Samuelson [90], the rational price of a warrant, as a function of present stock price, x, time to run, T, and exericse price, a, becomes with $a = \beta$ and the log-normal distribution

$$W(X,T;\sigma^2,a,\alpha) = e^{-\alpha T}\int_0^\infty \text{Max}\,(0,xZ-a)L\,(dZ;T\mu,T\sigma^2) \tag{6.13}$$

$$= e^{-\alpha T}\int_{-\infty}^\infty \text{Max}\,(0,xe^Y-a)\frac{1}{\sqrt{2\pi}\sigma\sqrt{T}}$$

$$\exp\left[-\frac{1}{2}(Y-T\mu)^2/\sigma^2 T\right]dY$$

$$= xN\,[v] - ae^{-\alpha T}N\,[v-\sigma\sqrt{t}]\,,v = [\log\,(x/a)$$

$$+(\alpha+\frac{1}{2}\sigma^2)T]/\sigma\sqrt{T}$$

By substitution it is easy to show that this can be reduced to

$$W(x,T;\sigma^2,a,\alpha) \equiv ae^{-\alpha T}W(xe^{\alpha T},T\sigma^2;1,1,0) \tag{6.14}$$

where

$$W(Z,t) = W(Z,t;1,1,0) \tag{6.15}$$

$$= \frac{1}{\sqrt{2\pi t}}\int_{-\log Z}^\infty (Ze^Y-1)$$

$$\exp\left[-\frac{1}{2}(Y+\frac{1}{2}t)^2/t\right]dY$$

$$= ZN \left[(\log Z + \tfrac{1}{2}t)/\sqrt{t} \right] - N \left[(\log Z - \tfrac{1}{2}t)/\sqrt{t} \right]$$

can be tabulated once and for all for a convenient range of t values.

My version of the geometric Brownian motion based on the log normal rather than normal distribution does remove Bachelier's objectionable feature of having the warrant price grow indefinitely with T, since for my case

$$\lim_{T \to \infty} W(x, T; \sigma^2, a, \alpha) \equiv x \qquad (6.16)$$

But we still retain the advantage of Bachelier's behavior for short T, since

$$W(x, T; \sigma^2, a, \alpha) \sim \kappa \sigma \sqrt{T} \qquad (6.17)$$

for T sufficiently small, just as in (4.7).

The notion of skewness of price ratios is an old one in economics. A century ago when Jevons computed his first index numbers, the geometric rather than arithmetic mean suggested itself. Wesley Mitchell's extensive report on World War I price changes confirmed this asymmetry for all but the shortest-run price variations. The log-normal distribution, dependent on a law of "proportional effect," was popularly referred to in the economics literature of 30 years ago as Gibrat's Law, after the French engineer and econometrician Gibrat [34]. See Aitchison and Brown [1] for its properties.

Independently of my replacement of the absolute or arithmetic Brownian motion by the relative or geometric Brownian motion, the astronomer Osborne [76] noted the empirical tendency for (i) a cross-section of common stock prices to be approximately distributed by the log normal distribution, and (ii) for an even better approximation by that distribution to an array of price ratios of different stocks. Other investigators have found similar approximations to the price ratios of single stocks. To rationalize these empirical facts, Osborne made frequent reference to the Weber-Fechner law in psychology. The validity of that law in the field of psychology itself has perhaps been overrated: in any case I would regard Weber-Fechner analogies more as scientific metaphors for the prosaic fact of proportional effects than as independent rationalization. Where the poetry may have gotten in the way of the prose is in connection with Osborne's hypothesis [76, p. 108] that $E \left\{ \log(X_{t+1}/ X_t) \right\} = 0$, a logical deduction that I cannot follow and which is at some variance with his assumption two pages earlier that men act to maximize the first moment of money itself rather than of a strongly-concave function of money. Moore [75] gives a modified paraphrase of Osborne's argument, which depends upon the doubtful postulate that men generally have Bernoulli logarithmic utility, $U(W) \equiv \log W$, in which case an either/or choice of all cash or one stock would become a matter of indifference on Osborne's postulate. Actually if log (X_{t+1}/X_t) has a zero first moment for each stock, a combination of two stocks can be expected to have a positive first moment. Why neglect the opportunity of people to trade in paired units? I am afraid that the Weber-Fechner arguments lack economic cogency.

As will be seen in Section 9's discussion of possible martingale properties of prices, one cannot in economics insist upon necessary absence of price bias. (Osborne, in his taking note of inflation as a separate reason for price change, must ask himself whether in Germany's 1920-23 hyperflation, when interest rates were millions of percent per month, $\log \left\{ P_{t+1}/P_t \right\}$ was *ex`ante* or *ex post* a martingale? Let me add that the array of prices in Wall Street today depends upon how corporations choose to split their stock and pay stock dividends: if price-ratios, X_{t+1}/X_t, were otherwise log normal and all firms split every stock 4-to-1 when they reach 100 in price, the resulting distribution will be skew, but not log normal.)

My own preoccupation with price ratios rather than price differences came from the fact that, in an ideally competitive market, each small investor can, except for brokerage charges, do the same with one dollar as with a million. The homogeneity-of-degree-one property of investment opportunity, plus the simplification of stationarity of opportunity whether a stock is quoted in units of $20 or of $40, suggested the identity

$$P(X_T, X_0; T) \equiv P(X_T/X_0; T)$$

from which log-normality emerges as an asymptotic or instantaneous result.

Let me say a word about Lévy-Pareto alternatives to Gaussian distributions for X_t or X_{t+1}/X_t. Mandelbrot [61-64] and Fama [25-31] have found some evidence that Lévy-Pareto distributions with fat-tail parameters $a \cong 1.9 < 2$ of the Gaussian cases. All investigators have noted that there tend to be many more outliers than in the log-normal or other Gaussian approximations. On the other hand, as later sections will suggest, I am inclined to believe in Merton's conjecture that a strict Lévy-Pareto distribution on $\log(X_{t+1}/X_t)$ would lead, with $1 < a < 2$, to a 5-minute warrant or call being worth 100 percent of the common! Evidently the all-wise market does not act as if it believes literally in Lévy-Pareto distributions, even though it may sense that there is some validity to the alternative notions of "subordinated processes" discussed by Clark [14], Press [80], and Feller's classic text, and which also lead to fat tails with abnormally-many outliers.

7. General case where warrant and stock expected yields differ. The above analysis, which agrees with results of Sprenkle [106] and other writers, assumed the special case of $\beta = a$, for which one can easily prove that conversion will never take place prior to expiration of a warrant, so that there is no advantage over a European warrant (that must be exercised only at the end of the T period) for an American warrant with its privilege of exercise at any time at the option of the holder.

Since warrants may be more volatile in price than stocks, concave utility maximizers might require that they have $\beta > a$. Certainly in real life perpetual warrants do not sell for as much as the common stock itself, as (6.16) of the $\beta = a$ theory requires. In any case, if the common is paying out a dividend at an instaneous percentage rate of its market value of $\delta > 0$, at the least we should expect

$$\beta = \alpha + \delta > \alpha \geqq 0 \tag{7.1}$$

Hence, in my 1965 paper [90], I tackled the tougher mathematical problem of $\beta > a$, for which conversion of a warrant with T periods to run becomes mandatory when

$$X_t/a > c(t; \beta, \alpha, \sigma^2) \;,\; \lim_{t \to \infty} c(t; \beta, \alpha, \sigma^2) = c(\beta, \alpha, \sigma^2) < \infty \tag{7.2}$$

Some very hard boundary problems to the partial-differential heat equations arise, as the reader can verify by referring to the mathematical appendix to [90] that H.P. McKean, Jr., generously provided in [68]. Exact solutions for the W function are known only for the perpetual log-normal and Poisson cases, and for warrants of all time periods in the rather special case where

$$\text{Prob} \left\{ X_t/X_0 = e^{gT} \right\} = e^{-bT} \tag{7.3}$$

$$\text{Prob} \left\{ X_T/X_0 = 0 \right\} = 1 - e^{-bT}$$

However, Robert Merton and I have made good computer approximations to the general solution and hope some day to publish abbreviated tables.

Dividends aside, the need for the difficult $\beta > a$ case has been lessened by the alternative theory of warrant pricing that Merton and I worked out in [95], based upon utility maximization.

More important, a fundamental paper by Black and Scholes [8] restores the $\beta = a$ case's mathematics to primacy. My 1965 paper had noted that the possibility of hedging, by buying the warrant and selling the common stock short, should give you low variance and high mean return in the $\beta > a$ case. Hence, for dividendless stocks, I argued that the $\beta - a$ divergence is unlikely to be great. I should have explored this further! Black and Scholes show that, if the

posited probabilities hold, transaction costs aside, in a world where all can
borrow and lend at a riskless interest rate r, by instantaneously changing hedging
proportions in an optimal way, one could make an infinite arbitrage profit over
the period to expiration unless warrants get priced according to the (6.13) $\beta \equiv a$
formula

$$W(x,T;\sigma^2,a,r) = xN\left(\frac{\log{(\frac{x}{a})} + (r + \frac{1}{2}\sigma^2)T}{\sigma\sqrt{T}}\right) - ae^{-rt}N\left(\frac{\log{(\frac{x}{a})} + (r - \frac{1}{2}\sigma^2)T}{\sigma\sqrt{T}}\right)$$

This is indeed a valuable breakthrough for science.[6]

Since my audience includes mathematicians, I have asked Robert Merton to
sketch in the Appendix the continuous-time Brownian-motion aspects of the
warrant problem. Merton deduces the Black-Scholes solution in elegant form.

8. Speculative price a "fair game"? Why should the spot price of wheat in
Chicago have a zero mean change? At harvest time, price should be low; to
motivate people to store it through the months after harvest and before the next
harvest, its spot price ought to rise systematically—and it does! With price
indexes showing inflation predominantly throughout this century, indeed
throughout the history of capitalism and for that matter the preceding centuries
of recorded history, is there any jury which believes or will act upon the belief
that the observations of spot-wheat price changes to come over the eons of time
ahead always have a first moment of zero?

If Kendall's serial correlations in [48] do not pick up any systematic
movements in spot prices, so much the worse for the power of such short-run
statistical methods. Had Kendall's observations been on "wheat futures" (i.e.,
the price changes of a contract to deliver spot wheat at some one specified
future date) rather than on spot or actual physical wheat at *different* dates, that
would have been quite a different matter, as I shall show. Then there are some
new and different reasons to expect an approach to fair-game or martingale
properties. Aside from experience with spot prices, think of their theoretical
causation. Wheat price will depend on, inter alia, the weather and the business
cycle. Causes of changes in the weather are numerous but they are surely not
independent through time. Persistence patterns of positive autocorrelation are
commonplace. Business cycle components, such as GNP or price levels, are not
themselves serially-independent series—far from it—even if some of the exogenous shocks that the endogenous system cumulates may approximate to such
patterns of independence.

Everything that I have said of a price like that of spot wheat can be equally
said of the quantity of wheat produced, consumed, sold, or stored. If these
magnitudes are random variables, there is no reason why at every time scale they
should follow probability distributions that lack dependence through time.

However, returning to price—particularly to the speculative price of a common stock or a commodity future, quoted in competitive markets in which there are many buyers and sellers, each free to buy and sell at posted prices without having to worry that his actions will greatly alter quoted prices—we find repeatedly in the literature a special reason why expected price change should be zero or small. The argument goes as follows.

Argument. Expected future price must be closely equal to present price, or else present price will be different from what it is. If there were a bargain, which all could recognize, that fact would be "discounted" in advance and acted upon, thereby raising or lowering present price until the expected discrepancy with the future price were sensibly zero. It is true that people in the marketplace differ in their guesses about the future: and that is a principal reason why there are transactions in which one man is buying and another is selling. But at all times there is said to be as many bulls as there are bears, and in some versions there is held to be a wisdom in the resultant of the mob that transcends any of its members and perhaps transcends that of any outside jury of scientific observers. The opinions of those who make up the whole market are not given equal weights: those who are richer, more confident, perhaps more volatile, command greater voting power; but since better-informed, more-perceptive speculators tend to be more successful, and since the unsuccessful tend both to lose their wealth and voting potential and also to lose their interest and participation, the verdict of the marketplace as recorded in the record of auction prices is alleged to be as accurate *ex ante* and *ex post* as one can hope for and may perhaps be regarded as more accurate and trustworthy than would be the opinions formed by governmental planning agencies.

The above long paragraph is purposely made to be vague, in faithful reproduction of similar ideas to be found repeatedly in the literature of economics and of practical finance. For sample passages dealing with the notion that competitive anticipations must, or often do, make price changes a fair game, the reader may dip into the Cootner symposium [16], where views of such diverse writers as H. Working, Taussig, Cootner, A.B. Moore are to be found. More recently, Samuelson [90], Mandelbrot [62, 64], Fama [31], and many others have grappled with this same notion of "efficient markets." This Fama reference gives a valuable survey.

The discussion has come full circle. The economists who served as discussants for Kendall's 1953 paper [48] were outraged, as he expected them to be, at the notion that there is no economic law governing the wanderings of price, but rather only blind chance. Such nihilism seemed to strike at the very heart of economic science. But more recently there have been plenty of economists to aver that, when speculation is working out its ideal purpose, the result must be to confront any observer with a price-change pattern that represents "pure white noise."

Sometimes competitive-discounting-leading-to-fair-game-price-changes is deemed to be practically a tautology, based upon definitions of competition. Actually, I would argue, the purported assertion is empirically untrue. Yet what we have here is a suggestive, heuristic principle. Most passages dealing with this problem, you will find when you put magnifying glasses on them, are quite unclear as to what theorems are being stated and what modes of proof or validation are being proposed.

Recall that spot wheat price series. Better still, concentrate on non-storable fish or sweet corn. Suppose everyone knew that next year fish will be more plentiful and its price lower. How could anyone arbitrage out that insight in order to bring fish price today, when the catch is small, into equality with next year's price? Or with the next decade's price? (My final section will discuss commodity models where spot prices are anything but martingales.) Similarly any economist who stops to think about the matter will realize that there is nothing anomalous about a low-coupon bond, say one now paying 3 percent a year, being confidently expected to rise in every period from now until its maturity date if during that period the market rates of interest are expected to stay far above the bond's coupon rate. Not only can such a discount bond have a positive first moment of price change: arbitrage equilibrium requires its price to rise. So it may be with common stocks. If inflation raises index numbers of goods' prices by 10 percent per year and can be expected to do so, no doubt the safe interest rate will have the expected 10 percent built into it; and anyone who expects a common stock to form an unbiased random walk, lest he be able to arbitrage out the expected price rise, would be crazy in view of the fact that the interest cost or "opportunity cost" of buying stocks now for resale later will no doubt involve interest rates and needed stock-price appreciation rates of at least 10 percent to make the venture worth while.

And which is zero, absolute price change, or logarithmic price change? Why not the change in $f(X_t)$, where $y = f(x)$ is a monotone two-way mapping of x and y? Most writers do not even think to ask these questions, being content with the primitive notion that if you can buy a thing at one price and know with certainty you can sell it at a higher price, then there is a patent contradiction. This kind of classical sure-thing arbitrage is portrayed by the following infinite-value linear programming problem:

You can exchange gold at the U.S. mint for silver in a 17-1 ratio; with the silver achieved, you can go to the Asian mint and get gold at a 1-16 ratio; thus your terminal gold can become an infinite amount X_1, namely the solution to the trivial problem

$$\text{Max}\,(17 - 16)\,X_1 \ \text{s.t.}\ X_1 \geqq 0 \tag{8.1}$$

Commodity and stock markets offer no such easy arbitrage to the speculator, save in singular cases not germane to the present discussion.

Mandelbrot, one of the few authors who attempts a serious discussion of advanced discounting, in [64] couples with an arbitrary time series $P_0(t)$, a new arbitraged time series $P(t)$, where

$$E\left\{P(t + T) - P(t)\right\} \equiv 0 \qquad (8.2)$$

and where $P(t)$ is "constrained *not* to drift from $P_0(t)$ without bound." Actually, he concentrates mostly on cases where $P_0(t) - P_0(t - 1) = \Delta P_0(t)$ is itself generated as a linear function of a series of past random variables ("innovations") which are of finite variance and serially uncorrelated:

$$\Delta P_0(t) = \sum_{-\infty}^{t} L(s)N(t - s) \qquad (8.3)$$

When the $L(s)$ coefficients are suitably convergent and the underlying probability distributions are subject to suitable restrictions, the new arbitraged $P(t)$ sequence can be defined so that $\Delta P(t)$ is proportional to $N(t)$, or what is the same thing to a calculable linear sum of present and past $[P_0(t)]$ values, the coefficients to be selected so as to minimize the mean least-squares drift of $P(t) - P_0(t)$.

I have not done justice to Mandelbrot's discussion, nor of his extension to imperfect arbitraging, both because of space limitation and the imperfection of my understanding of how his mathematics relates to economic models. So let me in the final section give an economist's version of what can be expected to be arbitrageable in an idealized commodity market. In concluding this section, I shall sketch briefly my own deductive derivation of the martingale property of competitively–anticipated prices. This is the only unambiguous statement known to me of what seems to be the root notion in the long passage labeled Argument.

Let a spot price, say of wheat, be designated as $P_0(t)$ and let it be subject to any known stochastic process, which need not even be a stationary one. Examples are the following:

$$P_0(t + 1) = .5P_0(t) + u_{t+1} \quad , \quad u_t \text{ an independent} \qquad (8.4)$$
$$\text{random variable}$$

$$\text{Prob}\left\{P_0(t + 1) = j \mid P_0(t) = i\right\} = a_{ij} \qquad (8.5)$$

where $[a_{ij}]$ is a Markov transitional probability matrix with non-negative coefficients and row sums that add up to unity.

In the first of these cases

$$Y_T = E\left\{P_0(t + 1 + T - 1) \mid P_0(t)\right\} \qquad (8.6)$$

$$= (.5)^T P_0(t) + E\left\{\sum_0^{T-1} (.5)^t u_t\right\}$$

$$= (.5)^T P_0(t)$$

if the expected values of the error terms are always zero. At the end of one period, we shall have

$$Y_{T-1} = E\left\{P_0(t + 1 + T - 1) \mid P_0(t + 1)\right\} \qquad (8.7)$$

$$= (.5)^{T-1} P_0(t + 1)$$

$$= (.5)^{T-1}(.5)P(t) + (.5)^{T-1} u_1$$

$$E\left\{Y_{T-1} - Y_T\right\} = (.5)^{T-1} Eu_1 = 0 \qquad (8.7)$$

Similarly

$$E\left\{Y_{t-1} - Y_t\right\} = 0 \ , \ (t = T, \ldots, 1) \qquad (8.8)$$

making the sequence $[Y_t, Y_{T-1}, \ldots, Y_0 = P_0(t + T)]$ a martingale. Note that the Y's are a new time series, $P(t)$, distinct from $P_0(t)$ but related to it.

In the second example

$$Y_T = E\left\{P_0(t + T) \mid P_0(t) = i\right\} = \sum_1^n a_{ij} T_j \qquad (8.9)$$

where

$$a^T = a.a^{T-1} = [a_{ij}{}^T] \qquad T = 1, 2, \ldots$$

Note that Y_T is a random variable taking on different values for each ($i = 1, \ldots, n$).

Also

$$Y_{T-1} = E\left\{P_0(t + 1 + T - 1) \mid P_0(1) = i\right\}$$

$$= \sum_1^n a_{ij}{}^{T-1}{}_j$$

$$E\left\{Y_{T-1} - Y_T \mid P_0(t) = i\right\} = \sum_{k=1}^{n} a_{ik} \sum_{j=1}^{n} T^{-1}j - \sum_{1}^{T} a_{ij}j \qquad (8.10)$$

$$= \sum_{j=1}^{n} (a_{ij}^{T} - a_{ij}^{T})j$$

$$\equiv 0$$

Again the market price quoted for the future contract payable at fixed time T from now will oscillate through the sequence $[Y_0, Y_1, \ldots, Y_T = P_0(t+T)]$ but as a martingale

$$E\left\{Y_{t-k} - Y_t\right\} = 0 \qquad (8.11)$$

This is evidently a general principal, as embodied in the following theorem.

Theorem on driftless anticipative speculative price. Let

$$\mathrm{Prob}\left\{P_0(t+T) \leqq x_T \mid P_0(t) = x_0, P_0(t-1) = x_{-1}, \ldots\right\}$$

$$= F_T\left[x_T; x_0, x_{-1}, \ldots\right]$$

$$Y_T \stackrel{\mathrm{def}}{=} E\left\{P_0(t+T) \mid x_t, x_{t-1}, \ldots\right\} \qquad (8.12)$$

$$\cdot \quad \cdot \quad \cdot \quad \cdot \quad \cdot \quad \cdot \quad \cdot \quad \cdot \quad \cdot$$

$$Y_{T-k} \stackrel{\mathrm{def}}{=} E\left\{P_0(\{t+k\} + \{T-k\}) \mid x_{t+k}, x_{t+k-1}, \ldots\right\}$$

Then

$$E\left\{Y_{T-1} - Y_T \mid x_t, x_{t-1}, \ldots\right\} \equiv 0 \qquad (8.13)$$

By induction

$$E\left\{Y_k - Y_j\right\} = 0, \quad (k, j = 0, 1, \ldots, T) \qquad (8.14)$$

The proof is immediate from repeated use of the identity

$$F_T\left[x_T; x_0, x_{-1}, \ldots\right] = \int_0^\infty F_{T-1}\left[x_T; x_1, x_0, \ldots\right]$$

$$F_1\left[dx_1; x_0, x_{-1}, \ldots\right] \qquad (8.15)$$

as in Samuelson [89], where it is shown that $P_0(t)$ and x_t can be given a vector interpretation so that price changes of wheat may depend on price data for corn and on weather elements of the vector.

The strict martingale property is more than one can expect to occur economically when there is a cost (interest, psychic disutility of bearing risk, etc.) to maintaining a position. In that case, rather than equalling the $[Y_{T-i}]$ sequence, the futures price, $P(t)$, may instead be related to a transformed variable $[Z_{T-i}]$, where

$$Z_0 \quad = \quad Y_0 \tag{8.16}$$

$$Z_1 \quad = \quad \lambda_1^{-1} Y_1$$

$$Z_2 \quad = \quad \lambda_1^{-1} \lambda_2^{-1} Y_2$$

$$\cdot \quad \cdot \quad \cdot \quad \cdot \quad \cdot \quad \cdot \quad \cdot$$

$$Z_T \quad = \quad \lambda_1^{-1} \ldots \lambda_T^{-1} Y_T$$

These present-discounted-values have the quasi-martingale property, for Z_t known

$$E\{Z_{t-1} \mid Z_t\} \quad = \quad \lambda_t E\{Y_{t-1} \mid Y_t\} \tag{8.17}$$

$$= \quad \lambda_t$$

Here $\lambda_t = 1 + \rho_t$ is kind of an interest premium that the risky futures price must yield to get it held. (Remark: unless something useful can be said in advance about the $[\lambda_{T-i}]$ —as for example $\lambda_t - 1$ small; or λ_t a diminishing sequence in function of the diminishing variance to be expected of a futures contract as its horizon shrinks, subject perhaps to a terminal jump in λ_1 as closing-date becomes crucial—the whole exercise becomes an empty tautology.)

I leave this subject of perfect discounting of price changes by "perfect speculation" with some needed remarks about the benefits and losses from speculation. Populist electorates often regard speculation as sharp-dealing at worst, as gambling at best. Apologists for bourses and for *laissez faire* by contrast regard the speculator as a noble and nimble operator who takes on his shoulders the irreducible risks of society for zero or little risk-premium: successful speculation, and the apologists think this to be dominant in the long run, enriches the speculator only by virtue of the fact that it enriches society even more.

Briefly, let me state what correct analysis suggests.

1. To the degree that speculation brings about an equilibrium pattern of intertemporal prices, society benefits in the Pareto-optimality sense: in the absence of equilibrium, there exists in principle a movement that could simultaneously make everybody better off. See, for example, a textbook discussion like that in Appendix Chapter 21 of Samuelson [82], or see Samuelson [87, 99].
2. There is some empirical evidence, as already mentioned in connection with Working and others, that some organized commodity markets approximate to equilibrium intertemporal price patterns.
3. The conclusion does not follow that the speculator necessarily "deserves" his gains. As demonstrated in Samuelson [87, p. 209], a man who is quicker in his response reflexes to new information by only epsilon microseconds might capture 100 percent of the transfer rents created by the new data. He would become rich as Croesus but, in this strong case will have conferred only an epsilon degree of benefit to society—say a nickel's worth.
4. Some speculators can be destabilizing; and, where imperfections of competition prevail or where self-fulfilling processes are possible (as in the case of exchange rate speculation that depreciates a currency and induces the increase in central-bank money supply that "justifies" the depreciation), these destabilizing speculations can be profitable. Also, existence of speculative markets can serve as an attractive nuisance to cause those who are over-optimistic to incur losses, to incur deadweight brokerage charges, and to hurt themselves and their families.
5. Finally, as in Samuelson [101], it can be proved that, under specifiable general conditions, the unsuccessful speculator, in hurting himself, does add benefit to the rest of the community—but in amount less than the hurt to himself. This sounds as if the utilities of incommensurable minds are being compared. But, actually all that is being asserted is that unsuccessful speculation destroys Pareto-optimality: if it could be reversed, everyone could be made potentially better off. (Indeed, in the commodity model of my last section, mistaken carryover of grain by half the identical population, under the mistaken belief that next year's crop will be definitely short, will do first-order harm to the speculators and confer infinitesimal benefit—i.e., benefit of a second-order of smallness—on the rest of the community.)

A fair conclusion is that *a priori* dogmatism in this matter is unwarranted. Pragmatic evaluation of the costs and benefits of empirical speculation institutions and their alternatives is needed for eclectic decision and opinion making.

We have seen that much of the vague discussion about "random walks" of stock or commodity prices does not distinguish closely between processes involving independent increments of price changes or price ratios and unbiassed martingales. In the language of autocorrelation, an independent-increment process will involve zero serial correlation of lagged price ratios or differences. For this there is some evidence. Against this, some evidence has been marshalled. One attempt, that partially misfires, is that by Shelton [104]. He points out that the universe of entrants to this Value Line contest, in which each entrant selects a portfolio of 25 stocks out of a much longer list, end up with a subsequent distribution of portfolio gains that has a mean greater than the mean of a portfolio made up of the larger universe of eligible stocks. The difference in means could not remotely arise by pure chance. I do not regard this as a cogent refutation of the hypothesis that each and every stock is subject to an independent increment random process. Shelton's findings are consistent with the alternative hypothesis: Volatile, high-variance stocks require a higher mean gain than the rest; people who enter contests correctly go for volatility in terms of that game's payoff function; this explains why Shelton's observations have such high variance, and could explain their superior mean performance.

In very short periods, there is weightier evidence in favor of some negative serial correlation. Thus, if by chance, more people want to sell GM today than buy it, the specialist in GM will oblige them, but at lower and lower prices. Tomorrow, when by chance, more people want to buy than sell, the specialist will oblige them on an up scale, perhaps returning to his same normal inventory, but having made an adequate profit by virtue of having bought cheaper than he sold.

Mathematically, this kind of negative serial correlation would occur in the first differences of prices (or, better, their logarithms) as a result of an assumption that the levels of prices are subject to a uniformly and independently distributed probability. Thus, replace

$$\text{Prob} \left\{ X_{t+1} - X_t \leqq \Delta x_t \mid x_{t-1} \right\} = F(\Delta x_t) \qquad (8.18)$$

by

$$\text{Prob} \left\{ X_{t+1} \leqq x_t \mid x_{t-1} \right\} = G(x_t) \qquad (8.19)$$

Then Prob $X_{t+1} - X_t \overset{<}{=} \Delta x_t \mid \Delta x_{t-1}$ will increase as Δx_{t-1} grows, in the same way that my electric bill tends to be lower in a month after it has been high when random errors in meter reading are involved.

This negative serial correlation is presumably weak and confined to short periods. It presumably gives the specialist, scalper, or floor-trader his raison d'être. This simplest model of this process I can describe as follows.

Suppose that the net algebraic amount that people want to sell of a stock in any period, X, is a random variable with a systematic part that is a weakly increasing function of its price above some perceived normal level, e.g., is proportional to $P_t - P^* = p_t$, plus a purely random-noise component with zero mean, fixed variance, and zero serial autocorrelation. Suppose that the specialist lowers (or raises) his price in proportion to algebraic net sales X_t. Then our stochastic equation becomes

$$p_t - p_{t-1} = -aX_t = -abp_t - au_t \qquad a > 0, b > 0 \qquad (8.20)$$

$$p_t = cp_{t-1} + v_t, \ 0 < c = (1 + ab)^{-1} < 1, \ v_t = -a(1 + ab)^{-1}u_t$$

Price will then perform a Brownian-like vibration around the normal level P^*, and there will be an ergodic probability

$$\text{Prob} \left\{ P_{t+T} \leqq y \mid P_t \right\} = Q_T(y;P_t) \qquad (8.21)$$

$$\lim_{T \to \infty} Q_T(y;P_t) = Q(y), \ \text{independently of } P_t$$

The specialist stands to make a mean profit per unit time, subject to finite variance, and proportional to $a\sigma_X^2$. What determines a is not clear: perhaps the specialist stands to lose his monopoly position if he makes a too large.

The above presupposes that the specialist is not unpleasantly surprised by an unperceived permanent change in the P^* level. Thus, if P^* rises permanently for some fundamental reason and the specialist does not recognize that this is going on, he will be selling out his normal inventory at too-low prices and be able to replenish it only at a loss. There seems to be a basic conflict of interest: the specialist is a small and steady winner from purely random fluctuations, but stands to be a big loser if he bucks unforeseen fundamental trends. (I am indebted to an unpublished Bell Laboratory memorandum of February 1971 on related matters by Kreps, Lebowitz and Linhart [50].)

9. Portfolio optimization. The 1965 theory of economic Brownian motion sketched in the last section might explain how, if we had futures markets for stocks, the *futures* price quoted October 11, 1971, for General Motors common to be delivered on October 11, 1972, might fluctuate like a quasi-martingale for the 12 months between now and then. In the notation of the last section, we would be talking about a $P(t)$ or (Y_{T-k}) of GM futures price and not a $P_0(t)$ or X_t of GM common stock. None of the last section's content touches the question of the probability laws that the common stock might *itself* be expected to satisfy. In the present section I cannot hope to outline a complete general equilibrium theory of stock pricing, since that subject is still in its infancy. For a start on such a complete theory, see Lintner [59, 60], Sharpe [103], Fama [27], Hirshleifer [39], Merton [72], and Samuelson and Merton [95]. To salve my conscience, I do present in the final section one complete general equilibrium model of stochastic speculative price, namely one for a commodity market.

In the present section I shall merely sketch some typical models of portfolio decision making. I do this with the thought that such models provide some of the indispensible building blocks out of which a complete theory will have to be built.

First, it is common to assume that a decision maker facing stochastic uncertainty acts to maximize the expected value of the concave utility of his wealth (or of the outcomes he faces), namely

$$\overline{U} = \int_0^\infty U(W)dP(W) = E\left\{U(W)\right\} < U(E\left\{W\right\}) \quad (9.1)$$

where $U(\cdot)$ is a concave von Neumann utility function. (After all, von Neumann's work does apply!) The von Neumann and Morgenstern classic [113] revived interest in notions which have been endemic in economics since the eighteenth-century days of Daniel Bernoulli [7], Laplace, and Bentham, and many others. I have a slight preference for the axiomatic approach of Ramsey [81], Marschak [66, 67], and Savage [102], as I have discussed in [85]. A good general reference is Arrow[4].)

It was long known that in choosing between safe cash and a zero-mean asset with positive variance, all of one's wealth would be put into cash if $\overline{U}$ is to be maximized. Pioneering work by Domar and Musgrave [23], Markowitz [65], and Tobin [111,112], turned economists' attention to models involving two parameters: a mean of money gain and a measure of riskiness, or in the case of the last two, mean and variance

$$\mu = \int_0^\infty WdP(W) \quad (9.2)$$

$$\sigma^2 = \int_0^\infty (W - \mu)^2 \, dP(W)$$

$$\overline{U} \cong f(\mu, \sigma^2) \text{ with } \partial f/\partial W > \partial f/\partial \sigma^2$$

In Markowitz's valuable version, let a dollar invested in each of ($i = 1, 2, \ldots, n$) securities give rise respectively to the random variables ($Z_1, \ldots Z_n$) with joint probability distribution

$$\text{Prob } Z_1 \leqq z_1, \ldots, Z_n \leqq z_n = P(z_1, \ldots, z_n). \quad (9.3)$$

with probability density

$$p(z_1, \ldots, z_n)dz_1 \ldots dz_n = (\partial^n P/\partial z_1 \ldots \partial z_n)dz_1 \ldots dz_n \quad (9.4)$$

Then the terminal wealth W_1, will have the probability density

$$d(W_1 W_0^{-1}) f(W_1 W_0^{-1}; w_1, \ldots, w_n) \qquad (9.5)$$

$$= d(W_1 W_0^{-1}) \int_0^\infty \ldots \int_0^\infty w_1^{-1}$$

$$p(w_1^{-1} W_1 W_0^{-1} - w_1^{-1} \sum_2^n w_j z_j, z_2, \ldots, z_n) dz_2 \ldots dz_n$$

with mean and variance

$$E\left\{ W_1 W_0^{-1} \right\} = \mu(w_1, \ldots, w_n) = \sum_1^n w_j E\left\{ Z_j \right\} \quad (9.6)$$

$$V\left\{ W_1 W_0^{-1} \right\} = \sigma^2(w_1, \ldots, w_n) = \sum_1^n \sum_1^n w_i \sigma_{ij} w_j \qquad (9.7)$$

where

$$\sigma_{ij} = E\left\{ (Z_i - E\left\{ Z_i \right\})(Z_j - E\left\{ Z_j \right\}) \right\} \qquad (9.8)$$

If p were a joint normal distribution, the solution to the maximum expected utility problem would have to involve a (μ^*, σ^*) choice that represents a solution of the following quadratic programing problem

$$\operatorname*{Min}_{w_i} \sigma^2(w_1, \ldots, w_n) \text{ s.t. } \mu(w_1, \ldots, w_n) \geqq \mu^* \qquad (9.9)$$

This defines an "efficiency frontier" $\sigma^* = M(\mu^*)$, and depending upon one's degree of risk aversion one will pick the best of these frontier points, with its implied (w_i^*) strategy.[7]

It is absurd to expect p to be literally a joint normal distribution since that would violate the axiom of limited liability. An alternative defense of this Markowitz-Tobin procedure is possible in the case where $U(W)$ is quadratic. However, this assumption is known to lead to the odd result that, as I become wealthier, I become *more* rather than less risk averse. See Samuelson [91, 98], Borch [9], and Feldstein [32] for critiques of mean-variance analysis. The best defense of it, I think, is as a good approximation when the probability distributions are relatively "compact," as discussed in Samuelson [98]. For in such cases, the true solution (w_i^{**}) to the general problem

$$\operatorname*{Max}_{w_i} \overline{U}(w_1, \ldots, w_n) = \operatorname{Max} \int_0^\infty \ldots \int_0^\infty \qquad (9.10)$$

$$U(W_0 \sum_1^n w_j z_j) p(z_1, \ldots, z_n) dz_1 \ldots dz_n$$

$$= \overline{U}(w_1^{**}, \ldots, w_n^{**})$$

Many of the results that the mean-variance analysis can establish can be also established by rigorous analysis for any strictly-concave $U(W)$ with convergent first moment. Here are a few representative theorems.

THEOREM 1. As (i) between safe cash or holding a safe security with yield $1 + r$ and (ii) holding a risky security with positive variance, one will never hold the risky security if its mean return is not greater than $1 + r$. If its mean return, μ_i, is greater than $1 + r$, one must prefer to hold some of it, i.e., $w_i^{**} > 0$, to holding cash alone.

THEOREM 2. A risky security, with mean greater than that of a safe security and not less than that of any other security, and which is not perfectly correlated (in a non-linear or linear sense) with any other security, must be held in positive amount.

THEOREM 3. If a group of securities are independently distributed with a common mean greater than that of the safe security being held, all must be held in positive amount.

THEOREM 4. If security i has a greater mean that any other security, and it is independently distributed from all other securities, it must be held in positive amounts.

THEOREM 5. If all risky securities are subject to a probability distribution symmetric as between securities

$$P(z_1, z_2, z_3, \dots) \equiv P(z_2, z_1, z_3, \dots) \equiv P(z_3, z_2, z_1, \dots) \equiv \dots \quad (9.11)$$

they must be held in the same proportions, $w_i^* = 1/n$.

On the other hand, special $U(W)$ functions, which satisfy the condition

$$\frac{U'}{U''} = a + bW \quad (9.12)$$

are subject to some special decomposition theorems as discussed in Tobin [112] and Cass and Stiglitz [11]. Included are the important cases

$$U = \log W, \quad U = W^{\gamma}/\gamma, 0 \neq \gamma < 1 \quad (9.13)$$
$$U = -e^{-\gamma W}, \quad U = a^2 W - b^2 W^2$$

Often analysis is wanted for maximization of terminal wealth, W_T, after $T > 1$ periods of time, during which the probabilities repeat themselves independently. Thus, we are sequentially to pick vectors $[w_i(1)]$, $[w_i(2)]$, $\dots, [w_i(T)]$ to give the greatest $E\left\{U(W_T)\right\}$ where W_T is the random variable defined by

$$W_T = W_{T-1} \sum_1^n w_j(1) Z_j(T) \tag{9.14}$$

$$W_{T-1} = W_{T-2} \sum_1^n w_j(2) Z_j(T-1)$$

$$\cdot \quad \cdot \quad \cdot \quad \cdot \quad \cdot \quad \cdot \quad \cdot \quad \cdot \quad \cdot \quad \cdot \quad \cdot$$

$$W_1 = W_0 \sum_1^n w_j(T) Z_j(1)$$

where the vectors $[Z_i(t)]$ are for $t = 1, \ldots, T$ all independently distributed according to a common probability distribution, namely

$$P[z_1(1), \ldots, z_n(1)] \, P[z_1(2), \ldots, z_n(2)] \ldots P[z_1(T), \ldots, z_n(T)] \tag{9.15}$$

The exact solution is given by the Bellman-like dynamic programming sequence

$$\underset{w_i(1)}{\text{Max}} \int_0^\infty \ldots \int_0^\infty U(W_{T-1} \sum_1^n w_j(1) z_j) p(z_1, \ldots, z_n) dz_1 \ldots dz_n \tag{9.16}$$

$$= \int_0^\infty \ldots \int_0^\infty U(W_{T-1} \sum_1^n w_j^*(1) z_j) p(z_1, \ldots, z_n) dz_1 \ldots dz_n$$

$$= U_1(W_{T-1}) \text{ , a concave function}$$

$$\underset{w_i(2)}{\text{Max}} \int_0^\infty \ldots \int_0^\infty U_1(W_{T-2} \sum_1^n w_j(2) z_j) p(z_1, \ldots, z_n) dz_1 \ldots dz_n$$

$$= \int_0^\infty \ldots \int_0^\infty U_1(W_{T-2} \sum_1^n w_j^*(2) z_j) p(z_1, \ldots, z_n) dz_1 \ldots dz_n$$

$$= U_2(W_{T-2}) \text{ , a concave function}$$

$$\cdot \quad \cdot \quad \cdot \quad \cdot \quad \cdot \quad \cdot \quad \cdot \quad \cdot \quad \cdot \quad \cdot \quad \cdot \quad \cdot \quad \cdot \quad \cdot \quad \cdot \quad \cdot \quad \cdot$$

$$\underset{w_i(T)}{\text{Max}} \int_0^\infty \ldots \int_0^\infty U_{T-1}(W_0 \sum_1^n w_j(T) z_j) p(z_1, \ldots, z_n) dz_1 \ldots dz_n$$

$$= \int_0^\infty \cdots \int_0^\infty U_{T-1}(W_0 \sum_1^n w_j{}^*(T)z_j)p(z_1,\ldots,z_n)dz_1 \ldots dz_n$$

$$= U_T(W_0)$$

Note that this yields a best portfolio strategy at each instant of time in function of that period's initial wealth.[8]

$$w_i{}^*(T-t) = f_i(W_t; T-t) \quad (i = 1,\ldots,n) \tag{9.17}$$

May I call attention to the fact that, when all the probability distributions are symmetric in the various securities, the optimal portfolio shares will involve equal dollar investments in all securities.

THEOREM. The optimal T-period solution to (9.16), when $P(z_1, z_2, \ldots) \equiv P(z_2, z_1, \ldots) \equiv \ldots$, the symmetric case, involves

$$w_i{}^*(T-t) = (1/n)W_t \tag{9.18}$$

The proof is immediate. Concavity of U guarantees that any local extremum is a global maximum. By a legitimate use of the Principle of Sufficient Reason, a deductive symmetry argument, we know there is no reason to invest more in one security than another. Q.E.D.

Finally, mention may be made of the special case where

$$U(W) = W^\gamma/\gamma, \quad 0 \neq \lambda < 1, \text{ or} \tag{9.19}$$

$$U(W) = \log W$$

This is the family of constant-relative-risk aversion, as discussed by Pratt [79] and Arrow [3], a special case of (9.12) that leads to portfolio fractions and other decisions that are proportional to the wealth level. I.e., in (9.17)

$$w_i{}^*(T-t) \equiv f_i(1;1) \quad (t = 0,\ldots,T-1) \tag{9.20}$$

Warning: $f_i(1;1)$ will, generally, be different for each different γ. Only for $\gamma \to 0$, will $f_i(1;1)$ approach the solution given by the case where $E\{\log W\}$ is the maximand. Hence, the Williams [114], Latané [54], Kelley [47], Brieman [10], Markowitz [65], Hakansson [38], and Throp [110] discussions which seem almost to recommend that, for $T \to \infty$,

$$f_i(W;T) \equiv f_i(1;1)_{\log W} \qquad\qquad (9.21)$$

which are the portfolio weights that maximize $E\left\{\log W_t\right\}$ at each single stage—such proposals cannot be valid for rigorous $E\left\{U(W_T)\right\}$ maximizers. Such "Latané-Kelley" strategies do, for T sufficiently large, give a result that is with indefinitely great probability, i.e., $P \to 1$, going to be better than the results of any other uniform strategy. But that is another matter, quite difference from expected utility maximizing, as Samuelson [88, 100] has argued. Note that, for general $U(W)$ and $P(z_1, \ldots)$, no *uniform* w_i^* strategy is optimal at every time period.

Let me put this apparatus to work to discuss a problem relevant to a more-complete general-equilibrium determination. Jen [42] reviews writings by those such as Jensen [43], Cheng and Deets [12], Evans [24], Latané and Young [55], devoted to the question:

Suppose you begin by putting equal dollars in all securities. At the end of one period, should you just continue to hold the now-unequal dollar amounts? Or transaction costs aside, is it better to rebalance your portfolio back to equal proportions? Which is better, buy and hold, BH, or continual rebalancing of portfolio to equal proportions, CRE?

This question can be given a definite answer in that one case where equal proportions are to be recommended in the beginning, namely when the joint distribution of price ratios is *symmetric* in the different stocks in each period and, for simplicity independent of earlier period outcomes. As was shown earlier in (9.18), under these circumstances CRE is better than any other strategy for a concave utility maximizer. Thus, CRE does beat buy and hold, BH.

However, the asserted primacy of equal-proportions proves too much. How can everybody hold as much of dollars in General Motors as in Ford? One company is bigger than the other and there will not be enough to go around for equal-proportions holding. The set up, looked at from a general equilibrium view in which everybody acts the same way, is self-contradictory. Even if Ford and GM start out with equal total values, under a symmetric $P(z_1, \ldots, z_n)$ distribution they must be expected to become unequal after one period, and increasingly unequal as T becomes large. Clearly the assumption of $P(z_1, \ldots, z_n)$ as a symmetric function has got to go in a good general equilibrium model.

Of course, in real life people differ: perhaps risk-averse widows will begin to buy the big and sluggish AT&T's and young[9] M.D.'s with sporting blood and fat prospects will buy the small and volatile stocks; and securities will get *repriced* so as to make them *all* be held.

However, if we seek a general equilibrium model of rock-bottom simplicity, it will involve all investors being alike. And then each will want, in effect, to pursue a buy and hold strategy, each of N people owning $1/N$ of all there is to be held. Is there any model which can rationalize such a buy-and-hold philosophy? (Note: I rule out the merits of buy-and-hold when you are *learning* inductively which stocks have the better expected values and are astutely letting your winners ride and become an increasing fraction of the total. I shall pretend that all similar men *know* the $P(z_1, \ldots)$ functions that each faces.)

Here then is a new idealized model which does seem to meet the challenge of making buy-and-hold motivated even in a world where people are alike in their information and probability expectations but possibly different in their wealths and degree of risk-aversions.

AXIOM: Call all outstanding shares of each company one unit, so that the prices of such units $\left\{ X_t \right\}$ are merely the total outstanding values of those stocks. (Splits are ignorable as dividends will be for the present terse exposition.)

I posit that each price, the high price for large GM or the low price for American Motors or some new firm, is proportional to the number of independent "profit-centers" or "molecules" in the firm. Each price changes as each molecule or profit-center in that firm proliferates into $(0,1,2,\ldots)$ succeeding molecules according to probability laws which are the *same* for every molecule in society *regardless of in which firm any one molecule may happen to belong.*

"What," you will ask, "could the size of an auto firm grow indefinitely, going beyond that fraction of the capitalized wealth of society that auto capacity could ever hope to attain under present tastes for autos and non-autos?"

Such a question holds no terror for the present model. If the age of conglomerates had not already dawned, the notion of companies which have profit centers that are not tied to any one industry but are free to go everywhere and to compete in search for a share of the consumer's dollar wherever spending tastes may direct such dollars—such a notion would have had to be invented to dramatize the present firm-as-collection-of-unrelated-molecules model. In the present model we are back to symmetry of results to be expected, but the symmetry is not with respect to equal dollars invested in each security, but is rather nicely gauged so that, by the Principle of Sufficient Reason, every concave utility maximizer will be motivated to make all of his portfolio proportions faithfully mirror all that there is to buy of total social wealth. If GM is three times the size of Ford, each of us will want to hold three times as much of GM as Ford: i.e., $w_i/w_j = 3$, and each w_i is directly proportional to the total values of outstanding stocks.

Call Z_j the number of new profit-centers or molecules that the jth present molecule will give rise to: then, independently of in which firm any molecule may be, we face a symmetric probability distribution

$$P(\ldots,Z_i,\ldots;\ldots,Z_j,\ldots;\ldots;\ldots) \equiv P(\ldots,Z_j,\ldots;\ldots,Z_i,\ldots;\ldots;\ldots)$$

where the placing of the semi-colons indicates the boundaries of the firms, GM, Ford, GE, etc. A special case of this symmetry would be where each molecule is subject to an *independent* distribution similar to that of any other molecule, whether inside the same firm or outside of it; or, perhaps, the case where each such molecule is subject to independent variation except for a common business-cycle component of the Sharpe type. In the case of complete independence, consider two firms of unequal size, one containing say M_1 molecules and the other M_2 molecules. Let Y_1 and Y_2 represent respectively the random variables depicting the ratio of X_{t+1}/X_t for the respective firms. Then in terms of the following notational convention, we can prove the theorem that the portfolio proportions will indeed be proportional to outstanding market value:

$$P_1(y) = P(y), P_2(y) = P_1(y) * P_1(y) = \int_0^\infty P_1(y - u)dP_1(u)$$

$$\cdot \quad \cdot \quad \cdot \quad \cdot \quad \cdot \quad \cdot \quad \cdot \quad \cdot \quad \cdot \quad \cdot \quad \cdot \quad \cdot \quad \cdot \quad \cdot \quad \cdot \quad \cdot$$

$$P_M(y) = P_1(y) * P_{M-1}(y) = \int_0^\infty P_1(y - u)dP_{M-1}(u)$$

In terms of this notation the probability distribution for $(Y_1, Y_2, \ldots)$ pertaining to firms of respective number of molecules and respective market values $(M_1, M_2, \ldots)$ will be of the form

$$P_{M_1}(Y_1)P_{M_2}(y_2)\ldots$$

And now it is easy to show that the resulting optimal proportions become proportional to firms' outstanding total market values or proportional to the M's.

This completes the description of the molecular model that can rationalize a buy-and-hold-all-there-is-to-hold philosophy. Rebalancing to equal proportions or adhering to any uniform proportions would definitely be sub-optimal. (Remark: A Latané-Kelley expected-log maximizer would, in this environment, not adhere to uniform proportions, but would rather do what every rational concave-utility maximizer would be doing even if his name were not Bernoulli or Weber or Fechner, namely he would be buying his quota of outstanding total market value.)

Is there not a possible objection to this model—I mean beyond the usual intrusions of the reality of market imperfections, transaction charges, informational disagreements, and so forth? What will happen to the size distribution of firms over time? One would have to work out the answer for each different kind of symmetric function. But it is intuitively evident that the spread of firm size would widen through time. An ergodic state would not be achieved, unless we altered some of the assumptions of the model. The reader must decide whether the bulk of the evidence suggests that a model of dispersing firm size should be admired or rejected, and must be referred to works on the stochastic dynamics of industry size, such as that by Steindl [107].

10. Speculative stochastic price. A survey cannot be encyclopedic. Let me bring this bird's-eye view to an end by discussing, all too briefly, one self-contained model which does settle the economic issue of whether or not prices form a martingale or merely a stationary time series with a well-defined ergodic state as the resultant of Brownian vibrations around a level of equilibrium.

I consider an idealized model of a single spot commodity, like that analyzed in Samuelson [86, 87, 99]. The crop comes in intermittently, say every autumn: at first we may ignore all stochastic variations and let the crop be an arbitrary time sequence $(\ldots, H_t, H_{t+1}, \ldots)$. At first we may ignore all storage and suppose that consumption, C_t does equal the harvest, H_t, in every period. Each C_t, so to speak, gets auctioned off for what price it will bring, along a conventional demand function

$$P_t = P[C_t] \quad , \quad P'[C] < 0 \tag{10.1}$$

Now let the crop be a stochastic variable, subject for simplicity to a time-independent uniform probability distribution

$$\text{Prob} \left\{ H_t \leqq h \right\} = F(h) \quad , \quad F(h_1, h_2, \ldots) = F(h_1) F(h_2) \ldots \tag{10.2}$$

Obviously price will vibrate stochastically around the mean level $P[E \ H \ ]$. Obviously, $P(t)$ will not be a martingale or, in any meaningful sense, a semi-martingale. Obviously, the conditional probabilities will be extremely simple, being of the form

$$\text{Prob} \left\{ P_t \leqq p \mid P_{t-1}, P_{t-2}, \ldots \right\} \equiv \pi [p], \pi [P(h)] = F(h) \tag{10.3}$$

Now let us introduce into the problem the possibility of storage and arbitrage through time. Suppose that there are interest costs reckonable at r per period and that all physical storage costs can for simplicity be subsumed under the assumption that if I carry over Q_t in grain from the end of t for use or sale in the period $t + 1$, only a fraction a of that will become available in the next period, namely aQ_t, to be added to the new harvest H_{t+1}.

Samuelson [87] shows by standard methods that, in the absence of stochastic variations, the equilibrium pattern of prices is determined by the following non-linear difference equations and inequalities

$$(1+r)^{-1}aP\left[H_{t+1} + aq_t - q_{t+1}\right] - P\left[H_t + aq_{t-1} - q_t\right] \leqq 0 \qquad (10.4)$$

$$q_t\left\{(1+r)^{-1}aP\left[H_{t+1} + aq_t - q_{t+1}\right] - P\left[H_t + aq_{t-1} - q_t\right]\right\} = 0,$$

$$(t = 0,1,2,\ldots,T),$$

$$(q_{-1}, q_t) \text{ specified}$$

with determinable solutions for the unknowns $(q_0, q_1, \ldots, q_{t-1}; p_0, p_1, \ldots p_T)$. Actually, if $U'[C] \equiv P[C]$, these conditions can be given a Kuhn-Tucker dynamic programing interpretation

$$\underset{q_0,\ldots,q_{T-1}}{\text{Max}} \quad \sum_0^T (1+r)^{-t} U\left[H_t + aq_{t-1} - q_t\right] \qquad (10.5)$$

$$\text{with } [H_0, H_1, \ldots, H_T; q_{-1}, q_T] \text{ prescribed}$$

It is further suggested how to handle the case of stochastic harvests. An obvious generalization of the non-stochastic programing problem of (11.5) is the following dynamic stochastic programing problem

$$J_T[H_0 + aq_{-1}] = \underset{q_0,\ldots,q_{T-1}}{\text{Max}} \quad E\left\{\sum_0^T (1+r)^t U\left[H_t + aq_{t-1} - q_t\right]\right\}$$

$$q_t \geqq 0, \quad (q_{-1}, q_T) \text{ prescribed} \qquad (10.6)$$

The solution to this is given by the usual Bellman recursive technique and leads to the following general type of conditions.

$$(1+r)^{-1}aE\left\{P_{t+1}\right\} - P_t = 0, q_t\left\{(1+r)^{-1}aE\left\{P_{t+1}\right\} - P_t\right\} = 0$$

$$(t = 0, 1, \ldots, T) \qquad (10.7)$$

More specifically, solving the optimal control problem gives us a decision function for optimal carryover strategy of the form

$$q_{T-n}{}^* = f_n(H_{t-n} + aq_{t-n-1}; q_T), \quad 0 \leqq \partial f(x; q_T/\partial x \leqq 1 \qquad (10.8)$$

$$\lim_{t\to\infty} f_n(x; q_T) \equiv f(x) \qquad , \quad 0 \leqq f'(x) \leqq 1$$

When we substitute these strategy functions f_n into the determining conditions of the problem, we emerge with a well-defined stochastic process. With $T \to \infty$, we can calculate the conditional probabilities

$$\text{Prob}\left\{ P_{t+1} \leqq p \mid P_t = p_0 \right\} = \pi_1(p; p_0), \dots,$$

$$\text{Prob}\left\{ P_{t+k} \leqq p \mid P_t = p_0 \right\} = \pi_k(p; p_0), \, (k = 1, 2, \dots)$$

$$\text{Prob}\left\{ P_{t+k} \leqq p \mid P_t = p_0, P_{t-j} = p_{-j} \right\} = \pi_k(p; p_0)$$

$$\lim_{k \to \infty} \pi_k(p; p_0) = \pi(p), \text{ an ergodic-state probability}$$

$$E_{k \to \infty}\left\{ P_{t+k} \mid p_0 \right\} = \int_0^\infty p \, d\pi(p)$$

This model portrays in a satisfying way many of the properties we should wish for a stochastic model of commodity prices. It fails to "explain" Keynes-Houthakker "normal backwardation" of futures prices; it fails to explain "convenience yields" of inventory and "negative carrying charges" for carryover. The first failure can be removed, I believe, as soon as we introduce the realistic fact that some people have a comparative advantage in producing and holding this grain; the rest of the community has an interest in consuming it. The diversity of their interests ought to lead to normal backwardation. Interestingly, the magnificent Arrow finding, that there must be as many "securities" as there are possible states of nature if Pareto-optimality is to hold, suggests that organized markets do not go all the way in doing the job of optimally spreading risks among producers, consumers, and well-informed speculators. See Arrow [2] and Debreu [21].

I have discovered inductively that one can only scratch the surface of stochastic speculative price in any one lecture.

Appendix: Continuous-time Speculative Processes

Robert C. Merton
Sloan School of Management, Massachusetts Institute of Technology

Let the dynamics of stock price, x be described by the stochastic differential equation of the Itô-type[A1]

$$dx = \alpha x dt + \sigma x dz \qquad (A.1)$$

where α is the instantaneous expected rate of return, σ is the instantaneous standard deviation of that return, and dz is a standard Gauss-Wiener process with mean zero and standard deviation one. It is assumed that α and σ are constants, and hence, the return on the stock over any finite time interval is log-normal.

Suppose we are in the world of the Samuelson 1965 theory [90] where investors require an instantaneous expected return, β, to hold the warrant and β is constant with $\beta \gtreqless a$. Let $W = F(x, \tau; \sigma^2, a, \alpha, \beta)$ be the price of a warrant with exercise price a and length of time until expiration τ. Using Itô's Lemma[A2], the dynamics of the warrant price can be described by the stochastic differential equation

$$dW = F_1 dx + F_2 d\tau + \frac{1}{2} F_{11} (dx)^2 \qquad (A.2)$$

where subscripts denote partial derivatives. Substituting for dx from (A.1) and noting that $d\tau = -dt$ and $(dx)^2 = \sigma^2 x^2 dt$, we can rewrite (A.2) as

$$dW = [\frac{1}{2}\sigma^2 x^2 F_{11} + \alpha x F_1 - F_2] dt + \sigma x F_1 dz \qquad (A.3)$$

where $[\frac{1}{2}\sigma^2 x^2 F_{11} + \alpha x F_1 - F_2]/F$ is the instantaneous expected rate of return on the warrant and $\sigma x F_1/F$ is the instantaneous standard deviation. Applying the condition that the required expected return on the warrant is β to (A.3), we derive a linear partial differential equation of the parabolic-type for the warrant price: namely,

$$0 = \frac{1}{2} \sigma^2 x^2 F_{11} + \alpha x F_1 - \beta F - F_2 \qquad (A.4)$$

subject to the boundary conditions for a "European" warrant,

(a) $\quad F(0, \tau; \sigma^2, a, \alpha, \beta) = 0$

(b) $\quad F(x, 0; \sigma^2, a, \alpha, \beta) = \text{Max } [0, x-a]$

Make the change of variables: $T \equiv \sigma^2 \tau; S \equiv xe^{\alpha\tau}/a; f \equiv Fe^{\beta\tau}/a$ and substitute into (A.4) to obtain the new equation for g

$$0 = \frac{1}{2} S^2 f_{11} - f_2 \qquad (A.5)$$

subject to

(a) $\quad f(0,T) = 0$

(b) $\quad f(S,0) = \text{Max}\,[0, S - 1]$

By inspection, f is the value of a "European" warrant with unit exercise price and time to expiration T, on a common stock with zero expected return and unit instantaneous variance, when investors require a zero expected return on the warrant. I.e.,

$$f(S, T) = F(S, T; 1,1,0,0) \tag{A.6}$$

which verifies the homogeneity properties described in (6.14). To solve (A.5), we put it in standard form by the change in variables, $y \equiv \log S$ and $\phi(y,T) \equiv f(S,T)/S$, to arrive at

$$0 = \frac{1}{2}\phi_{11} - \phi_2 \tag{A.7}$$

subject to

(a) $\quad |\phi| \lesseqgtr 1$

(b) $\quad \phi(y, 0) = \text{Max}\,[0, 1 - e^{-y}]$

(A.7) is a standard free-boundary problem to be solved by separation of variables or fourier transforms[A3]. Hence, the solution to (A.4) is

$$F = \frac{e^{-\beta\tau}}{\sqrt{\pi\sigma^2\tau}} \int_{\log(\frac{a}{x})}^{\infty} (xe^Z - a)\exp\left[-\frac{1}{2}\ \ Z - (\alpha - \frac{1}{2}\sigma^2)\tau\ ^2/\sigma^2\tau\right]dZ$$

$$= e^{-(\beta-\alpha)\tau}xN\left[\frac{\log(\frac{x}{a}) + (\alpha + \frac{1}{2}\sigma^2)\tau}{\sigma\sqrt{\tau}}\right] - ae^{-\beta\tau}N\left[\frac{\log(\frac{x}{a}) + (\alpha - \frac{1}{2}\sigma^2)\tau}{\sigma\sqrt{\tau}}\right] \tag{A.8}$$

which reduces to (6.14) – (6.15) when $\beta = \alpha$.

The analysis leading to solution (A.8) assumed that the warrant was of the "European" type. If the warrant is of the "American" type, we must append to (A.4) the arbitrage boundary condition that

$$F(x, \tau; \sigma^2, a, \alpha, \beta) \geqq F(x, 0; \sigma^2, a, \alpha, \beta) \tag{A.4.c}$$

It has been shown[A4] that for $\beta = a$, (A.4.c) is never binding, and the European and American warrants have the same value with (A.8) or (6.14) – (6.15) the correct formula. It has also been shown that for $\beta > a$, for every τ, there exists a level of stock price, $C[\tau]$, such that for all $x > C[\tau]$, the warrant would be worth more if exercised than if one continued to hold it (i.e., the equality form of (A.4.c) will hold at $x = C[\tau]$). In this case, the equation for the warrant price is (A.4) with the boundary condition

$$F(C[\tau],\tau;\sigma^2,a,\alpha,\beta) = C[\tau] - a \quad \text{appended and} \quad 0 \leq x \leq C[\tau] \quad (A.4.c')$$

If $C[\tau]$ were a known function, then, after the appropriate change of variables, (A.4) with (A.4.c') appended, would be a semi-infinite boundary value problem with a time-dependent boundary. However, $C[\tau]$ is not known, and must be determined as part of the solution. Therefore, an additional boundary condition is required for the problem to be well-posed.

Fortunately, the economics of the problem are sufficiently rich to provide this extra condition. Because the warrant holder is not contractually obliged to exercise his warrant prematurely, he chooses to do so only in his own best interest (i.e., when the warrant is worth more "dead" than "alive"). Hence, the only rational choice for $C[\tau]$ is that time-pattern which maximizes the value of the warrant. Further, the structure of the problem makes it clear that the optimal $C[\ ]$ will be independent of the current level of the stock price.

In attacking the difficult $\beta > a$ case, Samuelson [90] postulated that the extra condition was "high-contact" at the boundary, i.e.,

$$F_1(C[\tau],\tau;\sigma^2,a,\alpha,\beta) = 1 \tag{A.9}$$

It can be shown that (A.9) is implied by the maximizing behavior described in the previous paragraph. In an appendix to the Samuelson paper, McKean [68, p. 38-39] solved (A.4) with conditions (A.4.c') and (A.9) appended, to the point of obtaining an infinite set of integral equations, but was unable to find a closed-form solution. The problem remains unsolved.

In their important paper, Black and Scholes [8] use a hedging argument to derive their warrant pricing formula. Unlike Samuelson [90], they do not postulate a required expected return on the warrant, β, but implicitly derive as part of the solution the warrant's expected return. However, the mathematical analysis and resulting needed tables are identical to Samuelson [90].

Assume that the stock price dynamics are described by (A.1)[A5]. Further, assume that there are no transactions costs; short-sales are allowed; borrowing and lending are possible at the same risk-less interest rate, r, which is constant through time.

Consider constructing a portfolio containing the common stock, the warrant and the risk-less security with w_1 = number of dollars invested in the stock,

w_2 = number of dollars invested in the warrant, and w_3 = number of dollars invested in the risk-less asset. Suppose, by short-sales, or borrowing, we constrain the portfolio to require net zero investment, i.e., $\sum_1^3 w_i = 0$. If trading takes place continuously, it can be shown[A6] that the instantaneous change in the portfolio value can be written as

$$w_1 \left(\frac{dx}{x} - rdt \right) + w_2 \left(\frac{dW}{W} - rdt \right) \tag{A.10}$$

where the constraint has been eliminated from (A.10) by substituting $w_3 = -(w_1 + w_2)$, and so, any choice of w_1 and w_2 is allowed. We can substitute for dx/x and dW/W from (A.1) and (A.3), and re-arrange terms, to re-write (A.10) as

$$[w_1(\alpha - r) + w_2(\tfrac{1}{2}\sigma^2 x^2 F_{11} + \alpha x F_1 - F_2 - rF)/F]dt + [\quad \sigma + w_2 \frac{\sigma x F_1}{F}]dz \tag{A.11}$$

Note that w_1 and w_2 can be chosen so as to eliminate all randomness from the return, i.e., we can choose $w_1 = w_1{}^*$ and $w_2 = w_2{}^*$ where

$$w_1{}^* / w_2{}^* = -xF_1/F \tag{A.12}$$

Then, for this particular portfolio, the expected return will be the realized return, and since no net investment was required, to avoid positive, "arbitrage" profits, this return must be zero. Substituting for $w_1{}^*$ and $w_2{}^*$ in (A.11), combining terms, and setting the return equal to zero, we have that

$$0 = \frac{1}{2}\sigma^2 x^2 F_{11} + rxF_1 - F_2 - rF \tag{A.13}$$

(A.13) is the partial differential equation to be satisfied by the equilibrium warrant price. Formally, it is identical to (A.4) with "$\beta = a = r$," and is subject to the same boundary conditions. It is important to note that this formal equivalence does not imply that the expected returns on the warrant and on the stock are equal to the interest rate. Even if the expected return on the stock is constant through time, the expected return on the warrant will not be,[A7] i.e.,

$$\beta(x,\tau) = r + \frac{xF_1}{F}(\alpha - r) \tag{A.14}$$

Further, the Black-Scholes formula for the warrant price is completely independent of the expected return on the stock price. Hence, two investors with different assessments of the expected return on the common stock will still agree on the "correct" warrant price for a given stock price level. Similarly, we could have postulated a more general stochastic process for the stock price with a itself random, and the analysis still goes through.

The key to the Black-Scholes analysis is the continuous-trading assumption since only in the instantaneous limit are the warrant price and stock price perfectly-correlated, which is what is required to form the "perfect" hedge in (A.11).

Notes

1. Discovered simultaneously around 1929 by Tinbergen, Ricci and Henry Schultz, this has already reached the elementary textbooks as in Samuelson [82, p. 382].

2. Since illustrious French geometers almost never die, it is possible that Bachelier still survives in Paris supplementing his professorial retirement pension by judicious arbitrage in puts and calls. Buy my widespread lecturing on him over the last twenty years has not elicited any information on the subject. How much Poincaré, to whom he dedicates the thesis, contributed to it, I have no knowledge. Finally, as Bachelier's cited life works suggest, he seems to have had something of a one-track mind. But what a track! The rather supercilious references to him, as an unrigorous pioneer in stochastic processes and stimulator of work in that area by more rigorous mathematicians such as Komolgorov, hardly does Bachelier justice. His methods can hold their own in rigor with the best scientific work of his time, and his fertility was outstanding. Einstein is properly revered for his basic, and independent, discovery of the theory of Brownian motion five years after Bachelier. But years ago when I compared the two texts, I formed the judgment (which I have not checked back on) that Bachelier's methods dominated Einstein's in every element of the vector. Thus the Einstein-Folker-Planck fourier equation for diffusion of probabilities is already in Bachelier, along with subtle uses of the now-standard method of reflected images.

3. I say "in effect" because I write down cumulative probability distributions rather than his probability densities, which in my notation involve

$$F'(x;T_1 + T_2) = \int_{-\infty}^{\infty} F'(x - u;T_1)F'(u;T_2)\,du$$

Bachelier also assumes that the expected value of $X_T - X_0$ is by hypothesis zero, as in an unbiased random walk, an assumption I do not yet make. Note: all my page references are to the English translation in Cootner [16]. The Stieltjes integral that I write as $\int_{-\infty}^{\infty} f(x) P(dx)$ can also be written as $\int_{-\infty}^{\infty} f(x) dP(x)$.

4. Graduate students have a recurring nightmare that just as they are completing their Ph.D. theses with their stellar contributions, someone will turn up in the ancient literature many of their findings. This happened to Dr. Kruizenga when the Savage letter of inquiry arrived just as he was dotting the final i's on his own independent researches.

5. Bachelier, at p. 28 of [16], shows a guilty awareness of the defect in his model involving negative prices, as his translator, A.J. Boness, notes. Bachelier says, "We will assume that it [stock price, X_t] might vary between $-\infty$ and $+\infty$, the probability of a spread greater than X_0 [i.e., $|X_T - X_0| > X_0$, or $X_T < 0$] being considered completely negligible, *a priori*." For T large, this is a self-contradiction to his own absolute-Brownian-motion theory.

6. Under such pricing, the expected instantaneous percentage return on the warrant is no longer a constant β: instead β will grow when x/a is low and also when T is low, approaching down toward a as either of these gets large.

Warning: If the Black-Scholes pricing is violated, the universe will not explode as it would if (8.1)'s true-arbitrage situation were to hold. The market need not believe in the Black-Scholes formula in the way that it *must* believe in formulas that prevent (8.1) from being possible. Thus, how can a rational arbitrager "know with certainty" what the σ is that he needs to do the arbitrage? A more hypothetical arbitrage is involved in the Black-Scholes formalism, namely the following. Query: What pattern of pricing, *if* it were known to hold with certainty [if, if!], would prevent the possibility of arbitrage? What pricing pattern will yield no profits to locked-in arbitrage strategy that must be engaged in until expiration time? Answer: The Black-Scholes pattern of pricing and no other. See the Samuelson review [94] for a similar critique of the Thorp-Kassouf [109] allegedly sure-thing arbitrage in reverse-hedging of expiring warrants. That the Black-Scholes formalism cannot cover all cases is shown by the case where complete ruin is possible with finite probability. Thus, let $P(0; T) = 1 - e^{-bT}$ as in (7.3) and $P(0 + x; T) = (1 - e^{-bT}) + e^{-bT} L(x; T, \overline{T})$, so that only for $b = 0$ do we have (6.4). The possible discrepancy from Black-Scholes pricing, intuition suggests, must grow with b.

7. For the independence case where $p(z_1, \ldots, z_n) = q_1[z_1] \ldots q_n[z_n]$, and each $q_i[z]$ has the Lévy-Pareto distribution with the same q kurtosis and β skewness coefficient, being of the form, $q_i[z] = q[(z - \mu_i)/\epsilon_i]$, Samuelson [92] has shown how the Markowitz efficiency-frontier analysis of quadratic programing can be generalized to a solvable concave programing problem,

$$\underset{w_i}{\text{Min}} \sum_{1}^{n} w_j{}^{\alpha} \epsilon_j{}^{\alpha} \text{ subject to } \sum_{1}^{n} w_j \mu_j \geqq \mu^*, \sum_{1}^{n} w_j = 1, w_j \geqq 0$$

The resulting ϵ^* minimand forms with μ^* the efficiency frontier $[\mu^*, \epsilon^*]$ $= [\mu^*, f(\mu^*)]$, and the usual portfolio theorems follow. Because a joint L'one goes beyond independence assumptions, in the Sharpe [103] and Fama [25] way, by considering returns with a common component added to the Z_i, namely $Z_i + c_i Y$ and where Y satisfies the $q [(Y - \mu_0)/\epsilon_0]$ form.

8. The problem in which one maximizes consumption over time, subject to stochastic return was solved by Phelps [78]. Combining this with sequential portfolio making leads to problems like

$$\underset{w_i(t), c(t)}{\text{Max}} \quad \sum_1^T \lambda^{-t} u[c_t] + U(W_T)$$

where $\lambda \leqq 1$ and

$$c_t = W_{t-1} \sum_1^n w_j(t) z_j(t) - W_t$$

This has also been solved by Hakansson [36, 37], Leland [57], Mossin [74], Samuelson [96], and by Merton [70, 71] for the continuous-time version. The reader may be alerted to unpublished results concerning the case when T becomes large, done independently by Hakansson, Leland, and myself. The former has suggested the primacy that should be given to the mean and variance of average return per period; in my language, the mean and variance of the logarithms of portfolio change are "asymptotically sufficient" parameters for the decision process; in my rendering of the felicitous language of Leland, as T get large, the $[w_j(t)]$ decisions "most" of the time are indefinitely "near" to the $[w_j(t)]$ appropriate to some γ in W^γ/γ, namely the γ equal to the following limit, $WU''(W)/U'(W) + 1$, as $W \to \infty$. I am indebted to Professors Hakansson and Leland for permission to refer to their unpublished work.

9. In Samuelson [96], it was shown that "businessman's risk" cannot be explained by a tendency to be more venturesome when you maximize terminal W_T with T large, in the sense that one with $U(W) = W^\gamma/\gamma$ or $\log W$ will have uniform (w_i^*) unless inabilities to borrow or other realistic factors are introduced into the idealized setup.

Notes—Appendix

A1. For a complete discussion of Itô Processes, see the seminal paper of Itô [40], Itô and McKean [41], and McKean [69].

A2. See McKean [69, pp. 32-35 and 44] for proofs of the Lemma in one and n dimensions. For applications of Itô Processes and Itô's Lemma to a variety of portfolio and option pricing problems, see Merton [70], [71], and [73].

A3. For the separation of variables solution, see Churchill [13, pp. 154-6], and for the fourier transform solution, see Dettman [22, p. 390].

A4. Samuelson [90] gives a heuristic economic argument. Samuelson and Merton [95] prove it under more general conditions than those in the text. An alternative proof, based on mere arbitrage, is given in Merton [73].

A5. The assumptions and method of derivation presented here are not those of Black and Scholes [8]. However, the method is in the spirit of their analysis and it leads to the same formula. For a complete discussion of the Black and Scholes model and extensions to more general option pricing problems, see Merton [73].

A6. See Merton [70, pp. 247-8] or Merton [73, section 3].

A7. In this respect, the Black-Scholes result is closer to the Samuelson and Merton [95] case, where $\beta = \beta(x,\tau) \gtreqless a$ (and where no premature conversion takes place), than to the case of Samuelson [90].

Bibliography

1. J. Aitchison and J.A.C. Brown. *The Lognormal Distribution, with Special Reference to Its Uses in Economics*. Cambridge: Cambridge University Press, 1957.

2. K.J. Arrow. "The role of securities in the optimal allocation of risk-bearing." *Review of Economic Studies* 31 (1963-64), pp. 91-96; English translation of *Le rôle des valuers boursières pour la répartition la meilleure des risques*. *Econometrie*, Paris: Centre National de la Recherche Scientifique, 1953, pp. 41-48; reprinted in K.J. Arrow [4], pp. 121-33.

3. ——. *Aspects of the Theory of Risk-Bearing*. Helsinki: Academic Bookstore, 1965; reprinted in Arrow [4], pp. 44-120, 134-93.

4. ——. *Essays in the Theory of Risk-Bearing*. Chicago: Markham, and London: North-Holland, 1970.

5. L. Bachelier. *Théorie de la Speculation*. Paris: Gauthier-Villars, 1900.

6. E. Barone. "The ministry of production in the collectivist state." In F.A. Kayek, (ed.) *Collectivist Economic Planning*. London: Routledge and Kegan Paul, 1935, pp. 245-90.

7. D. Bernoulli. "Exposition of a new theory of the measurement of risk." *Econometrica* 12 (1954), pp. 23-36; English translation of "Specimen theoriae novae de mensura sortis," *Commentarii Academiae Scientiarum Imperiales Petropolitanae* 5 (1738), pp. 175-92.

8. F. Black and M. Scholes. "Capital market equilibrium and the pricing of corporate liabilities." Working paper 488-70, Sloan School of Management, M.I.T., January 1971.

9. K. Borch. "A note on uncertainty and indifference curves." *Review of Economic Studies* 36 (1969), pp. 1-4.

10. L. Brieman. "Investment policies for expanding business optimal in a long run sense." *Naval Research Logistic Quarterly* 7 (1960), pp. 647-51.

11. D. Cass and J.E. Stiglitz. "The structure of investor preferences and asset returns, and separability in portfolio allocation: a contribution to the pure theory of mutual fund." *Journal of Economic Theory* 2 (1970), pp. 102-160.

12. P.L. Cheng and H.K. Deets. "Portfolio returns and the randomly walk theory." *Journal of Finance* 26 (1971), pp. 11-30.

13. R.V. Churchill. *Fourier Series and Boundary Value Problems*. New York: McGraw-Hill, 1963.

14. P.K. Clark. "A subordinated stochastic process model with finite variance for speculative prices." forthcoming in *Econometrica*.

15. E.A. Coddington and N. Levinson. *Theory of Ordinary Differential Equations*. New York: McGraw-Hill, 1964.

16. P. Cootner, ed., *The Random Character of Stock Market Prices*. Cambridge, Mass.: MIT Press, 1967. (Revised Edition.)

17. A. Cowles. "Can stock market forecasters forecast?" *Econometrica* 1 (1933), pp. 309-324.
18. _____ and H.E. Jones. "Some *a posterior* probabilities in stock market action." *Econometrica* 5 (1937) pp. 280-94.
19. _____ . *Common Stock Indexes, 1871-1937.* Indiana: Principia Press, 1938.
20. _____ . "A revision of previous conclusions regarding stock price behavior." *Econometrica* 28 (1960), pp. 909-915.
21. G. Debreu. *Theory of Value.* New York: Wiley, 1962, Ch. 7.
22. J.W. Dettman. *Mathematical Method in Physics and Engineering.* New York: McGraw-Hill, 2nd ed., 1969.
23. E. Domar and R.A. Musgrave. "Proportional income taxation and risk-bearing." *Quarterly Journal of Economics* 58 (1944), pp. 384-22.
24. J.L. Evans. "An analysis of portfolio maintenance." *Journal of Finance* 25 (1970), pp. 561-72.
25. E.F. Fama. "The behavior of stock market prices." *Journal of Business* 38 (1965), pp. 34-105.
26. _____ and M. Blume. "Filter rules and stock market trading profits." *Journal of Business* 39 (1966), pp. 226-41.
27. _____ . "Risk, return and equilibrium." Report #5831, Center for Mathematical Studies in Business and Economics, University of Chicago, June 1968.
28. _____ and R. Roll. "Some properties of symmetric stable distribution." *Journal of the American Statistical Association* 63 (1968) pp. 817-36.
29. _____ ; L. Risher; M. Jensen; and R. Roll. "The adjustment of stock prices to new information." *International Economic Review* 10 (1969), pp. 1-21.
30. _____ . "Multiperiod consumption-investment decisions." *American Economic Review* 60 (1970), pp. 163-74.
31. _____ . "Efficient capital markets: a review." (Mimeograph), 1971.
32. M.S. Feldstein. "Mean-variance analysis in the theory of liquidity preference and portfolio selection." *Review of Economic Studies* 36 (1969) pp. 5-12.
33. F.M. Fisher. *Identification Problem in Economics.* New York: McGraw-Hill, 1966.
34. R. Gibrat. *Les Inegalités Economiques.* Paris, 1931.
35. T. Haavelmo. "The structural implication of a system of simultaneous equations." *Econometrica* 11 (1943), pp. 1-12.
36. N.H. Hakansson. "Optimal Investment and Consumption Strategies for a Class of Utility Functions, Ph.D. Dissertation, University of California at Los Angeles, 1966.
37. _____ . "Optimal investment and consumption strategies under risk for a class of utility functions." *Econometrica* 38 (1970) pp. 587-607.
38. _____ . "Multi-period mean-variance analysis: toward a general theory of portfolio choice." *Journal of Finance* 26 (1971) pp. 857-84.
39. J. Hirshleifer. "Investment decision under uncertainty: applications of the

state-preference approach." *Quarterly Journal of Economics* 80 (1966) pp. 611-72.

40. K. Itô. "On stochastic differential equations." *Mem. Amer. Math. Soc.* 4 (1951).

41. ____ and H.P. McKean, Jr. *Diffusion Process and Their Sample Paths.* New York: Academic Press, 1964.

42. F.C. Jen. "Multi-period portfolio strategies." Working paper #108, State University of New York at Buffalo, School of Management, May 1971.

43. M.C. Jensen. "Risk, the pricing of capital assets, and the evaluation of investment portfolios." *Journal of Business* 42 (1969), pp. 167-247.

44. ____. "The foundations and current state of capital market theory." In M.C. Jensen, (ed.) Studies in the Theory of Capital Markets. New York: Praeger Publishers, 1971.

45. S.T. Kassouf. "A Theory and An Econometric Model for Common Stock Purchase Warrants." Ph.D. Dissertation, Columbia University, 1965.

46. ____. Stock price random walks: some supporting evidence." *Review of Economics and Statistics* 50 (1968), pp. 275-78.

47. J.L. Kelley, Jr. "A new interpretation of information rate." *Bell System Technical Journal* 35 (1956) pp. 917-26.

48. M.G. Kendall. "The analysis of economic time-series—Part I: prices." *Journal of the Royal Statistical Society* 96, (1953), pp. 11-25; reprinted in P. Cootner, ed., [16], pp. 85-99.

49. J.M. Keynes. *General Theory of Employment, Interest and Money.* London: Macmillan, 1936, pp. 154-64.

50. D. Kreps; J.L. Lebowitz; and P.B. Linhart. "A stochastic model of a security market." AT&T memorandum, December 1971.

51. R. Kruizenga. "Put and Call Options: A Theoretical and Market Analysis." Ph.D. Dissertation, Massachusetts Institute of Technology, 1956.

52. ____. "Introduction to the option contract," and "Profit returns from purchasing puts and calls." Both in P.H. Cootner (ed.) [16], pp. 377-91 and 392-411.

53. O. Lange. "On the economic theory of socialism, part I and part II." *Review of Economic Studies* 4 (1936 and 1937), pp. 53-71 and 123-42.

54. H.A. Latané. "Criteria for choice among risky ventures." *Journal of Political Economy* 67 (1956), pp. 144-55.

55. ____ and W.E. Young. "Test of portfolio building rules." *Journal of Finance* 24 (1969), pp. 595-612.

56. W.W. Leontief. "Verzögerte Angebotsanpassung und partielles Gleichgewicht." *Zeitschrift für Nationalökonomie* 5 (1934), pp. 670-76.

57. H.E. Leland. "Dynamic Portfolio Theory." Ph.D. Dissertation, Harvard University, Cambridge, Massachusetts, 1968.

58. A.P. Lerner. "Economic theory and socialist economy." *Review of Economic Studies* 2 (1934), pp. 51-81.

59. J. Lintner. "The valuation of risk assets and the solution of risky investments in stock portfolio and capital budgets." *Review of Economics and Statistics* 47 (1965), pp. 13-37.

60. _____. "Security prices, risk, and maximal gains from diversification." *Journal of Finance* 20 (1965), pp. 587-615.

61. B.B. Mandelbrot. "The valuation of certain speculative prices." *Journal of Business* 36 (1963), pp. 394-419.

62. _____. "Forecasts of future prices, unbiased markets and 'martingale' models." *Journal of Business* 39, Special supplement (1966), pp. 242-55.

63. _____ and H.M. Taylor. "On the distribution of stock price differences." *Operation Research* 15 (1967), pp. 1057-67.

64. _____. "When can price be arbitraged efficiently? A limit to the validity of the random walk and martingale models." *Review of Economics and Statistics* 53 (1971), pp. 225-36.

65. H. Markowitz. *Portfolio Selection: Efficient Diversification of Investments.* New York: John Wiley and Sons, Inc., 1959.

66. J. Marschak. *Mathematical Thinking in the Social Sciences.* In P. Lazarsfeld, (ed.) "Probability in the Social Sciences." Glencoe, Illinois: Free Press, 1954, pp. 166-215.

67. _____. "Rational behavior, uncertain prospects, and measurable utility." *Econometrica* 18 (1950). pp. 111-41.

68. H.P. McKean, Jr. "Appendix: a free boundary problem for the heat equation arising from a problem in mathematical economics." *Industrial Management Review* 6 (1965), pp. 32-39.

69. _____. *Stochastic Integrals.* New York: Academic Press, 1969.

70. R.C. Merton. "Lifetime portfolio selection under uncertainty: the continuous-time case." *Review of Economics and Statistics* 51 (1969), pp. 247-57.

71. _____. "Optimum consumption and portfolio rules in a continuous-time model." *Journal of Economic Theory* 3 (1971), pp. 373-413.

72. _____. "A dynamic equilibrium model of the asset market and its application to the pricing of the capital structure of the firm." Working paper #497-70, Sloan School of Management, M.I.T., December 1970.

73. _____. "Theory of rational option pricing." Working paper #574-71, Sloan School of Management, M.I.T., October 1971; forthcoming, in M. Scholes (ed.) *Studies in the Theory of Capital Markets*, Volume II, New York: Praeger Publishers.

74. J. Mossin. "Optimal multi-period portfolio policies." *Journal of Business* 41 (1968), pp. 215-29.

75. A.B. Moore. "Some characteristics of changes in common stock prices." In P. Cootner, ed. [16], pp. 139-61.

76. M.F.M. Osborne. "Periodic structure in the Brownian motion of stock prices." *Operation Research* 10 (1962), pp. 345-79; reprinted in P. Cootner, ed., [16], pp. 262-96.

77. V. Pareto. *Cours d'Economie Politique*. 2 vols, Lausanne: Libraire de l'Université, 1897.
78. E.S. Phelps. "The accumulation of risky capital: a sequential utility analysis." *Econometrica* 30 (1962), pp. 729-43.
79. J.W. Pratt. "Risk aversion in the small and in the large." *Econometrica* 32 (1964), pp. 122-36.
80. S.J. Press. "A compound events model for security prices." *Journal of Business* 40 (1968), pp. 317-35.
81. F.P. Ramsey. Truth and probability. In his *The Foundations of Mathematics and Other Logical Essays*. London: Kegan Paul, 1931, pp. 156-98.
82. P.A. Samuelson. *Economics*, 8th ed. New York: McGraw-Hill, 1970.
83. *The Collected Scientific Papers of Paul A. Samuelson*, Vol. I and II, J.E. Stiglitz, ed., M.I.T. Press, Cambridge, Mass., 1966; hereafter abbreviated as CSP I and CSP II.
84. *The Collected Scientific Papers of Paul A. Samuelson* Vol. III, R.C. Merton, ed., M.I.T. Press, Cambridge, Mass., forthcoming 1972; hereafter abbreviated as CSP III.
85. P.A. Samuelson. "Probability, utility, and the independence axiom." *Econometrica* 20 (1952), pp. 670-78; reprinted in CSP I, Ch. 14, pp. 137-45.
86. _____ . "Spatial price equilibrium and linear programming." *American Economic Review* 43 (1953), pp. 283-303; reprinted in CSP II, Ch. 72, pp. 925-45.
87. _____ . "Intertemporal price equilibrium: a prologue to the theory of speculation." *Weltwirtschaftliches Archiv* 79 (1957), pp. 181-219; reprinted in CSP II, Ch. 73, pp. 946-84.
88. _____ . "Risk and uncertainty: a fallacy of large numbers." *Scientia* 57 (1963), pp. 1-6; reprinted in CSP I, Ch. 16, pp. 153-58.
89. _____ . "Proof that properly anticipated prices fluctuate randomly." *Industrial Management Review* 6 (1965), pp. 41-50; reprinted in CSP III, Ch. 198.
90. _____ . "Rational theory of warrant pricing." *Industrial Management Review* 6 (1965), pp. 13-32; reprinted in CSP III, Ch. 199.
91. _____ . "General proof that diversification pays." *Journal of Financial and Quantitative Analysis* 2 (1967) p. 1-13; reprinted in CSP III, Ch. 201.
92. _____ . "Efficient portfolio selection for Pareto-Lévy investments." *Journal of Financial and Quantitative Analysis* 2 (1967), pp. 107-22; reprinted in CSP III, Ch. 202.
93. _____ . "Two generalizations of the elasticity of substitution." In J.N. Wolfe, ed., *Value, Capital and Growth: Papers in Honour of Sir John Hicks*. Edinburgh: Edinburgh University Press, 1968, pp. 469-80; reprinted in CSP III, Ch. 133.
94. _____ . Book Review of E.O. Thorp and S.T. Kassouf [109]. *Journal of American Statistical Association* 10 (1968), pp. 1049-51.
95. _____ and R.C. Merton. "A complete model of warrant pricing that maxi-

mizes utility." *Industrial Management Review* 10, 2 (1969), pp. 17-46; reprinted in CSP III, Ch. 200.

96. _____ . "Lifetime portfolio selection by dynamic stochastic programming." *Review of Economics and Statistics* 51 (1969), pp. 239-46; reprinted in CSP III, Ch. 204.

97. _____ . "Classical orbital stability deduced for discrete-time maximum systems." *Western Economic Journal* 8 (1970), pp. 110-19; reprinted in CSP III, Ch. 158.

98. _____ . "The fundamental approximation theorem of portfolio analysis in terms of means, variances and higher moments." *Review of Economic Studies* 37 (1970), pp. 537-42; reprinted in CSP III, Ch. 203.

99. _____ . "Stochastic speculative price." *Proceedings of the National Academy of Sciences* 68 (1971) pp. 335-37; reprinted in CSP III, Ch. 206.

100. _____ . "The fallacy of maximizing the geometric mean in long sequences of investing or gambling." *Proceedings of the National Academy of Sciences* 68 (1971), pp. 2493-96; reprinted in CSP III, Ch. 207.

101. _____ . "Proof that unsuccessful speculators confer less benefit on the rest of society than their losses," to be published 1972.

102. L.J. Savage. *The Foundations of Statistics*. New York: John Wiley and Sons, 1954.

103. W.F. Sharpe. *Portfolio Theory and Capital Market*. New York: McGraw-Hill, 1970.

104. J.P. Shelton. "The Value Limit contest: a test of the predictability of stock-price changes." *Journal of Business* 40 (1967), pp. 251-69.

105. _____ . "Warrant stock-price relation." *Financial Analysts Journal*, Part I: May-June, 1967, and Part II: July-August, 1967.

106. C. Sprenkle. "Warrant prices and indicators of expectations and preferences." *Yale Economic Essays* 1 (1961), pp. 178-231; reprinted in P. Cootner, ed., [16], pp. 412-74.

107. J. Steindl. *Random Processes and the Growth of Firms: A Study of the Pareto Law*. New York: Hafner Publishing Co., 1965, pp. 157 and 160.

108. F. Taylor. "The guidance of production in a socialist state." *American Economic Review* 19 (1929), pp. 1-8.

109. E.D. Thorp and S.T. Kassouf. *Beat the Market: A Scientific Stock Market System*. New York: Random House, 1967.

110. E.D. Thorp. "Optimal gambling systems for favorable games." *Review of the International Statistical Institute* 37 (1969), pp. 273-93.

111. J. Tobin. "Liquidity preference and behavior towards risk." *Review of Economic Studies* 25 (1958), pp. 65-86.

112. _____ . "The theory of portfolio selection." In F. Hahn and F. Brechling eds., *The Theory of Interest Rates*. London: Macmillan, 1965.

113. J. von Neumann and O. Morgenstern. *Theory of Games and Economic Behavior*, 2nd. ed. New Jersey: Princeton University Press, 1947.

114. J.B. Williams. "Speculation and the carry-over." *Quarterly Journal of Economics* 50 (1936), pp. 436-55.

115. H. Working. "Theory of inverse carrying charge in future markets." *Journal of Farm Economics* 30 (1948), pp. 1-28.

116. _____. "Future trading and hedging." *American Economic Review* 43 (1953), pp. 314-43.

117. _____. "New ideas and methods for price research." *Journal of Farm Economics* 38 (1958), pp. 1427-36.

118. _____. "A theory of anticipating prices." *American Economic Review* 48 (1958), pp. 188-99.

119. _____. "Note on the correlation of first differences of average in a random chain." *Econometrica* 28 (1960) pp. 916-18; reprinted in P. Cootner, ed., [16], pp. 129-31.

4

A New Look at the Capital Asset Pricing Model

Marshall Blume and Irwin Friend

In a recent paper in the *American Economic Review*, we presented strong empirical evidence that the relationship between rate of return and risk implied by the market-line theory is unable to explain differential returns in the stock market. As a result, the risk-adjusted measures of portfolio performance based on this theory yield seriously biased estimates of portfolio performance.[1] We advanced, but did not test several tenable reasons for these observed biases, which included differences between *ex ante* or expected and *ex post* or realized returns and "risks,"[2] and the inability of investors to borrow large amounts of money at the same risk-free interest rate at which they can lend.

The differences between *ex ante* and *ex post* values of returns and risks would create biases in the one-parameter performance measures based on the market-line theory. The direction of these biases would in the short run hinge upon the nature of stock market developments, but hopefully in the long run these biases will average out to zero. The gap between borrowing and lending rates, we argued, would consistently bias these performance measures in favor of securities or portfolios of low risk and against those of high risk. A recent paper by Fischer Black[3] presents a theoretical model which suggests that the breakdown of the borrowing and lending mechanism would be expected to bias these measures, but not for the explicit reasons we gave. More will be said of the Black paper later.

The purpose of this paper is to examine both theoretically and empirically in greater depth than was done previously the reasons why the market-line theory does not adequately explain differential returns on financial assets. The first section of the paper briefly reviews the salient points of the market-line theory and analyzes the more obvious failures of the theory. The second section estimates the risk-return tradeoff implied by securities on the New York Stock Exchange for three different periods after World War II. The third section shows that the empirical results cast serious doubt on the validity of the market-line theory in either its original form or as recently modified. They provide evidence that the market for seasoned stocks such as those listed on the New York Stock Exchange is segmented from the bond market as well as from the market for unseasoned stocks. This has important implications for both the measurement of portfolio performance and the determination of optimal corporate financing.

The authors wish to thank the Rodney L. White Center for Financial Research of the Wharton School for financial support.

97

I. Possible Failures of the Theory

Under the assumptions underlying the market-line theory,[4] including the possibility of unlimited borrowing and lending at the same risk-free rate, it can be shown that the *ex ante* expected return for any asset or portfolio i, $E(R_i)$, is related to the *ex ante* expected return on the market portfolio, $E(R_m)$, by the equation

$$E(R_i) - R_f = \beta_i [E(R_m) - R_f] \tag{1}$$

where R_f is the risk-free rate assumed to be the same for both borrowing and lending and β_i is a measure of the non-diversifiable risk for asset or portfolio i.[5] In words, equation (1) says that the risk premium on asset or portfolio i is proportional to the risk premium on the market portfolio, the constant of proportionality being the beta coefficient.

Based upon the market-line theory embodied in equation 1, the expected return on a security is easily shown to be a linear function of beta. Solving equation (1) for $E(R_i)$ yields

$$E(R_i) = a + b\,\beta_i \tag{2}$$

where

$$a = R_f$$

$$b = E(R_m) - R_f$$

Since the coefficients a and b are independent of asset i, equation (2) should, according to the market-line theory, hold for any individual asset as well as any portfolio of assets. Any departures from equation (2) would be inconsistent with the market-line theory.

The *AER* paper indicates that the market-line theory, as re-expressed in equation (2), is seriously deficient as an explanation of the actual risk-return tradeoff in the market place. There are two possible deviations from equation (2) which *ex ante* would account for the biases which have been observed in the risk-adjusted measures of performance based upon the market-line theory. First, the coefficient a may not be equal to the risk-free rate and the coefficient b may not be equal to the risk-premium on the market, but may be equal to some other constants. In this case, the *ex ante* risk-return tradeoff would be linear, but not that which is implied by the market-line theory. Second, the *ex ante* tradeoff between risk and return may be non-linear and must be approximated by a more complex function.

Fischer Black has recently suggested that if there were no risk-free asset,[6] equation (2) would still hold in its linear form except that the intercept a would equal the expected rate of return on a portfolio which was uncorrelated with the market, a so-called zero-beta portfolio, and the slope b would be the expected return on the market portfolio less this zero-beta expected rate of return. Conceptually, the zero-beta portfolio takes over the function of the risk-free asset in the traditional model: It allows the individual investor to adjust the risk of the market portfolio to that which would maximize his expected utility. He can increase the risk of the market portfolio by shorting the zero-beta portfolio and investing the proceeds of the short sale in the market portfolio. Likewise, he can decrease the risk of the market portfolio by investing part of his wealth in that portfolio and part in the zero-beta portfolio.

Black's argument assumes among other things that short sales take place perfectly in the sense that an investor can with no transaction costs use the proceeds of a short sale to purchase additional assets and that there is no limit to the quantity of short sales allowed. In fact, an investor because of institutional restrictions[7] generally cannot use the proceeds from a short sale to purchase another security, and further the transactions costs are big.[8]

Two characteristics of the zero-beta portfolio as developed by Black will aid in a further discussion of the properties of this portfolio. First, its expected return must be less than the expected return on the market portfolio. Second, of all feasible zero-beta portfolios, the actual zero-beta portfolio used by investors in constructing their own portfolios will be the one with minimum variance. In Black's theory the zero-beta portfolio could possibly have a variance even larger than that of the market portfolio. Yet in practice it would probably have a variance very much smaller than that of the market. For an investor with an horizon of one month, treasury bills with three months to maturity held one month would almost certainly constitute a near zero-beta portfolio with a small variance whether returns were measured in real or nominal terms.[9]

One can conceive of other types of zero-beta or near zero-beta portfolios, but they would only be acceptable as zero-beta portfolios in Black's theory if they have the same or smaller variances. Thus, Black's zero-beta portfolio would have a very small or zero variance whether it consists only of Treasury bills or of some more complicated mixture of assets. This conclusion, though not developed by Black, appears to be a logical corollary to his argument. Further, if the market for Treasury bills is in equilibrium, the expected return on the zero-beta portfolio must be very close to the Treasury bill rate.

If there are differences between the borrowing or lending rates or if the short sales mechanism fails, the *ex ante* tradeoff between risk and return may be non-linear. If investors can borrow large amounts of money at an interest rate somewhat larger than the lending rate,[10] the *ex ante* risk-return tradeoff would be expected to be two straight lines (resulting from lending and borrowing opportunities) connected by a curve which is concave with respect to the risk axis (resulting from the set of efficient risky portfolios for which lending and borrowing opportunities would not improve an investor's position). Other assumptions about the borrowing and lending mechanism, implying substantially higher borrowing costs, would yield a linear relationship between return and risk for securities of relatively small risk and a curvilinear relationship thereafter which again is concave with respect to the risk axis.

Though arguments can be made that the *ex ante* risk-return tradeoff would be linear or non-linear and concave, the observed or *ex post* relationship may theoretically take any form. This statement however is true of most any economic theory. What is generally assumed is that over a long enough period of time the *ex ante* expectations are realized *ex post*, so that observed data can be used to make inferences about the *ex ante* relationship. The crux of the problem is how long is long enough. An answer to this question is very important in testing the market-line theory, but it should be noted that it is not important in measuring performance *ex post*. Here one is interested in a comparison of the actual return realized with that which should have been realized for the risk borne. For such a comparison, the *ex post* tradeoff between risk and return is pertinent, so that an analysis of the econometric problems in estimating this tradeoff is of interest in its own right.

II. The Risk-Return Tradeoff

The obvious way to estimate the risk-return tradeoff would be to collect the realized returns and beta coefficients for a large group of assets, which would typically be common stocks because of the readily available data. The next step would be to regress these realized returns on the corresponding betas to estimate the tradeoff. This procedure would be deficient for several reasons. First, the estimated betas may differ substantially from the true underlying coefficients, resulting in possibly large measurement errors and therefore biases in the regression coefficients. Second, the realized returns for individual securities will be poor estimates of the *ex ante* expected returns. Third, to preserve comparability among securities, the realized returns would have to be estimated over the same period of time. This restriction would introduce a survivorship or post-selection bias of unknown magnitude. The procedures used in this paper attempt to avoid these problems.

To cope with the measurement error problem, a technique discussed in Malinvaud[11] was used because of its intuitive appeal and its ability to deal with the other two problems mentioned above. First, beta coefficients were estimated by regressing monthly investment relatives, properly adjusted for capital changes and cash dividends, upon the corresponding values of the Fisher Combination Link Relatives, a measure of dividend-adjusted return on the market portfolio. These beta coefficients were, for instance, estimated for each stock listed on the New York Stock Exchange during the entire five year period January 1950 through December 1954.

Second, ten or so portfolios of roughly eighty securities apiece were formed on the basis of these estimates. No two portfolios contained any securities in common. The first portfolio consisted of those eighty or so stocks which had the lowest estimates of beta. The second portfolio consisted of those eighty or so securities with the next lowest estimates, and so on.

Third, monthly returns for each portfolio for the January 1955 through December 1959 period were calculated under two different assumptions concerning the initial investment in each security: (1) an equal investment in each security, and (2) an amount in each security proportional to the market value of the shares outstanding (authorized less Treasury) on December 31, 1954. Cash dividends were assumed reinvested in the security which paid them. Securities which were delisted were treated as follows: The security was assumed to be sold at the closing price of the last trading day of the month preceding the delisting or the closing price of the month if the stock were delisted on the last day. The proceeds were distributed over the remaining securities in proportion to their market values in the portfolio constructed in step 2 at the time of delisting.[12] Other than delistings, there were no redistributions among securities.

Fourth, these monthly returns for, say, 1955 through 1959 were averaged for each portfolio to obtain the portfolio monthly returns[13] and were then regressed upon the corresponding values of the Fisher Combination Link Relatives to yield an estimate of the beta for the portfolio. Finally, these arithmetic average returns were regressed on the beta coefficients in both linear and quadratic forms. All of these steps were repeated to yield similar regressions for January 1960 through December 1964 and January 1965 through June 1968. In both cases, the monthly returns for the five years previous to the initial date were used to assign the securities to the portfolios. These regressions are presented in Table 4-1 and will be discussed below.

These rather complicated procedures are an attempt to minimize the statistical problems of merely regressing realized returns of individual securities on the corresponding betas. The use of portfolios has several purposes. Although the estimated betas for individual securities may contain big measurement errors, the estimated betas for portfolios, which are merely weighted averages of the estimates of the betas for the individual securities, will tend to have substantially smaller measurement errors.[14] If the measurement errors for individual securities are independent and an equal investment is assumed in each of eighty securities, the variance of the measurement errors for portfolios will be one-eightieth of the variance for individual securities. Further, the realized returns for portfolios will tend to be less affected by the vagaries of individual securities and therefore may give a better *ex post* estimate of the *ex ante* expected return. Finally, the use of portfolios provides a convenient way of adjusting for delistings.

The regression results (Table 4-1) are presented in the usual format with *t*-values and coefficients of determination adjusted for degrees of freedom.[15] Because returns of individual securities were not simply regressed upon the

Table 4-1
Average Monthly Returns as a Function of Risk

Period and Portfolio											
A. 1/55-12/59											
Equal Weight	(1)	R =	1.0117	+	0.0002	β				$\overline{R}^2$ =	0.00
			(881.6)		(0.2)						
	(2)	R =	1.0063	+	0.0123	β	−	0.0061	β^2	$\overline{R}^2$ =	0.22
			(389.3)		(2.3)			(−2.3)			
Value Weight	(1)	R =	1.0118	+	0.0004	β				$\overline{R}^2$ =	0.00
			(506.4)		(0.2)						
	(2)	R =	1.0061	+	0.0140	β	−	0.0072	β^2	$\overline{R}^2$ =	0.00
			(215.8)		(1.6)			(−1.3)			
B. 1/60-12/64											
Equal Weight	(1)	R =	1.0205	−	0.0124	β				$\overline{R}^2$ =	0.68
			(412.0)		(−5.0)						
	(2)	R =	1.0268	−	0.0254	β	+	0.0064	β^2	$\overline{R}^2$ =	0.66
			(78.7)		(−1.0)			(0.5)			
Value Weight	(1)	R =	1.0199	−	0.0124	β				$\overline{R}^2$ =	0.58
			(360.8)		(−4.1)						
	(2)	R =	1.0447	−	0.0655	β	+	0.0273	β^2	$\overline{R}^2$ =	0.65
			(71.0)		(−2.1)			(1.7)			
C. 1/65-6/68											
Equal Weight	(1)	R =	0.9980	+	0.0197	β				$\overline{R}^2$ =	0.95
			(732.6)		(15.2)						
	(2)	R =	0.9933	+	0.0293	β	−	0.0046	β^2	$\overline{R}^2$ =	0.95
			(163.9)		(2.4)			(−0.8)			
Value Weight	(1)	R =	0.9930	+	0.0219	β				$\overline{R}^2$ =	0.65
			(254.1)		(4.7)						
	(2)	R =	0.9937	+	0.0201	β	+	0.0010	β^2	$\overline{R}^2$ =	0.61
			(92.0)		(0.8)			(0.1)			

corresponding betas and in fact a much more complicated procedure was used, these ancillary statistics will not be used here. Rather, the regressions were analyzed mainly by visual examinations of the scatter plots of the actual data[16] superimposed upon the graph of the regression lines. These plots are presented in Figures 4-1a-c and 4-2a-c.

During the 1965-68 period, the quadratic model almost coincides with the linear model over the observed range of betas for the value-weighted portfolios, and the data points appear randomly distributed about the regression lines. Thus, for this set of portfolios the linear model gives as adequate a description of the data as the quadratic. For equal-weighted portfolios during the 1965-68 period, there is somewhat more difference between the linear and quadratic models, but the differences are so small that the linear regression should be judged an adequate model.

Unweighted Estimates

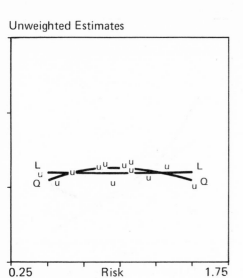

Linear (LL) and Quadratic (QQ) Regressions
of Unweighted Returns on Risk for January
1955 to December 1959

Figure 4.1a

Unweighted Estimates

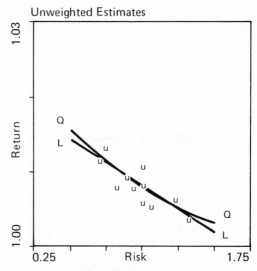

Linear (LL) and Quadratic (QQ) Regressions
of Unweighted Returns on Risk for January
1955 to December 1959

Figure 4.1b

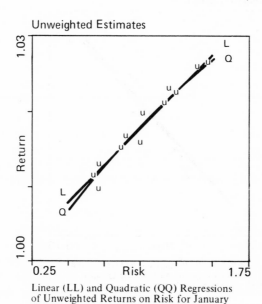

Linear (LL) and Quadratic (QQ) Regressions
of Unweighted Returns on Risk for January
1955 to December 1959

Figure 4.1c

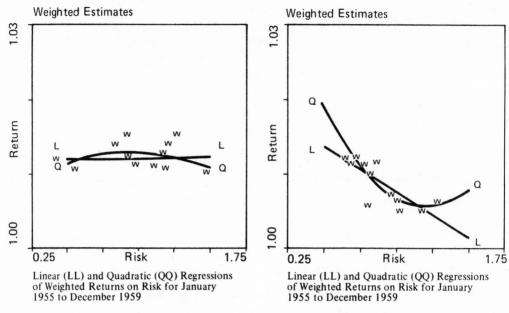

Weighted Estimates

Linear (LL) and Quadratic (QQ) Regressions
of Weighted Returns on Risk for January
1955 to December 1959

Figure 4.2a

Weighted Estimates

Linear (LL) and Quadratic (QQ) Regressions
of Weighted Returns on Risk for January
1955 to December 1959

Figure 4.2b

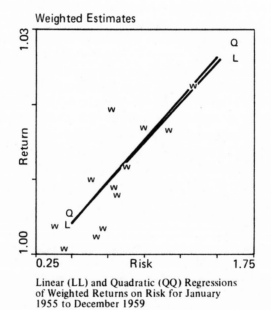

Weighted Estimates

Linear (LL) and Quadratic (QQ) Regressions
of Weighted Returns on Risk for January
1955 to December 1959

Figure 4.2c

During the 1960-64 period, the linear model appears adequate for the unweighted portfolios, but the quadratic model appears better than the linear for the weighted portfolios. This latter conclusion is evidenced by the obviously non-random distribution of the data points about the linear relationship and the more random distribution about the quadratic. For the linear model, the portfolios with the lower betas tend to be graphed above the regression line and those portfolios with moderate levels of beta below the line. This non-random pattern is somewhat mitigated with the quadratic.

During the 1955-59 period, the quadratic model appears slightly superior to the linear for both the weighted and unweighted portfolios. These results suggest that it is indeed a long period of time before one can assume that *ex ante* expectations are fulfilled. In the 1955-59 period, the quadratic model implies that securities of moderate risk returned more than either securities of low or high risk—a relationship which would not be expected to hold *ex ante* if investors were risk averse. Even the linear model is inconsistent with a risk averse *ex ante* world.

During 1960 through 1964, the negative relationship of return to risk is again certainly inconsistent with *ex ante* expectations if the beta coefficient is in any sense a valid measure of risk. In the period from 1965 through 1968, we have previously argued[17] that the rapid growth of institutional investments in common stock and the increased awareness of the power of diversification may have driven up the prices of the more risky issues relatively faster than those of the less risky issues. If this argument is correct, the *ex post* relationship between return and risk will exaggerate the *ex ante* relationship. Therefore, over these three non-overlapping periods it is quite likely that *ex ante* expectations were not realized.

Even though the regressions in Table 4-1 are based upon *ex post* data, they can in some circumstances be used to make inferences about the market-line theory, a theory stated in *ex ante* terms. One method of determining the validity of the market-line theory would be to examine the *ex post* data in different periods and then to suggest plausible reasons for the differences between the *ex ante* magnitudes of the theory and the *ex post* realizations. If one can always find such plausible reasons, the theory would be supported; otherwise, it would not be supported.

In the 1955 through 1959 period, the *ex post* magnitudes are such that there are probably no reasonable explanations for the differences between the *ex post* data and the *ex ante* expectations of the traditional theory which assumes the existence of a risk-free rate. The tradeoffs during this period are roughly flat for both the equal and value-weighted portfolios of common stocks with some evidence that the moderate risk assets realized the largest returns. The actual market return which can be estimated from the linear regressions in Table 4-1 as the return on a portfolio with a beta of one is between 1.19 percent per month for an equally weighted portfolio and 1.22 percent per month for a value-weighted portfolio. Since these percentages probably exceed the *ex ante* expected return, the high risk portfolios would be expected to return more than the low risk. This phenomenon did not occur, and there seems to be no reasonable explanation.

In the modified theory, it is possible that the *ex post* value of the relevant zero-beta portfolio exceeded the *ex post* value of the market in which case the tradeoff would be downward sloping. This explanation seems far-fetched when the realized return on the market was probably greater than expected if, as argued above, the zero-beta portfolio has a small variance and an expected return close to the bill rate.

Another method of examining the validity of the traditional market-line theory is to compare the actual risk-free rate which occurred during some period of time with the intercepts of the regressions during the same period. Large differences would be interpreted as evidence contrary to the theory. The rationale of this test is that the *ex ante* risk-free rate is identical to the *ex post* rate. Then, the *ex post* tradeoff, if it can be assumed a continuous function in risk, must emanate from the risk-free rate. As risk increases from a beta of zero into the range of betas for common stocks, the *ex post* tradeoff would be expected to approximate the tradeoffs as estimated in Table 4-1. The use of the intercepts in the regressions as estimates of the risk-free rate assumes that the functional forms which fit the data adequately for common stocks do not change markedly over a somewhat broader range of risk.

Using this approach the *ex post* relationship of return to risk in the 1955-59 period if it were judged to be quadratic would imply a risk-free rate of between .61 percent to .63 percent per month—somewhat over 7 percent per year. If the linear model were accepted, the rate would range from 1.17 percent to 1.18 percent per month. During the 1960-64 period, the implied rate would vary from 1.99 percent to 4.47 percent per month depending upon whether weighted or unweighted portfolios are used and whether a linear or quadratic model is employed. During the 1965-68 period, the estimated rate varied from −.20 percent to −.70 percent per month.

These rates of return are not even close to any risk-free rate observed during these periods. These results are obviously inconsistent with the original market-line theory. One might argue that, since the regressions in Table 4-1 are based upon only New York Stock Exchange common stocks, extrapolation of the lines to obtain the implied risk-free rate is incorrect. If however one supports this line of argument, one is forced into the unattractive position of concluding that the *ex post* relationship of return to risk is clearly non-linear. Thus the values of the implied risk-free rates contradict the original market-line theory.

These rates of return do not even lend support to Black's theory in which the risk-free rate of return is replaced with a rate of return on a so-called zero-beta portfolio. It was argued in the previous section that the actual zero-beta portfolio implied by this modified theory would most likely have a very small variance and an expected return very close to those in the short-term money market. Here again the implied rates from Table 4-1 are generally inconsistent with any observed in the market place. In the first two periods, they are much too high; and in the last, too low, at least for Treasury bills.[18]

Though not readily apparent, the regressions in Table 4-1 in addition disclose substantial differences between the returns on equal-weighted and value-weighted portfolios. Table 4-2, which is derived from Table 4-1, highlights these differences by evaluating the estimated regressions at various levels of risk. For example, the quadratic model in the 1955-59 period for unweighted portfolios would imply an *ex post* expected monthly return of 1.09 percent if beta were 0.50 and 1.21 percent if beta were 1.25.

From 1955 through 1959, value-weighted portfolios yielded a higher return than equal-weighted portfolios, although the differences were small, never being more than .04 percent per month. After 1959, equal-weighted portfolios outperformed value-weighted portfolios by increasingly greater amounts based on the linear model. Using the linear model, the returns on equal-weighted portfolios exceeded the return on value-weighted portfolios from 1965 through June 1968 by from .22 percent to .38 percent over the beta range of 0.5 to 1.5. When one remembers that these percentage differences are monthly, the large magnitude of these figures becomes apparent.

Table 4-2
Risk-Return Tradeoff Evaluated at Various Risk Levels

Period	Type of Portfolio	Monthly Relatives Implied by Linear Regressions for Beta Coefficients of				
		0.5000	0.7500	1.0000	1.2500	1.5000
1/55-12/59	Equal Weight	1.0118	1.0119	1.0119	1.0120	1.0120
1/55-12/59	Value Weight	1.0120	1.0121	1.0122	1.0123	1.0124
1/60-12/64	Equal Weight	1.0143	1.0112	1.0080	1.0049	1.0018
1/60-12/64	Value Weight	1.0137	1.0106	1.0075	1.0045	1.0014
1/65-6/68	Equal Weight	1.0078	1.0127	1.0177	1.0226	1.0275
1/65-6/68	Value Weight	1.0040	1.0095	1.0149	1.0204	1.0259

Period	Type of Portfolio	Monthly Relatives Implied by Quadratic Regressions for Beta Coefficients of				
		0.5000	0.7500	1.0000	1.2500	1.5000
1/55-12/59	Equal Weight	1.0109	1.0121	1.0125	1.0121	1.0109
1/55-12/59	Value Weight	1.0113	1.0125	1.0129	1.0123	1.0108
1/60-12/64	Equal Weight	1.0157	1.0114	1.0078	1.0051	1.0031
1/60-12/64	Value Weight	1.0188	1.0110	1.0065	1.0055	1.0079
1/65-6/68	Equal Weight	1.0068	1.0127	1.0180	1.0227	1.0269
1/65-6/68	Value Weight	1.0040	1.0094	1.0149	1.0205	1.0263

Part of this gap may be due to unanticipated capital gains on smaller issues as institutional investors and the investing public became more and more aware of the power of diversification and the recognition that the smaller issues were under-priced relative to their relevant risk characteristics. Part of this gap— though we suspect a lesser part—may stem from the attractiveness of larger issues to big institutions, which, because of their greatly increased trading activity during the 1960s or their concern with potential problems of control, may favor the larger issues.[19] Whether the gap in return between small and large issues will continue depends upon whether the behavior of returns in the sixties represents an adjustment in the relative prices of assets which has been completed or whether it represents a change in the institutional structure of the market.

III. Conclusion

The empirical evidence in this paper seems to require a rejection of the market-line theory either in its traditional or in its recent modified form. This theory in its traditional form assumes the existence of a risk-free rate of interest at which an individual can borrow or lend in unlimited quantities. The implied risk-free rates from the estimated risk-return tradeoffs could not be construed as even poor estimates of any observed risk-free rates. These implied rates are so far afield that they are even inconsistent with the weaker market-line theory recently developed by Black. The market-line theory, in its traditional or weaker form, therefore does not yield a satisfactory description of the pricing of capital assets.

Even though the market-line theory does not hold, the beta coefficient, the measure of risk inherent in this theory, can still be interpreted as a measure of risk if distributions of returns for portfolios are held to be symmetric and investors exhibit diminishing marginal utility of wealth. In this case, the *ex ante* expected returns would be positively, although possibly non-linearly, related to beta. *Ex post* the relationship could theoretically take on almost any form. The scatter plots show that from January 1965 through June 1968 the relationship was linear, but with an implied negative risk-free or zero-beta rate of return. During the two earlier non-overlapping five year periods, the relationships were close to linear, but quadratic forms generally offered slightly better fits. The apparent superiority of the quadratic might well result from differences between *ex ante* and *ex post* magnitudes. The implied risk-free rates in these earlier two periods were ridiculously large.

Since the analysis included only common stocks, the risk-return tradeoffs were estimated only over part of the range of total risk. The smallest beta for a portfolio considered in the analysis was 0.38. Therefore, the implied risk-free or zero-beta rate was derived by extrapolation, which, except for the obvious statistical problems, should have yielded estimates close to actual risk-free or zero-beta rates. If near zero-beta risky assets such as long-term corporate bonds were included in the analysis, the risk-return tradeoff over the entire range of risk would certainly have been highly non-linear in all periods.[20] In the 1955-59 period, the graph of realized return versus risk would be increasing for low levels of beta and then leveling off. In the 1960-64 period, the graph would be very rapidly increasing for low levels of beta and then decreasing for moderate levels of beta and increasing again if the quadratic form is believed. In the 1965-68 period, the graph would be decreasing and then increasing.

There is also evidence that it is not only the risk-free or low risk yields which cannot be explained by the market-line theory: For the 1926 to 1960 period published results indicate that the riskiest New York Stock Exchange stocks, as measured by their quality rating at the beginning of the period, tended to have the same or a somewhat lower rate of return than NYSE stocks of intermediate risk.[21] This same type of analysis, updated through 1967, yields comparable findings regardless of whether risk is measured by quality rating, or by beta or variance measures. Moreover, studies of the rates of return realized on new stock issues, covering roughly this same period, indicate that except for the transitory short-run gains associated with "hot-issue" periods, the rates of return on unseasoned new issues are on the average appreciably below those on seasoned NYSE stocks.[22] Thus, the traditional or modified market-line theory does not adequately explain the returns of different financial assets.

Nonetheless, it is intriguing that the relationship of average realized returns for NYSE-listed common stocks to their corresponding betas appears very close to linear in each of the three periods analyzed, and one is tempted to try to explain this phenomenon. A possible explanation is that the market for reasonably well-seasoned common stocks is at least partially segmented from the markets for other financial assets such as bonds or new issues. There is some independent, but not very strong empirical support for such segmentation.[23]

If such segmentation exists, there may be some mechanism which tends to produce a close to linear relationship of the realized average returns to the corresponding betas for well-seasoned common stocks like those analyzed in this study. An obvious candidate for such a mechanism is Black's modified market-line theory if it be applied only to these types of stocks. Then the portfolios of holders of these assets could be viewed as linear combinations of the market portfolio and some zero-beta portfolio which would only include such stocks and no other financial assets. The plausibility of this explanation hinges upon the variance of the returns on the zero-beta portfolio. The wide range of the implied rates of return for the zero-beta portfolio, from $-.70$ percent to 4.47 percent per month in this study, would require a very large variance of returns for this portfolio.

It does not seem likely that this zero-beta portfolio would have a variance large enough to explain the empirical facts. Because the beta of this portfolio is zero, the market factor, that is the factor common to all securities, will cause no variation. Further, since the zero-beta portfolio consists in Black's theory of virtually all common stocks, it would be well diversified so that very little variation would be caused by factors other than the market. Only in the case in which there was more than one important common market factor or in which the common market factor explained virtually none of the variation of the returns of individual securities, and most of the variation was due to a small group of industry factors, that is factors affecting the returns of subsets of all securities, could one conceive of a zero-beta portfolio with a sufficiently large variance to explain the empirical results. But this is contrary to the empirical evidence of Benjamin King and Stephen Meyer.[24]

Yet, if one can assume market segmentation, and if contrary to the above reasoning, the zero-beta portfolio does have a large variance, Black's theory would explain for well-seasoned common stocks the close to linear relationships observed in this study. It should be noted however that in this case any linear relationship, whatsoever, would support his theory. A more meaningful test of Black's theory would be to specify *ex ante* the composition of the zero-beta portfolio, and then to determine the *ex post* return realized by this portfolio. The line passing through this zero-beta return and the realized return on the market should almost coincide with the risk-return tradeoff as estimated in this paper, but this is virtually the same tack that was taken here in arguing that the zero-beta portfolio, consisting only of common stocks, would have a very small variance.[25]

The results of this paper together with independent evidence[26] strongly suggest that the markets for different types of financial assets are segmented even though there are few legal reasons for such segmentation. It is possible to explain the risk-return tradeoffs for the well-seasoned stocks analyzed in this study by Black's theory if his zero-beta portfolio has a large variance, but this seems implausible.[27] Until such segmentation vanishes, if it does indeed exist, and until more comprehensive and more satisfactory theories are developed,[28] the best and safest method to formulate the risk-return tradeoff is to estimate it empirically over the class of assets and the period of interest.

Finally, it should be pointed out that many of these findings about rates of return on different types of assets have implications for the cost of capital. By far the most important of these implications evolves from the evidence of market segmentation between the bond and stock markets. The required rate of return on bonds appears much lower than that of common stock on a risk-adjusted basis. This conclusion suggests that even without allowing for the tax advantages of debt financing, the cost of bond financing may have been substantially smaller than the risk-adjusted cost of stock financing and probably smaller than the risk-adjusted cost of internal financing. Considering the big tax advantage of bonds, the question arises why corporations did not place even more reliance on financing. One answer may be that corporate management, in its attempt to avoid the risk of bankruptcy and to preserve its own position, has shied away from debt financing, a risk readily diversified by individual investors. There is some evidence that the historically large-risk premium rquired on stock as compared with bonds may have diminished in recent years.[29]

Notes

1. Irwin Friend and Marshall Blume, "Measurement of Portfolio Performance Under Uncertainty," *American Economic Review*, September 1970. A subsequent paper by Fischer Black, Michael Jensen, and Myron Scholes, "The Capital Asset Pricing Model: Some Empirical Tests," in Michael C. Jensen, ed., *Studies in the Theory of Capital Markets* (New York: Praeger Publishers), forthcoming, further confirms the inability of the market-line theory to explain differential returns in the stock market. They use our earlier cross-sectional analysis over a longer period of time as well as a new time series analysis to arrive at this conclusion.

2. To be precise, the difference between the *ex ante* and *ex post* returns and "risks" is not a meaningful concept in the market-line theory. Rather, one should speak of the difference between the investors' *ex ante* subjective distributions of returns and the corresponding *ex post*, or in some sense objective, distributions of returns.

3. Fischer Black, "Capital Market Equilibrium With Restricted Borrowing," *Journal of Business* (forthcoming).

4. These assumptions will not be enumerated here. The interested reader is referred to Friend and Blume, op. cit., for a succinct discussion.

5. Statistically, the beta coefficient is defined as $Cov(R_i, R_m)/Var(R_m)$.

6. Black, op. cit. Black's argument initially assumes that only risky assets exist, but he then relaxes this assumption to include the possibility of riskless lending but not borrowing. He concludes that expected return will still be a linear function of the beta.

7. Generally in short sales the seller cannot use the proceeds for purchasing other securities. In addition, he has to deposit cash margin equal currently to 65 percent of the market value of the sales, unless he deposits securities which he owns with a market value roughly three times the cash margin which would otherwise be required. This obviously places a fairly severe wealth constraint on his short sales.

8. On the surface, the requirement for a perfectly functioning short sales mechanism may seem more restrictive than the standard assumption that an individual can borrow or lend at the risk-free rate. Margin accounts allow at least some borrowing at rates slightly above the risk-free lending rate and there are virtually no institutional barriers to the lending mechanism. Yet Black's theory may be robust to violations of the short sales assumption if it so happened that each investor's optimal portfolio involved no negative or short holdings. In this

case, one could think of an investor's portfolio as consisting of a linear combination of the market portfolio and a zero-beta portfolio. Such a zero-beta portfolio might require short sales if it were actually to be held. However, if in combination with the market portfolio there were no net short positions, no actual short sales need to have taken place. Thus, it is theoretically possible that the short sales assumption may be less restrictive than the usual risk-free rate assumption.

9. A newly issued treasury bill held one month would seem to constitute a risky asset in Black's theory, for which infinite short sales are allowed. Even a three month bill held to maturity would be risky if returns were measured in real terms.

10. The regulations of the Federal Reserve Board pertaining to margin requirements on common stocks cast doubt on this assumption. Only if these regulations are deemed ineffective, could this assumption hold.

11. E. Malinvaud, *Statistical Methods of Econometrics* (Chicago: Rand McNally and Co., 1966).

12. Since closing prices are not always realizable or investors may not always have had advanced information of a delisting, it would have been preferable to use the first realizable price after delisting, but this would have been prohibitively expensive.

13. Geometric returns were also calculated for each portfolio and the statistical analysis presented subsequently in this paper was replicated using these returns rather than the arithmetic averages. Although the geometric returns were of course slightly less than the arithmetic averages, there were no substantive differences in the implications of the analysis and so the analysis using geometric returns is not presented.

14. The use of betas estimated from one period to form portfolios and different betas estimated from a later period to determine the average betas for the portfolios was employed in the preparation of Marshall Blume, "The Assessment of Portfolio Performance: An Application of Portfolio Theory," Ph.D. dissertation, University of Chicago, March 1968. The primary conclusions based in most part on a time series analysis were unaffected whether portfolios and their average betas were determined from betas estimated in different periods or in the same period; therefore, only the simpler procedure was used. In this paper, which uses a cross-section analysis, only the more complicated procedure was used.

15. In estimating these regressions, it is implicitly assumed that the process generating these returns is stationary over time. For the short periods used in this paper the assumption appears plausible and further, the empirical evidence of Black, Jensen, and Scholes, op. cit., confirms that the generating process after World War II and through 1966 is remarkably stationary.

16. The letter U and W in the charts are centered over the actual point.

17. Irwin Friend, Marshall Blume, and Jean Crockett, *Mutual Funds and*

Other Institutional Investors: A New Perspective (New York: McGraw-Hill Book Company, 1970).

18. M.J. Brennan in "Capital Asset Pricing and the Structure of Security Returns," unpublished manuscript, May 1971, argues that empirical tests, like those in this paper, are very likely to suggest the breakdown of the market-line theory purely because of statistical reasons. The reason is that if there are two or more factors common to all securities which have a substantial effect in determining returns, the estimated regressions would be more than likely to differ from the true relationships. His empirical analysis in support of this hypothesis assumes the validity of the market model, but other statistical studies such as that of Stephen Meyers, "A Factor Analysis Approach to Studying the Structure of the Stock Market," Ph.D. dissertation, University of Pennsylvania, September 1970, and to some extent of Benjamin King, "Market and Industry Factors in Stock Price Behavior," *The Journal of Business*, January 1966, Part II, which do not assume the validity of the market model, have suggested that there is only one important factor common to all securities. The studies of King and Meyer differ however from that of Brennan in that their analyses are based upon individual securities rather than portfolios, so that there may be some question as to the applicability of their conclusions to Brennan's study. Nonetheless, Brennan's statistical hypothesis seems less plausible than the hypothesis of the breakdown in the market-line theory. Until he can provide more robust tests and a stronger economic argument, his explanation of our empirical results must await a definitive evaluation.

19. There is, of course, reason to believe that at least some of the major groups of institutional investors were showing an increased tolerance towards smaller and less marketable issues over this period, presumably reflecting the recognition of the underpricing of the smaller issues referred to above and perhaps also a greater ability to favorably affect prices of such issues.

20. This statement is based upon the observation that risk-free investment opportunities would have a beta coefficient of zero and upon an analysis of twenty year AA corporate bonds held one quarter. Regressing the quarterly market rate of return for these bonds on the Standard and Poor's 500 adjusted for dividends over the period 1960 through 1970 yields a beta coefficient of 0.126 (with a *t*-value of 2.57) which is only moderately larger than zero. However, the beta coefficient was insignificantly different from zero in the early 1960s. The data used in these calculations were provided by the Portfolio Evaluation Service of Merrill Lynch.

21. Irwin Friend and Paul Taubman, "Risk and Stock Market Performance," *Proceedings of the Center for Research in Security Prices*, University of Chicago, Nov. 1966, p. 11.

22. Irwin Friend and J.R. Longstreet, "Price Experience and Return on New Stock Issues," in Friend et al., *Investment Banking and the New Issues Market* (The World Publishing Company, 1967).

23. For instance, in 1967, households including personal trusts and non-profit institutions owned 83.9 percent of all corporate stocks, 4.5 percent of corporate and foreign bonds, 35.2 percent of state and local obligations, 29.8 percent of U.S. government securities, and 2.7 percent of mortgages. For more detail about the holdings of different groups, the reader is referred to Friend, Blume, and Crockett, op. cit.

24. Benjamin King and Stephen Meyer, op. cit.

25. One could argue that the variance of returns is small but that the expected return on the zero-beta portfolio shifts over time, so as to explain the observed tradeoffs. This argument is no theory at all unless the process causing the shifts is specified.

26. Cf. note 23.

27. Another possible explanation of the observed phenomenon is that the beta coefficient has no relationship to what investors mean by risk, but there is evidence that the stated risk objectives of mutual funds are related to the beta coefficients for their portfolios. (Cf. Friend, Blume, and Crockett, op. cit.)

28. A promising approach to explain the results of this paper is that all well-seasoned stocks, even though of different cyclical variability as measured by the beta coefficient, command the same risk premiums and that the slope of the risk-return tradeoffs in this paper result primarily from differences between *ex post* and *ex ante* magnitudes.

29. See Friend, Blume, and Crockett, op. cit.

Part III:
Information, Expectations and
Investment Decisions

5 Information Flow and Stock Market Price Changes

Oskar Morgenstern

There have been many high-powered talks using very advanced methods which will make what I have to say seem very coarse, unrefined and strictly verbal.

I shall start with a quotation from Samuelson. Somewhere in his textbook I looked up what he said about the stock market. It is in general a fair description of what goes on, and this is already remarkable because most books on economic theory have not a word to say about the stock market; so in that sense it is distinctive.

After having given this general description with which I agree, he states that there isn't any question but that prices on the stock market obey a random walk. But at the very end, he says, "Investing is an art." Now to my mind, that seemingly innocuous statement has to be analyzed, because what is art?

"Art" simply means that you don't know how to describe how things are done. So "investing is an art" means that you do not know how to invest, what the right principles and techniques are. Painting, making a great painting, is an art; ask the artist how he does it and he cannot explain it to you. That is why it is an art.

When it is a matter of *action*, of the application of a principle, then we remove ourselves from the intuitive notion of "art" by applying scientific principles. But in order to do so, we must possess these principles, be able to describe with their aid completely the process involved in regard to which an action is to be undertaken. When I cannot give a complete description of a scientific character as to how a particular painting is made—which in theory is, of course, imaginable—then this simply states that science has not penetrated as far as it would be necessary, and that the nature of the process discloses itself only to the intuition of the artist. It is questionable that investing is an art in that sense because the process is entirely differently structured from writing a piece of music or painting a great painting. The parallel therefore does not hold except for the fact that one is not explaining good investing if one merely says that it is an art.

Let me go into certain matters related to the problem of information and information flows. I published a book with Clive W.J. Granger[1] only last November and since that time nothing much new has occurred to me regarding investment or the stock market. So you cannot expect me to say anything really different from what is in essence contained in that particular work.

117

However, it may still be useful to bring some of these matters up for discussion. First, let us start with the fact that we would all like to have a theory of the stock market which would have an operational value, which would allow us really to use it in a practical sense. It is generally assumed that it is the final test of any theory that it can be used in a predictive manner.

But when we ask that question, we must also realize that, as had been pointed out many times and in many fields, for example in physics by Eugene Wigner, that false theories have sometimes very high predictive power. That is a very important point. So prediction is not absolutely the sole final proof.

For example, take the old Ptolemy Theory of the solar system. We know that it is totally false, but with elaborate computations you can nevertheless predict exactly the next occurrence of a solar eclipse, i.e., on the basis of a false theory.

Now that is as interesting as important. So we know that a false theory can do this, but still we reject it and replace it by a better theory, which will make the same prediction in a simpler manner and in addition other predictions which the false theory cannot make. That may also be the case in regard to the stock market. We sometimes have theories which allow us to predict and we may still be able to prove that they have no value in a scientific sense.

So we must search for a theory which really stands unchallenged, and by unchallenged I mean that the theory by its being used, by its being convincing as a theory ought to be, will not abolish itself and contradict itself.

The only mechanism which one can state about the stock market which fulfills this criterion is that the market is a random walk with certain qualifications which are not important. The fact that prices obey the rules of a random walk has been established without any doubt by means of spectral analysis, the most powerful mathematical technique with which to investigate the behavior of time series. Any other mechanism that is announced and analyzed, should it exist, once it becomes part of the information of a large set of operators in the stock market, will abolish itself. It is simply a manifestation of the well-known fact that certain predictions when they become effective may be self-fulfilling and therefore make the prediction wrong, indeed impossible.

That is a point to which I shall return. In the discussions I have heard so far about expectations, there is one thing that was not mentioned at all, namely that expectations are interdependent among people, which seems to me to be an absolutely fundamental fact.

So the random walk thesis is not self-destroying. Facts which become known certainly have an influence on the stock market, but facts have to be interpreted and interpretation of a fact which becomes common knowledge may be subject to many interpretations. Communication as well as lack of information are some of the principle sources of errors. One might say, although this is probably something horrible for humanists and philosophers to hear, that most of the dramas we go and enjoy looking at are based on the fact that there is a lack of information or that information becomes available.

Romeo and Juliet, the poor, would not have died if there had been a telephone or if the horse had been a little faster to come and bring the information that it was not necessary for them to poison themselves. That is tragedy. Of course, it goes farther back. For example, sometimes it is not the fact that communication did not work, but that the communication was wrongly interpreted. You remember the case of the Argonauts, when Jason went to the Black Sea. It had been agreed with his father that if a black sail would be hoisted, it would indicate that Jason was dead.

Somehow they forgot this, hoisted the black sail, and the father seeing this ship come in, killed himself in despair over the alleged death of his son. So there was a fact, a misrepresentation, and the "correct" interpretation of the misdirected fact by the father—another tragedy. And so you could go through literature and find that repeated; but I think it is not nice to interpret tragedy just in terms of flows of information.

Sometimes the tragedy is, of course, that the information does flow. I mean that is pretty clear, e.g., when the husband hears that his wife had been deceiving him. And there are other instances.

The next point is that the knowledge of the theory itself will have an influence on the behavior, even when the "theory" is incorrect. Let me give you an illustration. If you have inflation in a country, it is clear that it will make a whale of a difference whether the country has an understanding of what inflation means, or whether it experiences inflation for the first time.

The fact that beliefs or theories, whether false or true, held by the participants in an economy have an influence on the working of the economy is a fundamental matter. For nature it does not matter at all whether or not we know the structure of nature, have a complete understanding of all physical processes, because these processes will not change in response to our knowledge. Yet we will be able to interfere with them and use them to our advantage or disadvantage as the case may be. However, in the social field, it is clear that a very different situation obtains: if a theory is known and is, as was stated above, absolutely convincing, which means that the agent feels compelled to act according to the theory, then the degree of spread of knowledge of that theory among all agents is of fundamental importance. This is a very basic and important factor and ought to be considered carefully in methodological studies of the social sciences.

For example, after the great inflation in the 1920s, in Germany, Austria, or Hungary, those governments were restrained from making new inflationary policy by the very fact that the country was inflation-experienced and would have reacted in a way to a new inflation so as to speed up the process of inflation very considerably. Therefore, it was virtually impossible to produce even a modest expansionist policy because it would rapidly have led to catastrophe or to a degree of inflation which the government never wanted. That is a very different course of events compared to, let us say, naive countries like the United States, which has had no such (recent) experience, where you therefore can make inflation as at present, provided it is creeping and stays on creeping, and people still go on lending money and saving when in fact the only thing to do in inflation is to borrow money, for the obvious reasons.

As I have said, expectations or information flow is very dependent on how people are related to each other. Certainly in the stock market most are related to each other. Hardly anyone acts independently, without looking at the others, as to what the others do, and this is a fundamental characteristic of the market. Little attention is paid to this fact.

I suggest that we briefly look at the meaning of the presence of "others" for an individual in various typical situations. There are four of these. The first is roulette. In the case of roulette, it is totally irrelevant for the individual player, whether any others are also playing or not. That is of course important for the bank because the bank wants to have as many playing as possible, since that is what makes their money.

But my payoff, even when I am the only one to play, is totally independent of the activity or presence of the others who are also playing roulette. That is a very interesting phenomenon.

Take the second case, playing the horses. Here it is already different, and quite a bit more complicated. If I am betting on a horse that wins, and others are present who bet on horses that do *not* win, then they are friendly to me because they increase my payoff. And the more who do this, the better it is for me.

If the others also bet on the same winning horse, then they are hostile to me because they reduce my payoff, and of course, if we all bet on the wrong horse, that's not a good idea for anybody. So they can be friendly or unfriendly, depending on the orientation of their acts.

Third, take the activities of others in the Walrasian equilibrium system. If I am a seller and the others are selling also (of course the same commodity), then they are unfriendly, because by being also sellers, they depress my price. If they are on the other side, i.e., buyers, they're friendly—they drive up the price.

Fourth, look at the stock market, and there we have a different situation. A new factor enters, namely, time, or rather the timing. If I buy a stock, the others who buy the same stock *after* I have bought mine are friendly. If they buy other stocks, or buy mine before I have been able to buy it, they are unfriendly. Their actions then are inimical to me. And the same can be reversed. Of course, if I should sell short, etc., these statements have to be adjusted accordingly.

So you see, here it is again as in "toto": a matter of classification as to *what* they do, but the timing element enters which is absent in toto, because the time curtain falls for all at the same moment.

If this analysis is correct—and I think it is true—the stock market is clearly one in which the sequences of operations are of the essence. Now we come to the point, which of course has been made many times and which by necessity we make again in our book, and that is—if one has information, what is the value of the information? Assuming the information is correctly described and interpreted?

I think there are two kinds, two categories, of what we would call "inside information." The one is the ordinary method of becoming acquainted, before others do, with some material event, political, economic or what have you. And, what is important to possess is some sort of theory, which is, of course, merely an abbreviation for experience. And it may be a very wobbly theory, but it must be a particular one, namely, how the other people will react to this event when this event becomes known to them.

If I know about that type of reaction, and I am in possession of the information about the occurrence of this event, then I am able to profit from this situation. Of course, it is entirely irrelevant whether the reaction of the others makes any sense in any objective or moral or political manner whatsoever. This is totally irrelevant. And we have hundreds of cases which prove this.

For example, when President Eisenhower had a heart attack, people sold stock—for heaven knows what reason. If I know that the president has a heart attack, before the others, and if I am in possession of that theory concerning the others, namely that this somehow has a bad influence on stock prices, however nonsensical the connection may be, that is information which has investment value. There are many such cases.

If I find out before others that a company has discovered a gold field, for example, then that clearly is inside information; it will affect my behavior if I am in the position financially to profit from this, and therefore that kind of inside information is something to strive for, and to make an effort to get and hold.

In this case it also makes some sense, of course, because the gold field will increase the earning power and therefore the value of that particular company. So, sense is a relative matter and need not be further analyzed in this respect.

There is a second category of inside information. That would be, for example, that there exist economic reasons why certain stock price movements are to occur. If I know that the government is making inflation, or increases the quantity of credit, or certain international phenomena occur which have a bearing, which eventually always affect the stock market, and I am powerful enough to analyze them while they occur or are about to occur, that is then inside information of the second or higher type. And that is the point, of course, where the economist might enter, provided he can prove, which is not so obvious, that many of these associations actually work.

For example, it would mean that one really could show that an increase in the supply of money in the economy would drive up the stock prices—which is not necessarily the case. This is an area where real economic analysis is possible and would provide information which might have operational value.

In that category is, for example, that one observes that the price of shares has gone up for companies which had increasing earnings. So what is more natural than to look for the change in earnings? If discovered, that would constitute inside information, which would have operational value.

But the record is that earnings cannot be predicted, that the prediction of earnings is as weak and poor as the prediction of stock market prices themselves. And even if you can predict, there is uncertainty. There is a company called Mohawk Data Sciences; recently when it was reported that their earnings had risen by some spectacular 25 or 30 percent, the stock dropped very severely on exactly the same day, and on the basis and because of this announcement.

What is the explanation? Very simple: people had expected even greater increases in earnings and they were anticipated in the stock price movement. So the fact that one is getting hold of a correct fact, which has a correct relationship in the very long run with price formation may not at all work in the concrete situation, and investment, it must be remembered, is in the overwhelming number of cases a matter of concrete decisions and not of decisions in the abstract or in the very long run.

Decisions must be made in the short run, and therefore this is an illustration of how things may go wrong. To bring out the fact of expectations in a somewhat different light, let us assume the following case.

Imagine you have a community in which there is only one single investment advisor, and we can certainly construct such a case. That is, his advice becomes known to everybody and is believed by everybody. There are three conditions. Singularity, complete information distribution, and belief of this information. (Not every advice is believed.) What are the consequences?

The consequences are that he can never say "now is the time to sell stocks," because nobody would buy. Who would be the buyers? He would never be able to say: "now is the time to buy stock Y," because there will be no sellers. He can only say one thing, which will lead to a change, and that is: "now is the time to buy the *new* stock of company Z," because it is not yet on the market!

That is the only possible operational function that a single, well-informed, and completely believed advisor can possess. When you have two advisors, and their advice differs, then you have different information patterns in the economy, or different patterns in the economy, or different patterns as to who knows these advices and who believes them. Among those who know them, not all will believe them, not all are capable of acting, and then it becomes unpredictable as to what the reactions of the investors or stockholders will be.

And so you go on and finally come to the present situation. You find you have a multitude of information of this type injected into the market. It is clear that this corresponds really to the fact we observed, namely that there is a continuous turnover of stock which is an expression of the fact that the opinions and the expectations of price changes in the possession of different people differ.

I have already said what is crucial in the matter, and that in order to get transactions at all on the stock market, it is necessary to have differences of opinions about the same stock, except for the case—which may be a borderline case—when, for example, a forced sale has to take place, when cash has to be raised, etc. We can neglect these as being negligible items in the total volume of transactions.

So there have to be differences in expectations, differences in judgment. Now that is very interesting because that is due to what I would call multidirectional transactions, due to the fact that the flow of the object which is being traded on the stock market is not unidirectional as distinguished from any physical production or the rendering of services.

For example, a motor car producer has no other intention except to sell the motor car. Whether you say motor cars or food or no matter what it is, that is being produced, the purpose is only to get rid of it, to put it into the hands of the next—until it reaches the final consumer.

But on any speculative market, the same commodity may flow in all directions. In fact, I may buy a stock I have recently sold, I may buy it back again. I may sell it again, and so on. There is, therefore, no unidirection and consequently also no clear association between the amount of price change and the amount or the volume of transactions.

The fact that every sale is also a purchase and vice versa is of course a trivial observation. But like basic and even trivial matters, it is often forgotten, especially in discussing price changes on the stock market, whether up or down. When advice is given "now is the right time to sell," that means there must be somebody there who will buy at that price or at a very near price. If that assumption does not hold the advice is worthless. And we have to understand that on the stock market everything is dependent on expectations of a very special kind, namely as a rule involving at least the maintenance, presumably however, the change of the price either upward or downward. In the purchase of ordinary commodities, say of an automobile, the seller is merely selling an automobile and the purchaser is buying a commodity which he will put to particular uses. The motivation for the transaction is a totally different one than when stock transactions are considered. This point cannot be stressed enough because it reveals a significant and fundamental difference in various kinds of economic activity.

It becomes difficult, if not impossible (and in fact I believe it to be impossible), to use standard demand theory for explaining price changes and volume movements on the stock market, which is an interesting limitation of the tool of current demand analysis. Very often the demand for a stock will rise when prices are rising, but not for the ordinary reasons when we have shifts in the demand functions. This may happen, of course, with commodities and not speculative commodities, too, but not in this manner. All this makes it very difficult to claim that current demand analysis is a general way of approaching all price phenomena.

That is perhaps of some interest for economics in general. When you have this lack of unidirection in a market—always eliminating the case I mentioned of any forced situation, when a sale occurs simply for legal or other reasons, let us say having to pay taxes or having to pay death duties—a sale of stock means that there is no confidence in a future price rise on the part of the seller, or that there is knowledge, or assumed knowledge, of a better rise or other advantage in another stock, and therefore a switch occurs.

The purchase is simply the reverse of this. And these two conditions must be met, otherwise there will be no transactions. And that is, I think, quite different from the price formation of ordinary commodities and services which obey other laws.

I must mention the word: manipulation of information. But in addition, of course, there is also a *leadership* phenomenon. You see that one man or one group buys or does something, and the others follow; there is a herd instinct, and that certainly is terribly important.

If you watch this, you have inside information of the second kind, and when the herd is running wild, then you stay away from it, whichever way the herd goes.

Or, one may make some very basic assumptions, which may be perfectly justified. I have two particular cases in mind. Both were friends of mine. One was a banker in Zürich, who in 1932 or 1933, when everything was absolutely at the bottom here in the United States, said, "It is absurd to assume that the United States' economy will never recover, steel will be produced again and money will be made because profitability at such low prices and unemployment exists." So he bought heavily stock in 1933. You can imagine what happened to that investment.

Or, in the summer of 1947, I met a famous economist, L. Albert Hahn, in Zürich, and I asked "What are you doing here?" He said, "I'm buying German stocks." He was a wealthy banker, or rather ex-banker, and for several million dollars he bought Mercedes and I.G. Farben and Mannesmann, and heaven knows what other German companies.

I asked, "What is the basis for this operation?" He said, "It is extremely simple: either the Soviet Union will overrun the whole West, in which case everything is lost, or it will not happen and I don't expect this to happen, and therefore Germany will have to be reconstructed and all these stocks will rise in value." He took this money, put the shares in a holding company, in Liechtenstein, and later lived in peace in Paris. You can imagine what happened to those millions of dollars. This is the sort of investing that yields much more than portfolio analysis of the conventional kind.

Since information is so important and opinions and expectations matter profoundly, there is one point which has to be stressed once more, and that is that the field is wide open, as everybody knows, for fabrication of alleged information.

That means that speculative markets invite immorality. There can be no question about it, and therefore, one should take this into consideration, but I shall not discuss this any further. It is also clear that there is, given a free enterprise system, probably not immoral, interest, namely on the part of stockbrokers: these try to get as many transactions done as possible, because it is from the fees that they make their living. Otherwise, they would not bother to be stockbrokers anymore, or else they have got their money already into a safe harbor.

So there is manipulation and fabrication of news. We know that the law tries to prevent such things, but it is very difficult to imagine how that can be done effectively. If anybody wants information as to how that happens, I suggest reading the excellent studies by John Brooks, who wrote two books: *Once in Golconda* (1969)[2] and *Business Adventures* (1969).[3] He gives an excellent description of the Texas Gulf Sulphur Case, which is really a striking case of the difficulties the law has to know what it really wants to do in regard to preventing abuses or so-called abuses of possessing information.

This big, gray area is, of course, a very unpleasant thing to contemplate, because of the uncertainty that people have in not knowing how to behave.

If we look at facts, or alleged facts, I think we ought to realize that the stock market prices are probably the best data in economics. They are really known with very little error. The volume data are already much less certain, because it is known that the volume figures are, for purely mechanical reasons, often attributed to a somewhat different, later price of the same stock than when the actual transaction happened.

So the association of a particular price with a particular volume is already not necessarily very definite and good, but the prices are very well known, and from there on all economic data decrease in precision. Nevertheless, it is safe to conclude that great changes in prices are not always associated with great changes in volume of transactions and vice versa.

If anybody has read my book, *On the Accuracy of Economic Observations*,[4] you will see that there are countless examples of the widely varying uncertainty in economic data, though very little, if any, attention to this fact is paid by contemporary economic theory. One datum which is, however, particularly interesting in this connection, which is taken as one of the principle features of information, is profits.

I have recently studied a very interesting book by Professor Homer Kripke of the Law School of New York University and T.J. Filis of the Law School of the University of Colorado, which is called *Accounting for Business Lawyers* (1971).[5] It shows the absolute and incredible uncertainty in accounting procedures and confirms what I have long thought and known, that what are called profits are numbers which are not traduced by a uniform, strict procedure; they are very often only figures picked out when a balance sheet is made up. It seems mostly that first of all the question is raised: what profits should we show? And, from there on the balance sheet is set up. I cannot help telling a story which is from another country, but countries are not so different from each other.

In Switzerland, I have a friend who is on the board of a very large company, and when once he was going to a board meeting, I asked, "What goes on?" He said, "Well, we sit three days in a beautiful villa on Lake Geneva, and then we get the balance sheet, which has been made up for the Board." And I said, "That's fine. What then?" He said, "Then from that balance sheet we construct the second balance sheet on the basis of which we go to the Swiss Government, and negotiate the taxes. And then after that is done, we have a third balance sheet which is published." Then come the econometricians and take the third balance sheet, compare it with the other similar third balance sheets of other industries, and determine what the "profitability" of different industries is, the capital-investment ratios, and so the blackboard can be filled with interesting and very meaningful formulas.

Well, that is the reality. Now I am not saying that American corporations behave in the same way, but I have a suspicion that while we do not negotiate taxes with our Internal Revenue Department, there still is the ability to show one number as profit rather than another number. These numbers—estimated in advance—enter the information flow of stock market analysts and investors. They may become inside information, lead to stock market price changes and then the assertion is made that the stock market is the "optimal allocater" of investible funds. All that goes then over into the theory of the Pareto Optimum and similar beautiful theorems. So, we can leave it at that.

Now let me ask, what are the open problems, if what I have been saying is really true? Is the stock market an interesting field for research? I would say: certainly, unquestionably. We have seen many examples of this and there are terribly complicated problems there of a statistical nature, of evaluation of risk, etc., and all of this is very important and significant.

But one of the problems which I think has been neglected is the virtual impossibility of using standard demand analysis in the explanation of prices and therefore of price changes.

The fact is that the price of a stock is obtained by a process of auctions. It is a peculiarly complicated auction, because it is not only between the seller and the buyer, but involves a third party, the "specialist." The understanding of this process of auction, in which there is not only the interest of the seller and the willingness of the buyer, but also the specialist, who is not only a middle-man, but a third active party, is of great importance. The specialist is not involved in every transaction with his own funds, but in most transactions by virtue of being a dealer and having an inventory.

So this is a most interesting situation of price formation and I think that is a challenging problem for theoretical analysis to understand how this auction really works. Since we know that prices are changing and that they are moving between barriers and that the barriers are collapsible or movable, then this auction process becomes even more complicated than if it did not have this further characteristic.

Another problem would be, of course, to discover whether in the whole analysis of past prices one might get information about non-linear properties of prices and price relations to each other. (I think, however, its solution would have no practical value.)

I know of no particular studies of this problem, but I may not be fully informed. I would suspect that if they are found, they will be so small that such relationships would have no operational value, because of the expenses of putting such mechanisms to use. These expenses are the reason why whatever traces of cycles we find in spite of the random walk—like the very small monthly cycles Granger and I have noticed—are worthless so far as operational value is concerned, because of their expense.

So their existence would not contradict the statement which I made at the beginning, which is now quite obvious, of course, namely, that no mechanism which becomes known will survive, except the random walk. That refers to all those mechanisms which it is financially feasible to operate, and if they are not feasible, then they are only theoretically of interest. But they offer a scientifically legitimate field and might lead to very interesting results to satisfy the scholar.

To summarize, we know the fact that we have a random walk; we know that information flows are vital, that they can be manipulated, that the same facts lead to different interpretations, otherwise there would be no transactions, and that these are significantly different from what I have called the "unidirectional operation." Still unknown are the mechanisms which actually make the price in the concrete case.

That is all I want to say at this juncture. My last note is, however, the one that I had started with, "Investing is an art." We can well leave it at that, which means that most people do not know how to invest. Only those who have done it can tell us how they have done it, *ex post*, but they never can with assurance tell us how they should do it again.

Notes

1. Oskar Morgenstern and Clive W.J. Granger, *Predictability of Stock Market Prices* (Lexington, Mass.: Heath-Lexington, 1970).

2. John Brooks, *Once in Golconda*, New York, 1969.

3. John Brooks, *Business Adventures*, New York, 1969.

4. Oskar Morgenstern, *On the Accuracy of Economic Observations*, 2nd Edition, Princeton University Press, 1963.

5. Homer Kripke and T.J. Filis, *Accounting for Business Lawyers*, 1971.

6

The Assessment of Probability Distributions for Future Security Prices

Robert L. Winkler

1. Introduction

In countless situations in a wide variety of areas, individuals or corporations make inferences or decisions in the face of uncertainty about future events. Although deterministic models are sometimes applicable or may provide a reasonable first approximation, it is necessary in most cases to take account of uncertainty when modeling an inferential or decision making problem. Since probability can be thought of as the mathematical language of uncertainty, formal models for decision making under uncertainty require probabilistic inputs. In financial decision making, this is illustrated by the models that have been developed for the portfolio selection problem; such models generally require the assessment of probability distributions (or at least some summary measures of probability distributions) for future prices (or returns) of the securities that are being considered for inclusion in the portfolio (e.g., see Markowitz, 1959; Sharpe, 1970). In medical diagnosis, a physician (either explicitly or implicitly) formulates a probability distribution involving various possible diseases and uses this distribution in making decisions concerning treatment (e.g., see Lusted, 1968). In meteorology, weather forecasters prepare probability forecasts for various meteorological variables such as precipitation, and these forecasts are used by decision makers whose activities are sensitive to the occurrence of precipitation (e.g., see Murphy and Allen, 1970). In economics, probability forecasts of various economic indicators are of considerable interest to economists and to decision makers in both the public and private sectors of the economy. Although these examples represent only a small subset of the inferential and decision making situations in which probabilistic inputs are of interest, they provide an indication of the importance and usefulness of such inputs.

In this paper it is assumed that an individual faced with an inferential or decision-making problem (hereafter this individual is referred to as a decision maker) has access to information regarding future events that are related to the problem. Such information may include the output of models of the "system"

The research leading to this paper was conducted in part while the author was on leave and visiting the Graduate School of Business Administration, University of Washington, Seattle, for the 1970-71 academic year.

of concern (e.g., the stock market, the patient, the atmosphere, or the economy) and the results of highly-sophisticated statistical analyses of large amounts of data, or, at the other extreme, it may involve only informal observations by the decision maker or by an "expert" who is consulted by the decision maker. Whatever form the information takes, how to use this information in the formulation of a probability distribution is ultimately a subjective choice on the part of the decision maker, so the resulting distribution is a subjective probability distribution.

Ultimately, *all* components of the formal mathematical models underlying inferential and decision-theoretic procedures represent quantified judgments. Thus, the subjective, or personal, interpretation of probability, in which probability measures the confidence, or degree of belief, that a particular individual has in the truth of a particular proposition, appears to be the most useful interpretation of probability. This interpretation differs from other approaches by not attempting to specify a "correct" set of probabilities. All self-consistent, or coherent, sets of probabilities are admissible as long as the individual feels that they correspond with his judgments. It can be shown (de Finetti, 1937; Savage, 1954) that subjective probabilities assessed in accordance with certain plausible behavioral postulates of coherence must conform mathematically to a probability measure. In essence, the postulates of coherence (the term "consistency" is often used in place of "coherence") are such that if a person obeys the postulates, it is impossible to set up a "Dutch book" (i.e., a series of bets which guarantees that the person will lose money regardless of the outcomes of the events of interest) against him.

A brief discussion of the assessment and evaluation of probability distributions is presented in Section 2, some experimental results regarding the prediction of future security prices are reviewed and their implications are discussed in Section 3, and Section 4 concerns the choice of appropriate variables for inferential or decision-making models. Some potential Bayesian models are briefly presented in Section 5, and Section 6 contains a short summary and discussion. In a narrow sense, then, this paper is concerned with the assessment of probabilities for future security prices and with the development of models to be used in inferential and decision-making problems involving securities. In a much broader sense, however, the question of interest might be stated as follows: How can a decision maker best use all of the information available in a given situation, including the judgments of experts as well as any relevant data?

2. The Assessment and Evaluation of Probability Distributions

With regard to the use of probability distributions as inputs in inferential and decision-making problems, two considerations are of particular concern: the assessment, or formulation, of probability distributions and the evaluation of the distributions after the events of interest are observed. Of course, these considerations are by no means mutually exclusive, since evaluation may lead to more refined assessment techniques or to a re-examination by individuals of the relationship between their judgments and their assessed probabilities. However, for the purpose of exposition it is convenient to discuss assessment and evaluation separately, and this section contains a brief review of some of the work in this area.

Until recently, little attention had been paid to practical problems associated with the assessment of subjective probability distributions. "If certain structure axioms are satisfied, any rational man acts as if he had an a priori distribution on the states of nature. But what the rational man wants is a method for selecting that a priori distribution which best uses his a priori information." (Suppes, 1956, p. 72) Various procedures have been suggested to help an individual translate his judgments into probabilities, and many of these procedures might be classified as methods of direct interrogation.

In an earlier paper (Winkler, 1967a), several direct interrogation procedures were discussed and the results of a study designed to investigate these procedures were reported. The assessment techniques used in the study were divided roughly into four categories. Two of the techniques, involving questions about densities and cumulative probabilities, were concerned directly with the distribution being assessed, whereas the other two were indirectly related to the distribution (e.g., via questions about the effect of hypothetical sample evidence on the individual's probabilities). The study of these four techniques indicated that, by and large, it is feasible to question individuals about subjective probability distributions, although some instruction is required and different techniques may lead to different distributions.

Methods of direct interrogation provide a way for an individual's judgments to be expressed in probabilities or in some form that can be translated into probabilities. Such methods have been criticized on the grounds that there is no way of knowing if the resulting probabilities are actually in accordance with the individual's judgments. This criticism has played an important role in the development of the personalistic theory, leading to the development of techniques that are designed to provide some incentive for an individual to carefully translate his judgments into probabilities without "slanting" his probabilities. Good (1965, p. 49) states, "Probability judgments can be sharpened by laying bets at suitable odds. If people always felt obliged to back their opinions when challenged, we would be spared a few of the 'certain' predictions that are so frequently made."

An individual's choice of bets reveals certain features of his personal probabilities. In addition to bets, various "scoring rules," or "elicitation functions," have been developed to encourage an individual to make careful assessments that correspond to his judgments. These rules involve the computation of a score, or reward, which is a function of the assessed probabilities and of the event that actually occurs. A "strictly proper" scoring rule penalizes an individual (in terms of a lower expected score or reward) for any deviations from his actual judgments. General discussions involving scoring rules and reviews of the previous work in the area may be found in Winkler (1967b), Winkler and Murphy (1968), Staël von Holstein (1970b), and Savage (1971).

After the events of interest are observed, it is useful to evaluate the probability distributions that had been assessed prior to the occurrence of the events. Furthermore, evaluation may be approached from an inferential viewpoint or from a decision-theoretic viewpoint. From an inferential viewpoint, the association between the probabilities and the actual outcomes is of interest, and this association is sometimes referred to as "validity." The scoring rules mentioned above provide measures of validity (e.g., see Murphy and Winkler, 1970). For example, if one individual continually obtains higher scores than a second individual, then the first might reasonably be thought of as a "better" assessor than the second for the type of situation being considered. Of course, expertise may vary from situation to situation; A's probability forecasts of temperature (or of the future price of a particular security) may be "better" than B's, but B may obtain higher scores than A with regard to precipitation probabilities (or with regard to probabilities for the future price of a different security). If a decision maker repeatedly consulted a particular "expert" to obtain probability forecasts, he might want to calibrate the expert's probabilities on the basis of an evaluation of previous forecasts. Furthermore, if evaluation measures such as scoring rules are used as feedback to the individual making the probability assessments, they should help him to evaluate his past performance and to attempt to "improve" in the future. There is, of course, a direct analogy between this procedure and the use of measures of past performance to evaluate and to refine mathematical models in general.

From a decision-theoretic viewpoint, the relation of the assessed probabilities to a decision-making problem is of interest, and one way to evaluate the probabilities is in terms of the payoff obtained by the decision maker after using the probabilities as an input to his decision model (e.g., see Murphy, 1971). For example, if a security analyst assesses probability distributions for future security prices and these distributions are used as inputs to a portfolio selection model, his probabilities might be evaluated from a decision-theoretic viewpoint in terms of the actual rate of return on the portfolio chosen by the model. This form of evaluation is consistent with a suggestion of Savage (1971) that a decision maker should reward a probability assessor with a share of the decision-making problem.

3. The Assessment of Probability Distributions for Future Security Prices: Some Experimental Results

The use of probabilistic inputs in decision-making models concerning security investment has for the most part been confined to the consideration of certain summary measures of probability distributions rather than entire distributions. For example, the portfolio model developed by Markowitz (1959) requires only the mean and variance of the distribution of the price (or return) of each individual security and the correlations between prices (or returns). These inputs are sufficient for the calculation of the mean and variance of the return from any portfolio, and the model chooses an "efficient set" of portfolios on the basis of mean and variance. This implies somewhat restrictive assumptions concerning the decision maker's utility function (e.g., see Hakansson, 1971), so it might be useful to obtain summary measures other than (or in addition to) the mean and variance (Fama, 1965b; Jean, 1971). Of course, if an entire distribution is assessed, any desired summary measures can be determined from the distribution.

Several experiments have been conducted regarding the actual assessment and evaluation of entire probability distributions (e.g., see Winkler, 1967a; Alpert and Raiffa, 1969; Staël von Holstein, 1970a; and Winkler, 1971a). At this time, however, I am aware of only two studies concerning the assessment of entire probability distributions for future security prices. These two studies are reported in Bartos (1969) and Staël von Holstein (1970a, Chapter 10). Since both of these studies represent doctoral dissertations and are not readily available, the results are briefly summarized in this section. Further details, of course, can be obtained by consulting the original sources.

Bartos (1969) developed a questionnaire to elicit information in probabilistic form from security analysts regarding future prices of individual stocks. The questionnaire involved the use of direct interrogation techniques relating to the density function and to the cumulative distribution function. The density function was assessed by means of questions regarding relative densities and relative areas and by graphing the function. In assessing the cumulative distribution function, fractiles were assessed by means of direct questions and "successive subdivisions" (successively dividing intervals into two equally likely subintervals to find the .5 fractile, the .25 fractile, the .125 fractile, and so on) and by graphing the function. The predictions in Bartos' study were obtained from three security analysts employed by an investment company that would rank in the second quartile of a listing of mutual funds in terms of total funds available for investment. Each analyst chose five securities that were of particular interest to him at the time of the study, so the setting was clearly that of experts making predictions on the basis of a considerable amount of information. After an extensive "practice-instruction" session to acquaint the analysts with the assessment techniques, they made predictions once a month over a six month period, assessing probabilities at each session for the closing prices of their chosen securities one, three, and six months into the future. For each situation, the analyst assessed a density function and a cumulative distribution function and then reconciled any differences between these two functions.

After the practice-instruction session, the analysts seemed to understand the assessment techniques and appeared to be quite interested in the assessment task. The general shapes of the assessed distributions varied, with bimodal or multimodal distributions occurring most frequently. The analysts claimed that they found it easier to work with the density function than with the cumulative distribution function, and their "reconciled" distributions were generally closer to the distribution assessed by considering the density function than to the distribution assessed by considering the cumulative distribution function. As the lead time of the forecasts (the amount of time between the forecast and the event) increased, both the means and the variances (as well as the coefficients of variation) of the assessed distributions tended to increase. The increase in means was expected because the analysts selected securities that were included or were seriously being considered for inclusion in the firm's portfolio, and the increase in variances seems reasonable because "uncertainty about the future" should increase with lead time. A majority of the assessed distributions were asymmetric (negatively skewed more frequently than positively skewed), and the degree of skewness appeared to be a function of the individual security. Kurtosis measures indicated that the assessed distributions tended to be platykurtic, which is noteworthy in view of the considerable body of empirical results which indicate that distributions of changes in security prices are leptokurtic (e.g., see Fama, 1965a).

Bartos attempted to evaluate the analysts' probability distributions in two ways. First, he considered only the means of the assessed distributions and analyzed the relationship between the means and the actual prices of the securities. The means tended to be lower than the actual prices, and the distribution of the differences between the means and the actual prices was found not to be a good fit to a normal distribution because it was asymmetric and platykurtic. Second, he used scoring rules to evaluate the probability distributions. The continuous distributions assessed by the analysts were approximated by histograms with twelve class-intervals (the exact intervals differed among securities) for the purposes of the scoring rules. Comparing scores obtained by the analysts with scores obtained by using a uniform distribution over the twelve class-intervals in each case indicated that in almost half of the cases, the uniform distribution outperformed the analyst's distribution. Furthermore, for 19 percent of the predictions, the observation (i.e., the observed price) fell outside the interval from the .01 fractile to the .99 fractile (one would hope that, in the long run, the observation would fall in this interval about 2 percent of the time). These results, which would seem to indicate that the assessed distributions were too "tight," are consistent with experimental evidence in contexts other than the prediction of future security prices (Alpert and Raiffa, 1969; Staël von Holstein, 1970, Chapter 11).

In general, the results of the Bartos study indicate that with some training, analysts can assess probability distributions for future security prices to their own satisfaction without any assistance other than some initial instruction. Furthermore, the analysts all stated after the conclusion of the study that participating in the study had proved very useful with regard to their jobs as security analysts. They indicated that the assessment of probability distributions led them to analyze carefully their basis for predicting prices and to formalize their judgments regarding potential price movements. In general, the use of mathematical models and the determination of inputs to such models forces an individual to think carefully about the problem at hand and often leads to the consideration of factors that otherwise would be ignored. Thus, the process of model-building is often extremely useful to a decision maker, although more emphasis seems to be placed on "solving" the model once it has been developed.

One difficulty that arose in Bartos' study concerned the tails of the distributions. The analysts experienced some difficulties in the assessment of tail-area probabilities, which is comparable with the assessment of extremely small probabilities (e.g., probabilities for "rare events"). Such difficulties may account in part for the results discussed in the preceding paragraph. It is apparently more difficult to subjectively distinguish among probabilities such as .001, .005, .01, and .02 than it is to distinguish among, say, .4, .5, and .6. In terms of variables such as the future price of a security, however, the interval from the .005 fractile to the .02 fractile may be wider than the interval from the .4 fractile to the .6 fractile; for a standard normal distribution, the former interval has an approximate width of .50 and the latter has an approximate width of .53. With regard to investment decisions, moreover, the tails of the distribution may be of particular importance. If the decision maker is a risk-avoider, for instance, the tails of the distribution may be closely related to the "riskiness" of the security. Under certain utility assumptions, the distribution may be adequately summarized for decision-making purposes by its mean and variance, and the variance is quite sensitive to changes in the tails (if the distribution is asymmetric, the mean may also be quite sensitive to such changes).

Another difficulty encountered in Bartos' study concerned the notion of a "future price" of a security. Although the variable of interest was clearly defined as the closing price of the security on a specified date in the future, and this was identical to the definition used by the analysts' firm for future price estimates, the analysts claimed some vagueness regarding the variable. They thought of definitions of "price" such as "the price in the middle of May" or "the price for June." "When questioned on what they meant by a 'June price,' the analysts were unable to define it. They did admit that it was neither a high, low, nor closing price but were unable to say what it was. The best they could do was say it was an average or normal price over some undefined period of time. The more remote the prediction, the greater this period of time." (Bartos, 1969, p. 162) Such ambiguity is, of course, undesirable, and the question of what variables should be considered is discussed in Section 4.

Finally, the analysts felt that the time required to make assessments would make it impractical to make such assessments on a routine basis for all securities under consideration for the firm's portfolio. Various refinements, such as the use of time-sharing computers with appropriate display terminals and the use of families of distributions that allow the consideration of certain summary measures instead of entire distributions, should ease the time burden. Such refinements will be discussed in Sections 5 and 6.

A somewhat different study involving the assessment of probability distributions for future security prices was conducted by Staël von Holstein (1970a, Chapter 10). This study dealt with twelve securities on the Stockholm Stock Exchange, and the 72 subjects included stock analysts, statisticians, and students. Thus, in contrast to the Bartos study, in which all three subjects were expert stock analysts with exposure to one or two statistics courses, the subjects in the Staël von Holstein study possessed a wide variety of expertise with respect to the stock market and the securities in question and with -respect to probability and statistics. Instead of assessing continuous distributions, the participants in the Stockholm study assessed probabilities for five intervals (price decreases more than 3 percent, decreases more than 1 percent but at most 3 percent, changes at most 1 percent, increases more than 1 percent but at most 3 percent, and increases more than 3 percent). The forecast lead time was two weeks, and the class-intervals were chosen in order to make the past frequencies of occurrence of the five intervals roughly equal on the basis of the observed price changes for the two years preceding the study. The assessments were made every two weeks for a total of ten sessions.

Because the lead time equalled the time between assessments, the subjects were able to observe the relationship between their assessed probabilities and the actual prices before making the next set of assessments. In addition, they were presented feedback which included their assessed distributions and scores determined from a (quadratic) scoring rule, the average score and ranking for each assessor for the preceding session and for the entire study to date, the average score for each security for the preceding session and for the entire study to date, and the average probabilities assessed for each security by the participants. Such extensive feedback should be extremely useful to an individual in helping him to examine the relationship between his predictions and the actual scores and to compare his performance with the performance of the other participants, provided that he is willing to take the time to make a careful evaluation of the feedback.

An evaluation of the scores indicated that only 3 of the 72 subjects received a better average score than that attained by using a uniform distribution over the five class intervals. Because of the way in which the intervals were chosen, an assessor who chose to base his forecasts solely on the relative frequencies from the past two years would have assessed approximately a uniform distribution. Furthermore, there was a positive relationship between the average score and the average variance of the assessed distributions; those individuals assessing distributions with higher variances tended to have higher scores, and the average variance increased over the course of the study. Since this implies that "tight" distributions were associated with low scores, it may be related to the previously-mentioned tendency for the analysts in the Bartos study to assess distributions that were too "tight."

In both the Bartos and Staël von Holstein studies, then, the subjects apparently understood the assessment techniques and had little difficulty assessing probability distributions for future security prices. However, the results indicate that uniform distributions "outperformed" the subjects' distributions in a majority of cases. Only three analysts, five stocks per analyst, and six sets of assessments were considered in the Bartos study, and it is difficult to make generalizations on the basis of such a small sample. The results could have been dominated by the particular movements of the stock market during the period in question. The Staël von Holstein study involved a large number of subjects, but since many of these subjects had only a passing interest in the securities being considered, the degree of expertise may be questioned. In addition, while a lead time of only two weeks is ideal from the standpoint of providing rapid feedback, it may be an unfortunate choice because it is considerably shorter than the usual decision horizon. And as in the Bartos study, the particular movements of the stock market during the twenty week period in question may have dominated the results.

Despite their limitations, the two experiments discussed in this section provide useful guidelines for further study of the assessment of probability distributions for future security prices. They imply that it is feasible to have "experts" assess such distributions, although several problems need further investigation (e.g., the assessment of tail-area probabilities and the choice of variables to be predicted). It would be useful to have a record of assessed probabilities over a period of time of sufficient length to minimize the chance of the results being seriously contaminated by the particular time period. Unfortunately, data such as this would require an extensive experiment because in the few situations known to me in which probability assessments for future security prices are currently being made at an operational level, information regarding the probabilities is treated as confidential and is not publicly available.

4. What Variables Should Be Predicted?

In both of the studies described in the preceding section, the variable for which probability distributions were assessed was the closing price of a security on a specified date in the future, with lead times ranging from two weeks to six months. However, the closing price of a security on some future date does not seem to be a particularly useful variable for decision-making purposes. There may be few trades at the closing price, and the price fluctuation of a security during a particular day is not necessarily nonnegligible. Thus, perhaps the average price at which a security trades during a given day is a more reasonable variable to consider than the closing price. Other variables of possible interest include the average price over a period longer than a day or high and low prices during a day or during a longer period.

The fact that 19 percent of the observed closing prices fell outside the assessed .01 and .99 fractiles in Bartos' experiment suggests that the assessed distributions were too "tight." Given the ambiguity regarding the definition of price, this phenomenon might be explained in part by comparing the assessment of an "average price" with the assessment of a closing price. Suppose that $\tilde{p}$, the price of a security at any particular point of time during a certain day in the future, has a distribution with mean $E(\tilde{p})$ and variance $V(\tilde{p})$. (In this paper, tildes are used to indicate random variables.) The form of the distribution is irrelevant, as long as it possesses finite mean and variance. Moreover, suppose that n observations of price are made during the course of the day, beginning with the opening price and ending with the closing price, and let the "average price" be defined as the average of these n observations. If the observations could be considered to be independent, the distribution of "average price" would have mean $E(\tilde{p})$ and variance $V(\tilde{p})/n$. It is highly unrealistic to consider the observations (as contemplated some time in advance) as independent (although the random walk theory implies that price *changes* are independent); a much more realistic assumption would be that the n observations are positively (but not perfectly) correlated. As a result, the variance of the "average price," which is equal to $V(\tilde{p})/n$ plus a sum of covariance terms,

$$V(\tilde{\tilde{p}}) = [V(\tilde{p})/n] + 2 \sum_{\substack{i=1 \\ i<j}}^{n} \sum_{j=1}^{n} \mathrm{Cov}(\tilde{p}_i, \tilde{p}_j)/n^2$$

is greater than $V(\tilde{p})/n$ but less than $V(\tilde{p})$.

If the analysts in Bartos' study tended to think in terms of average prices rather than closing prices, then, their distributions might appear to be too tight when compared with actual closing prices, which is exactly what happened. If the analysts tended to think in terms of average prices over periods longer than a single day, this result would be magnified yet further. The mean of the distribution of the average price over a certain period is equal to the mean of the distribution of the price at the midpoint of that period provided that any expected price trend over the period in question may be assumed to be linear (other assumptions also lead to this result, but the linear assumption appears to be the most realistic assumption, especially if the period is not extremely long). The variance of the distribution of the average price, however, is generally smaller than the variance of the distribution of the price at any particular point within the period.

Most of the above variables concern the price of a security, whether it is a closing price, an average price, or some other price, on a specified date in the future. But the securities market is such that an investor need not specify in advance a particular date on which he will sell a certain security. Indeed, he would be foolish to do so, although he may wish to specify a rough time horizon for his investment decisions. For example, he might ask, "What will the average price of security X be next June?" or "What will the average price of security X be between now and next June?" He would *not* be as likely to ask, "What will the closing price of security X be on June 15?"

Thus, the investor is interested in the price movements of a security over some period of time. But average prices are not sufficient to describe price movements; the investor might react differently to two securities with identical expected average prices if one was expected to deviate little from the average price and the other was expected to be subject to wide swings around the average price. For example, the investor might ask, "What will the price range of security X be next June?", "What will the price range of security X be between now and next June?", or "What are the chances that the price of security X will be greater than $40 per share at any time between now and next June?" This suggests that it might be useful to assess probability distributions for high and low prices of a security over a particular period of time.

From an inferential standpoint, the closing price of a security on a particular date in the future may be of interest, and this variable is surely related to the average price during that day or during a longer period which includes that day and, probably to a lesser degree, to the high and low prices during that day or during a longer period including that day. From a decision-theoretic standpoint, the closing price does not seem to be a particularly compelling variable with respect to investment decisions. Even if it is granted that under certain conditions the mean of the distribution of a closing price will be equal to the mean of the distribution of an average price and will be related to the means of the distributions of high and low prices (hopefully the relationships are linear or approximately so, but this is by no means certain), the variances will usually be quite different. If the decision maker's utility function is linear, the variances are not of concern in the investment problem (although they may be of concern for related decisions such as whether or not to seek additional information). For nonlinear utility functions, the variances generally *are* of concern; for quadratic utility functions, for example, decisions depend directly on the means and variances of distributions of future prices. Therefore, if average prices or high and low prices are considered instead of closing prices, the differences in variances could significantly affect the investment decisions (e.g., in portfolio analysis, such differences could alter the composition of the "optimal" portfolio).

The point of this section is that it is not at all obvious what variables are most relevant with regard to investment decisions and that this in turn may affect the assessment of probability distributions for future security prices. For example, if closing prices are of limited practical usefulness in investment decision-making, then analysts may find it difficult to think in terms of closing prices. The resulting ambiguity may affect the analysts' probability assessments and the resulting inferences and decisions. Thus, it is important to give some consideration to the choice of variables and to carefully define these variables before assessing probability distributions.

5. Potential Bayesian Models

The question of what variables are relevant in a given inferential or decision-theoretic situation is closely related to the development of mathematical models to represent the situation. In general, there is a need for the development of models of security price movements that are realistic in an inferential sense *and* useful in a decision-theoretic sense. In particular, the previous sections have dealt with the assessment at a particular point in time of probability distributions for future security prices. As new information is obtained, it is necessary to reconsider the situation and to assess new probabilities. It would be more convenient if this revision procedure could be accomplished formally through the use of a model that would somehow reduce the assessment burden. The Bayesian framework, with its emphasis on the revision of probabilities, is well-suited to this situation.

In the Bayesian approach to problems of statistical inference and decision, probabilities are updated as new information is obtained. Such updating is a particularly desirable feature with respect to decision making because of the desire to base decisions on all available information. The models presented in this section, which are discussed in more detail in Winkler (1971b), represent an attempt to model the price movements of securities in a Bayesian framework.

Suppose that a particular security is under consideration, and let $\widetilde{x}_i$ represent the price of that security at time i, where $\widetilde{x}_i \epsilon X = (0,\infty)$, i is a non-negative integer, and $i=0$ corresponds to the current time. The length of the time interval from i to $i+1$ is unspecified (but independent of i); depending on the problem at hand, it could be taken as an hour, a day, a week, a month, a year, or any other convenient choice. To simplify matters, it will be assumed for the moment that the only relevant information available in the ith time period (the period from time $i-1$ to time i) is $\widetilde{x}_i$. If the decision maker is interested in the distribution of $\widetilde{x}_t$, he can assess $f(x_t | x_0)$ and revise it via Bayes' theorem as new information is obtained. (In this paper all variables are assumed to be continuous, and f is used to represent any density function; the corresponding development for discrete variables is analogous).

At time i $(0 < i < t)$,

$$f(x_t|x_0, x_1, \ldots, x_i) = \frac{f(x_t|x_0)f(x_i, x_2, \ldots, x_i|x_t, x_0)}{\int_X f(x_t|x_0)f(x_i, x_2, \ldots, x_i|x_t, x_0)dx_t}, \tag{1}$$

where $f(x_1, x_2, \ldots, x_i \mid x_t, x_0)$, considered as a function of $\tilde{x}_t$, is the likelihood function; $f(x_t \mid x_0)$ is the prior distribution of $\tilde{x}_t$, and $f(x_t \mid x_0, x_1, \ldots, x_i)$ is the posterior distribution of x_t. If this updating is performed each period, a series of distributions $f(x_t \mid x_0)$, $f(x_t \mid x_0, x_1)$, $\ldots$, $f(x_0, x_1, \ldots, x_i)$, $\ldots$ will result. Alternatively, it might be more convenient to work with price differences, logarithms of price differences, or rates of change of prices, which can in turn be manipulated to determine the distributions of interest.

The above approach requires a tremendous number of assessments, even for a single security, so it would be convenient to have a somewhat simpler model. The objective in developing such a model is to include restrictions that simplify the analysis without greatly limiting the realism of the model. As a starting point, a very simple model will be presented. The model deals with price differences, $\tilde{d}_i = \tilde{x}_i - \tilde{x}_{i-1}$, and assumes that the price differences are independent. In addition, the model is restricted further by assuming that the differences are identically distributed and that the distribution of $\tilde{d}_i$ belongs to a certain family of distributions which may be indexed by the parameter (or vector of parameters) $\tilde{\theta}$. Given a prior distribution $f(\tilde{\theta})$ over the parameter space Ω, the marginal distribution of $\tilde{d}_i$ at time 0, which is called a predictive distribution in Bayesian terminology, is

$$f(d_i) = \int_\Omega f(d_i|\theta) \, f(\theta) \, d\theta. \tag{2}$$

The predictive distribution of $\tilde{x}_t$ is

$$f(x_t|x_0) = \int_\Omega \int_{D_{0,t}} f(d_t|\theta)f(d_{t-1}|\theta)\ldots f(d_1|\theta)f(\theta)dd_1 \ldots dd_t d\theta,$$

where $D_{i,t} = \left\{ (d_{i+1}, \ldots, d_t) \mid x_i + \sum_{j=i+1}^{t} d_j = x_t \right\}. \tag{3}$

For example, suppose that $\tilde{d}_i$ is normally distributed with unknown mean $\tilde{\mu}$ and known variance σ^2 and that the prior distribution of $\tilde{\mu}$ is a normal distribution with mean m_0 and variance σ^2/n_0. Then at time 0, the marginal distribution of $\tilde{d}_i$ is a normal distribution with mean m_0 and variance (n_0+1) σ^2/n_0, and the predictive distribution $f(x_t \mid x_0)$ is a normal distribution with mean $x_0 + tm_0$ and variance $(n_0 + t)\sigma^2/n_0$. Note that the particular choice of distributions greatly simplifies matters. Since $\tilde{d}_i$ is normally distributed for each i, the sum of price differences $\sum_{j=1}^{t} \tilde{d}_j = \tilde{x}_t - x_0$ is also normally distributed, and (3) reduces to

$$f(x_t \mid x_0) = \int_{-\infty}^{\infty} f(x_t \mid \mu) f(\mu) \, d\mu. \qquad (4)$$

Given that $\tilde{\mu}$ is also normally distributed, the derivation of $f(x_t \mid x_0)$ is quite simple.

At time 1, the new information x_1 is used to revise the distribution of $\tilde{\theta}$:

$$f(\theta \mid x_0, x_1) = \frac{f(\theta) f(d_1 \mid \theta)}{\int_{\Omega} f(\theta) f(d_1 \mid \theta) \, d\theta}. \qquad (5)$$

If the investor wants to look t periods into the future, the distribution of $\tilde{x}_{t+1}$ at time 1 is analogous to the distribution of $\tilde{x}_t$ at time 0. It is interesting to consider time t as a fixed point of reference, in which case the relevant predictive distribution is

$$f(x_t \mid x_0, x_1) = \int_{\Omega} \int_{D_{i,t}} f(d_t \mid \theta) f(d_{t-1} \mid \theta) \ldots f(d_2 \mid \theta) \qquad (6)$$

$$f(\theta \mid x_0, x_1) \, dd_2 \ldots dd_t d\theta.$$

The uncertainty about $\tilde{x}_t$ has been modified in two ways: (1) there are only $t-1$ periods remaining until time t, and (2) the distribution of $\tilde{\theta}$ has been revised. An analogy may be drawn between this procedure and the Bayesian approach to inferences concerning a finite population. If the finite population is assumed to be generated by an underlying process with parameter $\tilde{\theta}$, sampling without replacement yields information about a portion of the population *and* information about $\tilde{\theta}$. Both types of information are useful in making inferences about the finite population, the former because it provides knowledge about part of the population and the latter because it is useful in making inferences about the rest of the population.

At time i ($0<i<t$), the distribution of θ is

$$f(\theta|x_0,x_1,\ldots,x_i) = \frac{f(\theta)f(d_1|\theta)f(d_2|\theta)\ldots f(d_i|\theta)}{\int_{\Omega} f(\theta)f(d_i|\theta)f(d_2|\theta)\ldots f(d_i|\theta)\,d\theta} \quad (7)$$

and the distribution of $\tilde{x}_t$ is

$$f(x_t|x_0,x_1,\ldots,x_i) = \int_{\Omega}\int_{D_{i,t}} f(d_t|\theta)f(d_{t-1}|\theta)\ldots f(d_{i+1}|\theta) \quad (8)$$

$$f(\theta|x_0,x_1,\ldots,x_i)\,dd_{i+1}\ldots dd_t d\theta.$$

For the example utilizing the normality assumptions, the distribution of $\tilde{\mu}$ at time 1 is normal with mean $m_1 = (n_0 m_0 + x_1 - x_0)/(n_0 + 1)$ and variance $\sigma^2/n_1 = \sigma^2/(n_0+1)$, and the predictive distribution of $\tilde{x}_t$ is a normal distribution with mean $x_1 + (t-1)m_1$ and variance $(n_1 + t-1)\sigma^2/n_1$. At time i $(0<i<t)$, $f(\mu|x_0,\ldots,x_i)$ is normal with mean $m_i = (n_0 m_0 + x_i - x_0)/(n_0 + i)$ and variance $\sigma^2/n_i = \sigma^2/(n_0 + i)$. The predictive distribution of $\tilde{x}_t$ at time i is normal with mean $x_i + (t-i)m_i$ and variance $(n_i + t - i)\sigma^2/n_i$.

Given a convenient set of assumptions, then, the updating procedure can be quite simple. The assumptions of the above model are as follows:

1. The price x_i is unambiguously defined (it may represent a closing price an average price, a high price, a low price, etc., as long as it is clearly defined; thus, the question of the appropriate "price" to consider is still open).
2. The only relevant information available in the ith time period is the price $\tilde{x}_i$.
3. The price differences are independent and identically distributed.
4. The distribution of $\tilde{d}_i$ is a member of a particular family of distributions (the normal family with known variance in the example), which is indexed by $\tilde{\theta}$.
5. A prior distribution is assessed for $\tilde{\theta}$. For the sake of mathematical tractability in the application of Bayes' theorem, it is convenient if this distribution is conjugate with respect to the family of distributions chosen in the preceding assumption (the concept of conjugate prior distributions is developed in Raiffa and Schlaifer, 1961). In the example, the normal distribution for $\tilde{\mu}$ is a conjugate prior distribution.

The model can be modified by weakening the assumptions, but such modifications are not without cost in terms of the manageability of the model. For example, empirical evidence (e.g., Fama, 1965a) suggests that the distribution of price changes of securities is non-Gaussian and can be represented most generally in terms of the family of stable distributions (which includes the normal distribution as a special case). The family of stable distributions has four parameters (a characteristic exponent, an index of skewness, a scale parameter, and a location parameter) and is more difficult to work with than the normal distribution (see, e.g., Fama and Roll, 1968, 1971). An important question in the choice of a family of distributions for $\tilde{d}_i$ is the sensitivity of the inferences and decisions produced by the model to variations in the distribution of $\tilde{d}_i$. If such inferences and decisions tend to be somewhat insensitive to moderate deviations from normality, then the normal family might be a useful approximation to use for the distribution of $\tilde{d}_i$. Incidentally, the extension to a normal family with unknown mean and unknown variance is straightforward and should cause no difficulties.

A generalization of the fifth assumption that could be quite useful is to let the prior distribution of $\tilde{\theta}$ be a mixture of conjugate distributions. For the normal model, this means that the prior distribution of $\tilde{\mu}$ is a mixture of K normal distributions,

$$f(\mu) = \sum_{j=1}^{K} f(\mu \mid \phi_j) P(\phi_j), \tag{9}$$

where $f(\mu \mid \phi_j)$ is a normal distribution with mean $m_{0,j}$ and variance $\sigma^2/n_{0,j}$, $P(\phi_j) \geqslant 0$, and $\sum_{j=1}^{K} P(\phi_j) = 1$. For example, $\phi_1, \ldots, \phi_K$ might represent K different sets of "economic conditions," or K different "states," relating to the stock market as well as the individual security, and $f(\mu \mid \phi_j)$ is the density function of $\tilde{\mu}$ conditional upon a particular state ϕ_j. The use of mixtures of conjugate distributions to represent the prior distribution increases the computational burden somewhat, but fortunately still leaves a reasonably "tractable" model. As new information is obtained, the revised distribution of $\tilde{\mu}$ is also a mixture of conjugate distributions, and the predictive distributions for future prices can be expressed as mixtures. The new information is used to revise the probabilities associated with $\phi_1, \ldots, \phi_K$ and to revise each conditional distribution $f(\mu \mid \phi_j)$. In general, a mixture of unimodal distributions is multimodal. As noted in Section 3, the majority of the distributions assessed by the analysts in the Bartos study were multimodal; mixtures may provide good fits to assessed distributions such as these. Of course, a single conjugate prior distribution is simply a special case of a mixture with $K = 1$.

The third assumption is not so easy to relax, but it is consistent with the random walk model and may be justified by the empirical evidence supporting that model (e.g., see Fama, 1965a). Relaxing the assumption by allowing the distribution of $\tilde{d}_i$ to change over time would imply that $\tilde{\theta}$ should be replaced by

$\widetilde{\theta}_1, \widetilde{\theta}_2, \ldots, \widetilde{\theta}_t$, which would necessitate a joint prior distribution for these t parameters. One way to handle this would be to assume a functional relationship among the $\widetilde{\theta}_i$'s and to assess a prior distribution for the parameters of that relationship (e.g., a linear regression model with a prior distribution for the regression coefficients).

In addition to the price $\widetilde{x}_i$, other information might be available during the ith period. For example, it might be worthwhile to consider various economic indicators, industry variables, and variables relating to the security in question (e.g., earnings per share). Formally, this necessitates a joint distribution of all of the relevant variables and parameters. One way to handle the additional variables is to treat each variable as a separate security, using the model presented above, and to include correlations among the parameters in the overall model. Another possibility is to assume a functional relationship among the variables and to deal with the parameters of this functional relationship. The latter approach was used by Sharpe (1963), who related security returns to a market index via a simple linear function.

Just as the model can be extended to include variables other than the price of a single security, it can be extended to include the prices of several securities, and the resulting framework can then be used to determine probability distributions that are useful for portfolio selection. Of course, depending upon the assumptions that are made about the decision maker's utility function, it may only be necessary to consider certain summary measures of the distributions. At any rate, a portfolio model utilizing a Bayesian model of security prices would have the desirable feature of revising the probability distributions on the basis of new information. Without this feature, it is necessary to assess an entirely new set of distributions each time portfolio revision is considered. Conceptually, the Bayesian framework should make it possible to consider potential revisions in advance and to treat the portfolio problem as a sequential decision-making procedure. Whether a tractable yet realistic model incorporating all of these features can be developed is yet to be seen.

6. Summary and Discussion

With regard to the assessment of probability distributions to be used as inputs in problems of inference and decision, recent experimentation in this area (including the two studies discussed in Section 3) points to the need for further refinement of assessment procedures. Such refinement might take the form of individual instruction and supervision, various "checks" on the assessments, extensive use of feedback, and so on. Of particular interest is the potential for the development of self-interrogation procedures for use with time-sharing computer systems. With appropriate display terminals and computer programs, an individual might be able to see the implications of his assessments and to investigate the possibility of using various models to approximate his assessed probability distribution. Such programs could not only ask questions and make helpful computations, but they could challenge the assessor on certain aspects of his assessments. For example, in response to an assessed probability of zero, the assessor might be asked, "Do you really believe that it is impossible for the price of Stock X to be greater than $50 per share one year from now, or do you want to modify your assessments?" It is hoped that the development of more refined assessment procedures will continue to cast light on the process of assessing probabilities, the evaluation and comparison of assessed probabilities with probabilities arrived at through other means, and the use of probabilities in actual decision-making situations.

An important issue with regard to the probabilistic prediction of future security prices appears to be the choice of an appropriate definition of price for predictive purposes. It is especially important for the definition to be realistic and useful from a decision-theoretic standpoint. As noted in Section 4, the choice among closing price, average price, high price, low price, or combinations thereof may have considerable effect on the assessed probability distributions. In addition, the models discussed in Section 5 raise the issue of whether it might be more useful to assess distributions directly for future security prices or to assess distributions for parameters such as $\tilde{\mu}$ and then use a model to determine distributions for future prices.

Models of security price movements, then, are related to the assessment of probability distributions for future security prices. The models presented in this paper are quite simple, but they may provide a basis for the development of more realistic models, and the suggestions in Section 5 regarding possible extensions should prove useful in this regard. The Bayesian framework is particularly appealing in that it makes provisions for revising probability distributions as new information is obtained, thereby making it possible to base any decisions on all available information without requiring new assessments each period.

As noted in the introduction, this paper is concerned in a narrow sense with the assessment of probabilities for future security prices and with the development of models to be used in inferential and decision-making problems involving securities. In a much broader sense, however, the issue is how a decision maker can best use all of the information available in a given situation, including the judgments of experts as well as any relevant data. Germane to this issue are the notions of clinical versus statistical prediction (e.g., see Pankoff and Roberts, 1968), the aggregation of information (e.g., see Winkler and Murphy, 1971), and man-machine systems in general. The problem is clearly of an interdisciplinary nature, and the need for further research is evident.

Bibliography

Alpert, M., and Raiffa, H. (1969) "A progress report on the training of probability assessors," unpublished manuscript, Harvard University.

Bartos, J.A. (1969) "The assessment of probability distributions for future security prices," Ph.D. dissertation, Indiana University.

de Finetti, B. (1937) "La prévision: ses lois logiques, ses sources subjectives." *Annales de l'Institut Henri Poincaré* 7, 1-68. English translation in Kyburg, H.E., Jr., and Smokler, H.E., eds. (1964), *Studies in Subjective Probability*. New York: Wiley, 93-158.

Fama, E.F. (1965a) "The behavior of stock-market prices." *Journal of Business* 38, 34-105.

Fama, E.F. (1965b) "Portfolio analysis in a stable Paretian market." *Management Science* 11, 404-419.

Fama, E.F., and Roll, R. (1968) "Some properties of symmetric stable distributions." *Journal of the American Statistical Association* 63, 817-36.

Fama, E.F., and Roll, R. (1971) "Parameter estimates for symmetric stable distributions." *Journal of the American Statistical Association* 66, in press.

Good, I.J. (1965) *The Estimation of Probabilities: An Essay on Modern Bayesian Methods*. Cambridge: M.I.T. Press.

Hakansson, N.H. (1971) "Capital growth and the mean-variance approach to portfolio selection." *Journal of Financial and Quantitative Analysis* 6, 517-57.

Jean, W.H. (1971) "The extension of portfolio analysis to three or more parameters." *Journal of Financial and Quantitative Analysis* 6, 505-515.

Markowitz, H. (1959) *Portfolio Selection: Efficient Diversification of Investments*. New York: Wiley.

Lusted, L.B. (1968) *Introduction to Medical Decision Making*. Springfield, Illinois: Charles C. Thomas.

Murphy, A.H. (1971) "On the relationship between the 'accuracy' and the 'value' of probability forecasts," *Proceedings, International Symposium on Probability and Statistics in the Atmospheric Sciences*, Boston, American Meteorological Society, 94-99.

Murphy, A.H. (1971) "Ordinal relationships between measures of the 'accuracy' and 'value' of probability forecasts." *Atmosphere* 9, in press.

Murphy, A.H., and Allen, R.A. (1970) "Probabilistic prediction in meteorology: A bibliography." Washington, D.C.: Environmental Science Services Administration, Weather Bureau, Technical Memorandum WBTM-TDL-35.

Murphy, A.H., and Winkler, R.L. (1970) "Scoring rules in probability assessment and evaluation." *Acta Psychologica* 34, 273-86.

Pankoff, L.D., and Roberts, H.V. (1968) "Bayesian synthesis of clinical and statistical prediction." *Psychological Bulletin* 70, 762-73.

Raiffa, H., and Schlaifer, R. (1961) *Applied Statistical Decision Theory*. Boston: Division of Research, Graduate School of Business Administration, Harvard University.

Savage, L.J. (1954) *The Foundations of Statistics*. New York: Wiley.

Savage, L.J. (1971) "The elicitation of personal probabilities and expectations." *Journal of the American Statistical Association*, in press.

Sharpe, W.F. (1963) "A simplified model for portfolio analysis." *Management Science* 9, 277-93.

Sharpe, W.F. (1970) *Portfolio Theory and Capital Markets*. New York: McGraw-Hill.

Staël von Holstein, C.-A.S. (1970a) *Assessment and Evaluation of Subjective Probability Distrbutions*. Stockholm: Economic Research Institute, Stockholm School of Economics.

Staël von Holstein, C.-A.S. (1970b) "Measurement of subjective probability." *Acta Psychologica* 34, 146-59.

Suppes, P. (1956) "The role of subjective probability and utility in decision-making," in J. Neyman, ed., *Proceedings of the Third Berkeley Symposium on Mathematical Statistics and Probability* 5. Berkeley: University of California Press.

Winkler, R.L. (1967a) "The assessment of prior distributions in Bayesian analysis." *Journal of the American Statistical Association* 62, 776-800.

Winkler, R.L. (1967b) "The quantification of judgment: Some methodological suggestions." *Journal of the American Statistical Association* 62, 1105-20.

Winkler, R.L. (1971a) "Probabilistic prediction: Some experimental results." *Journal of the American Statistical Association* 66, in press.

Winkler, R.L. (1971b) "Bayesian models for forecasting future security prices," in preparation.

Winkler, R.L., and Murphy, A.H. (1968) " 'Good' probability assessors." *Journal of Applied Meteorology* 7, 751-58.

Winkler, R.L.. and Murphy, A.H. (1971) "Information processing in probabilistic prediction," submitted for publication.

7

The Coming Revolution in Investment Management

Jack L. Treynor

This paper has three parts. The first considers the implication of investment risk for the investment management process and concludes that because of the problems introduced by risk an approach to security analysis independent of any explicit macroeconomic forecasting is highly desirable. The second considers whether such an approach to security analysis is theoretically possible and feasible. The third explores some of the practical consequences of separating security analysis from macroeconomic forecasting, including consequences for the way the investment-management task is organized.

I. The Implications of Risk

Exhibit I depicts in a summary way investment management as it is commonly practiced today. Macroeconomic forecasts logically precede industry forecasts, and industry forecasts logically precede sales forecasts for individual companies within the industry. Price estimates are derived largely independently of cost estimates and of sales volume projections. From these considerations the analyst projects the future cash flows; these are discounted to determine an estimate of the current worth of the company's shares. Comparison with current share price generates trading recommendations, which are then forwarded to the portfolio manager for a final decision. The main justification for the current procedure is that if the macroeconomic analysis, the analysis that translates macro forecasts into industry forecasts, and analysis of the company based on the industry forecast are all correct, then a recommendation based on a comparison of the resulting appraisal with current market price can scarcely fail to be correct in turn. This mode of investment management has one great advantage. At each stage the analysis builds unconditionally on the results of the previous stage. It is rarely necessary to take a backward look at the prior stages of analysis until the recommendation reaches the final decision maker. (At that point, of course, any step in the process may be called into question.) Because the analysis proceeds unconditionally from one stage to the next, the fruit of each stage can be expressed in numbers rather than algebra. This is a consequence with undeniable appeal for most practicing security analysts and portfolio managers.

The great disadvantage of the current procedure is that it is based on a faulty

149

premise: namely, that the forecasts generated at each stage of the process are certain. Wiesenberger's Mutual Fund Annuals used to carry (and perhaps still do carry) demonstrations of how rich one would become if he could anticipate and trade (at no cost) on daily fluctuations in the market averages. In a few years the man gifted with this kind of forecasting ability is richer than the richest men in history, and in a generation or two he owns the world. The consequences of perfect foresight contrast sharply with the actual record of professional investors. Professor Michael Jensen of the University of Rochester found, for example, that out of the several hundred mutual funds (chosen for study because their results are public knowledge) only two or three departed sufficiently far from neutral performance to defy an explanation on the grounds of mere good luck. Almost one-third of the time, price variations in over a year's time in NYSE common stocks exceed 20 percent of their initial value. If professional investors were able to anticipate even a fraction of price movements of this magnitude, their performance would improve significantly. One is forced to conclude that, of the price movement observed in the securities held in professionally managed portfolios, the great bulk is surprise—even to professional investors. These surprises are the fundamental source of investment risk. It is clear from the numbers already cited that the risks are large.

Broadly speaking, the risks are of two kinds: those specific to a single company or a few companies; and those shared by a large number of companies. The former obviously tend to be risks relating to market share and the success of new technologies. The latter tend by their nature to be the risks surrounding variables with broad economic impact.

There are two ways of eliminating the impact of a security on the riskiness of a portfolio (short of selling the security):

1. *Hedging.* Hedging works only for risks common to a large number of securities. In principle it is not difficult to take a position in a second security that will "cancel out" portfolio exposure to a given risk through a first security. In taking a position in the second security, however, the portfolio may become exposed to other sources of investment risk not shared in the same proportion by the first security. Thus hedging is practical only when it is possible to isolate a particular source of risk.
2. *Diversification.* Risks affecting large numbers of securities can be isolated through diversification. In portfolios containing large numbers of securities, common factors tend to become very important and factors unique to the individual securities relatively unimportant.

   Diversification can be used to minimize the contribution to portfolio risk of unique factors, but will not work for common factors; hedging can be very effective in eliminating common factors, but will not ordinarily work for unique factors. Used together, however, the two techniques represent powerful complementary instruments for focusing portfolio exposure on those risk factors a portfolio manager is most confident he can predict while minimizing the exposure to the others. To a remarkable degree, they transform the task of portfolio balancing from one of choosing among securities to one of choosing among causal factors. Securities are merely incidental vehicles for taking positions in underlying factors.

Conventional security analysis implies that if a recommendation to take a position in a security is accepted by the portfolio manager, his decision represents a commitment to expose his portfolio to the uncertainties surrounding variables at every stage of the analysis—even though the degree of confidence may differ radically from one variable to another. Hedging can focus on the specifics to the exclusion of the market. On the other hand, diversification used alone can emphasize a portfolio's exposure to market risk while minimizing all other sources of investment risk.

In order to take proper advantage of these possibilities, however, two things must be true: (1) The uncertainties surrounding point forecasts of both kinds of factors—systematic and unique—must be known and quantified. (2) It must be possible to estimate the difference between the portfolio manager's assessment of specifics for the company and the market's assessment.

Present investment management practice, as summarized in Exhibit I, frustrates both requirements. In particular, present practice tends to leave the portfolio manager unenlightened as to whether a buy recommendation is due to a bullish macroeconomic forecast, a bullish assessment of specifics, or both. Thus he has no basis for deciding that he might prefer to emphasize exposure to the specifics of the security in question, or the underlying economic factors. In effect, what is required is a comparison of the specifics implicit in current market price with the portfolio manager's (or perhaps more appropriately the security analyst's) assessment of the specifics.

It is of course impossible to know what specifics are assumed by the market. But a meaningful comparison can be made in the price domain—provided the macroeconomic assumptions underlying the analyst's appraisal are identical to the macroeconomic assumptions implicit in the market consensus. On the other hand, the market consensus regarding macroeconomic factors is not directly measurable, any more than the market consensus regarding specific factors.

Nevertheless, the task is far from impossible. It is obvious that there will always be some macroeconomic forecast so sanguine that the current price of almost any security sensitive to economic conditions can be shown to be underpriced in terms of that forecast; or some forecast so gloomy that the price of virtually any security dependent on economic conditions will be higher than the price warranted by the latter forecast. To define "underpriced" and "overpriced" in terms of the conventional appraisal procedure outlined in Exhibit I is clearly unsatisfactory. Although the prices of individual securities may be too high or too low at a point in time, the general level of security prices implies a certain economic outlook. A more meaningful definition for "under-priced" and "overpriced" is that the security in question is respectively under priced or overpriced in relation to the current market consensus regarding the outlook implicit in the observed prices of other securities.

II. A New Approach to Security Analysis

With this thought in mind, let us consider a highly schematic model—a model far too simple to capture those features of the real world of importance to the portfolio manager, but still perhaps complex enough for our immediate purposes. In this model the only uncertainty revolves around the future level of final demand, which is assumed henceforth to be constant as a function of time. The model is therefore a static model (ignoring any transients generated by initial conditions!) and avoids accelerator problems that are actually very important to the portfolio manager.

Let:

z_j = final demand on j industry.

c_{ij} = input-output coefficients (input from i industry required per unit of j industry output).

x_i = derived demand on the i industry.

v_i = $a_i + b_i x_i$ = gross market value of the i industry as a function of derived demand, where a_i and b_i are constants specific to the industry.

It is clear from these definitions that we have achieved a complete dichotomy between macroeconomic forecasts and forecasts of industry specifics. Dichotomy in this sense is very desirable, for reasons to be discussed in the next section. (The discounting process is submerged in the constants A and B.) The constants A and B incorporate everything specific to the i industry that determines what level of gross market value for an industry will correspond to a given level of derived demand. Under our assumptions, the macroeconomic forecasting problem is of course confined to the Z. No comment on the C seems necessary at this point, except perhaps to say that they are defined consistent with whatever dimensions we assign to the z and x.

It will be convenient to adopt the convention whereby capital letters represent vectors and matrices constructed from the corresponding small letters. Thus we have a final demand vector Z, a derived demand vector X, and a vector of equilibrium market values V. We also have a matrix C of input-output coefficients. Using these definitions, we arrive immediately at the relation between equilibrium market values and final demand.

$$V = A + B \ [I - C]^{-1} \ Z$$

There is no point of course to security analysis if market prices always satisfy the equilibrium relationships implied by one's model. In the unlikely case in which those relationships can be represented faithfully by the model under discussion, a vector P of observed market prices will differ from the vector V of equilibrium market values by a vector E of error terms.

$$P = A + B \ [I - C]^{-1} \ Z + E$$

At this point the task of security analysis can be restated as finding those values for the components of Z for which the difference between estimated V and the observed P is minimized—doubtless in terms of the traditional least squares metric. In effect the components of P are the dependent variable, the components of A and $B \ [I - C]^{-1}$ are respectively independent variables, and the components of Z representing the unknown market consensus regarding final demand play the role of undetermined coefficients. In this formulation it is quite clear that security appraisal (in the sense of what Wall Street calls fundamental analysis) is in fact a regression problem. It is a linear regression problem in my example only, because my model is so unrelentingly (and unrealistically) linear.

It should also be noted that, unless some constraints are imposed on the components of Z, no meaningful regression analysis is possible, since there are as many components of Z as there are observations. In general, the more severely the components of Z are constrained, the more accurately they can be estimated. The extreme would be a one-sector model in which final demand for each industry moves up and down in strict proportion with final demand for every other industry. It is of course more realistic to recognize several sectors including, for example, consumer durables, capital goods, defense spending, and so forth. The number of observations is limited only by the degree of disaggregation in the input-output data incorporated in the model. Since as a practical matter the data will provide several hundred observations, one can afford to distinguish several independent final demand sectors without encountering a real degrees-of-freedom problem.

A faulty model will lead to serious specification problems in estimating the market consensus of the Z, and this in turn will lead to serious errors in estimating the V. To put the same statement in terms that Wall Street can understand: You can lose a lot of money acting on security appraisals based on the wrong model. The writer expects, in particular, that a portfolio manager could lose money very rapidly relying on security appraisals derived using the purely schematic model presented in this paper.

Practical Consequences for Investment Management

The approach to security analysis described above has far-reaching consequences for the way security analysts and portfolio managers define their jobs and the way they organize to make portfolio decisions. The easiest way to see how sweeping the consequences will be is to refer once again to Exhibit I. As security analysis is conventionally practiced, the analyst's first step is to form a judgment regarding the underlying macroeconomic variables. He may of course listen to a large number of expert economists before arriving at his judgment; nevertheless, determination of the values of these variables for his purposes is unavoidably a matter of judgment.

When the analyst communicates his opinion of the security in question to the portfolio manager it is couched, more often than not, in terms of a recommendation. On the face of it a recommendation to buy, sell, or hold from the security analyst is absurd, since portfolio decisions can only be made in the context of information regarding other securities, many of which will commonly be outside the analyst's ken. The reason for couching the analyst's opinions in terms of recommendations seem to be that, if instead, the analyst's opinion were couched in terms of his opinion of the value of the security in question, it would be obsoleted almost before he could convey it to the portfolio manager by changes in the underlying macroeconomic variables.

More often than not, analyst's recommendations to portfolio managers are recommendations to buy rather than sell. On the face of it this is surprising because, if securities were being valued in practice in relation to the observed prices of other securities, one would expect to find roughly as many securities overpriced as underpriced. This curious practice stems from the portfolio manager's difficulty in measuring the quality of the individual analyst's advice.

The reason the quality is difficult to measure is that, in the conventional investment management process, there is no way for the portfolio manager to know what macroeconomic assumptions are underlying the analyst's advice. Nor, since the entire process is carried through in terms of numbers rather than algebra, is there any opportunity for the portfolio manager to determine what the analyst's recommendation would have been if his macroeconomic assumptions had been those which in hindsight turned out to be correct. Without such knowledge, however, the portfolio manager is powerless to determine whether the analyst's advice was good or bad. The practical consequence has been that the analysts who get recognized and rewarded are those who (1) succeeded in persuading portfolio managers to buy their recommendations, and (2) whose recommended securities appreciate.

The current mode of investment management has a number of practical consequences:

1. As just noted, it is impossible for portfolio managers to measure meaningfully the quality of the advice they get from individual analysts.
2. There is no way for a portfolio manager to make consistent comparisons between securities recommended by different analysts if the analysts are free to base their recommendations on different sets of macroeconomic assumptions.

3. Even if it were possible to appraise all securities on the basis of the same set of macroeconomic assumptions, the present approach would bias the selection process; some securities are more sensitive to the underlying macroeconomic assumptions than others and would thus benefit, for example, from assumptions more bullish than those implicit in current market prices.

4. Because analysts tend to communicate to portfolio managers primarily in terms of recommendations to buy and because, as explained above, the analyst often has little hope of recognition unless he succeeds in getting his recommendations accepted, the conventional investment management process transforms the various analysts supplying information to a portfolio manager into rivals. The portfolio manager typically has limited funds with which to buy, and acceptance of one analyst's recommendation is likely to preclude acceptance of another's. It is obvious from the nature of the rivalry that it encourages analysts to bias their recommendations upward. Although systematic means for adjusting for analysts' bias can be devised, the high probability that the degree of bias is changing over time leads, as a practical matter, to a very substantial degradation in the quality of the information reaching the portfolio manager. (The rivalry system is nevertheless popular with many portfolio managers, chiefly because it transforms the portfolio manager into an administrator adjudicating conflicts among his subordinates. The present system maintains and enhances the status of the portfolio manager even while it degrades the quality of his product.)

5. Measurement of the quality of analyst's advice is essential—not only for any just system for rewarding analysts and their employers, but also because these quality measurements play an essential role in deciding whether portfolio should be exposed to the unique risk associated with a given security. The fraction of price variance not anticipated by the analyst may of course vary over time, and the analyst himself may have an opinion whether it is currently higher or lower than his long-run batting average (that opinion may be termed "confidence" and can obviously be quantified). Unless the portfolio manager knows the analyst's long-run batting average, however, he is unable to apply the analyst's current confidence and estimate the current residual risk.

In the face of these problems it would be quite remarkable if conventional investment management were able to make any contribution to portfolio performance whatever.

It would be tedious to review the alternative approach suggested here, pointing out that in each case the problems raised by the conventional approach are absent. But it would be wrong to end this paper without pointing out that the approach suggested here will radically redefine the jobs of the security analyst and portfolio manager.

As noted above, the analyst's job becomes estimating the value of those factors specific to the company in question and its industry that have some demonstrated bearing on future rents. Because the determination of how the capital market discounts risky future rents can be done more efficiently once and for all by the portfolio manager rather than repeated for each individual security, and because consistency here is as important as consistency elsewhere, this burden will be removed from the security analyst and centralized with the portfolio manager. This is only the first step, however, in what the writer expects to become a trend. More and more, the analysts' task will be restricted to estimating or forecasting factors in non-financial terms, while leaving the determination of the financial significance to the portfolio manager. It is not clear that, when this trend has run its course, any special knowledge of economics or finance will remain that a security analyst will need to know in order to do his job.

Instead of challenging the assumptions made by individual analysts, the portfolio manager will be free to concentrate on perfecting the model that relates one industry to others, and all industries to the macroeconomy, and to perfect his model of how the capital markets value risky future rents. He will also be concerned with the larger system, in which this model is embedded, that measures the quality of analysts' advice, reports any bias and determines whether the portfolio in question is adhering to its stated objectives (quantified in terms of risk). The portfolio manager will finally become something more than an adjudicator and a kibitzer.

Portfolio management will have ceased to be an administrative art and will have become, instead, a technology.

Exhibit I

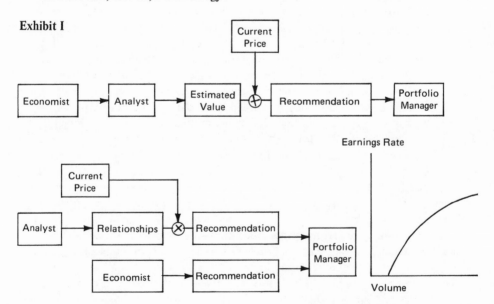

8 Expectations in Finance-Investment Theory

George C. Philippatos

Introduction

The formal transition between the economic and financial theories of the firm is normally obtained through the various structures of the traditional theory. For example, in the static certainty case, the expository structures of both theories employ marginal analysis and equilibrium techniques to emphasize regularity and ideal structure, which are implied by the stationarity assumption. Similarly, the normative and empirical structures of both theories retain the informational and organizational assumptions, respectively. On the other hand, the analytic structure of the financial theory of the firm alters both the motivational and the independence assumptions of traditional economic theory.

In the former case, profit maximization is replaced by market-value or shareholder-wealth maximization. In the latter, the independence assumption is modified to account for statistical interdependence in the single-period multi-project framework, thus yielding the case of static uncertainty. In the same vein, modifications of the basic assumptions lead to naive versions of dynamic uncertainty. In effect, financial theory departs from traditional microeconomic theory by its added concern for the following aspects of the entrepreneurial process: (a) size and composition of the firm's assets; (b) size and composition of the firm's liabilities; and (c) the effects of (a) and (b) upon the market valuation of the firm's equity.[1]

However, the delineation of the internal (organization) and external (market) social spaces of the financial theory of the firm requires knowledge of the futurity and uncertainty characterizing the budgeting and financing decisions of the firm. To wit, expectations and their realization in the market-place, in terms of forecasts and programs of economic activity, serve as the motivational framework that guides the intratemporal and intertemporal substitutions of consumption and investment goods.[2] The various theories of business behavior rely heavily (if not mechanistically) on the expectational framework, i.e., anticipations proper, forecasts and plans, for the interpretation of managerial activities. Expectations about the possible states of nature in the external social space condition the expectations about the viability and success of the organization and its participants. And, this overall pattern of behavior prevails whether we conceive of the firm as a holistic or as a behavioral organism, or any of the subdivisions within these concepts.[3]

157

The pivotal role of expectations in the theories of social behavior has been widely recognized. In particular, the economic disciplines abound with hypotheses regarding the logical formalization of expectations, thereduction of evidence to single-valued sure-prospect equivalents, as well as selective reductions to two-valued and strategy-dependent prospects.[4] In the same vein, related disciplines, concerned with the organizational and behavioral theories of the firm, have constructed elaborate subtheories of expectations that purport to explain the search procedures and information-gathering behavior of managerial groups.[5]

In perspective, it is apparent that if the financial theory of the firm is to be grounded on its economic counterpart, it will find a richly cultivated field of experience, which can be further developed and refined. Indeed, given the need for a unified theory of the firm, financial microtheory can benefit from a number of reliable sources. At the same time, the financial theory of the firm, which has been primarily concerned with the transformation of sources of funds into efficient uses in the short run and long run, must also adopt and modify an explicit expectational framework that is congruent with the behavioral assumptions employed, and must serve as the explanatory mechanism for the investment, financing, and valuation considerations.

Recent developments in the discipline notwithstanding, the theory of finance-investment has not explicitly acknowledged the importance of expectations in the budgeting, dividend, and financing decisions of the firm. Neither has it been particularly innovative in the area of equity valuation and portfolio selection, with its sole reliance on the certainty equivalence technique.[6] Specifically, the role of expectations in finance-investment theory has been primarily relegated to the analytic structure, where programed business decisions[7] are based on some formal transformation of the evidence into a sure-prospect. For example, given the motivational assumption of share-price maximization, and the relevant market structure in which the firm operates, managerial and shareholder expectations converge toward the posited goal.

However, the stress of finance-investment theory on the analytical structure has been achieved at the expense of the empirical and normative structures. That is, little attention has been paid to the shapes and regularities that describe the real world. For example, the behavioral and adaptive mechanisms that might be present in the perception, coding, and transformation of the evidence into a prospect have not attracted the attention of financial theorists. Similarly, the importance of institutions in the formation expectations and the stabilizing effects of expectations upon institutions have been assigned a lower status in the hierarchy of goals. In fact, a discipline that has only recently moved from the intuitive to the respectable stage, has also managed to preserve the old trichotomy of institutionalism, behaviorism, and analysis.

In line with earlier arguments the present methodological study constitutes a critical survey of some of the literature on expectations, with particular emphasis on the recent literature in finance-investment theory. Since the term "expectations" has been accorded the scarcity of an economic commodity in the legitimate literature in finance-investment,[8] it will become necessary to place the arguments in perspective by digressions into the economic literature proper. At the same time, the treatment of expectations will be primarily confined to microfinance decisions made by *holistic* units. Hence the stress will be restricted to the internal social space of the firm that operates within a known and specified external space.[9]

This paper is divided into four parts. Part I briefly outlines the formalization of expectations and the underlying logical relations. Part II reviews some of the hypotheses for the reduction of expected outcomes into single valued sure-prospects. Part III relates to the subjective content of expectations and some psychological theories. Part IV presents a framework of adaptive and heuristic search procedures that might be useful in explaining the process of expectational formation and change in financial decisions.

Causality, Teleology, and Logical Relations in Expectations

The nature and scope of expectations in explaining the behavior of *homo oeconomicus* have been surrounded by the type of intense controversy that typically results in bipolar views. Such disagreement has encompassed both the importance of expectations and the methodology employed in transforming the evidence into a comprehensive prospect.[10] One school of thought would argue that since the financial decisions of households and firms can be represented by a *causal* link between the evidence and the prospect, the available market data suffice to interpret the actions of investors.[11] The other school of thought would stress the importance of goal-oriented activity in financial decisions, and the need for a *teleological* theory that interposes expectations between the evidence and the prospect.[12]

Subscription to the causal theory nearly eliminates the expectational mechanism, and stresses a prescribed reactive behavior to a change in the evidence. Simple examples of such causal references in finance-investment theory can be found in the crude-acceleration principle, and the institutional regularities dealing with liquidity considerations and control of the enterprise. In the former case, capital stock adjustments to changes in demand are achieved through the technological relationship of the capital-output ratio,[13] while in the latter firms are mindful of their balance sheet positions; such firms attempt to strike a balance between the costs of liquidity decumulation and increased indebtedness.[14] More sophisticated versions of causal explanations can be found in the theory of games,[15] where the stategies are made within a set of well-defined rules, and the *homeostatic* overtones of the various approaches to the theory of the firm.[16]

A less restrictive version of the causal explanation of business behavior suggests that expectations about the future are ordinarily mere extrapolations of recent performance. An increase in the market value of an asset is expected to yield a similar change in the near future, until some exogenously determined reversal occurs. In its crudest form, the extrapolative approach to expectational formation seems to describe the behavior of many stock market technicians who make sport with charts and trading rules.[17] It also seems to approximate reasonably well the rationale of the various filter trading rules of the "one security and cash" type within a submartingale framework. Such filters have been used to test for non-linear dependence in stock price changes.[18]

An intermediate view on the expectational framework suggests that expectations are indeed very important, but they are not delineable and measurable scientifically.[19] In this vein it has been suggested that, as far as business theorists are concerned, expectations derive from complex emotional processes whose study lies outside the province of business disciplines.[20] Subsequently, research should be confined to the legitimate economic and financial variables whose values can serve as the realization of market expectations. Within this framework, all unexplained statistical variation can be attributed to excluded psychological variables and random factors.

On the other hand, subscription to the teleological theory requires the employment of expectations as the linkage between the evidence and the prospect. Within this framework, businessmen's behavior can be best explained by reference to their posited goals. It is, of course, this type of explanation that is of interest in the study of decisions that transform sources of funds into productive uses. That is, the motivational assumption in the theory of finance-investment posits a specific goal for the firm, and it is in the pursuit of this goal that expectations link the environmental conditions with the behavior of the market participants.

However, teleological explanations of business behavior have been characterized by the same controversy between analytic and behavioral researchers. The former stress the logical relations underlying the expectational mechanism and generally attempt to reduce the evidence to a single-valued sure-prospect or sure-prospect equivalent. The latter insist that expectations and their adjustment to changing evidence originate in a variety of personal and environmental developments. The difficulty is further compounded by the methodological arguments between the *subjectivists*, who stress *introspection* as the mode of such that, based on statistical inference, a hypothesis is either verification, and the *behaviorists*, who rely on laboratory and field experimentation.[21]

Expectations proper involve three interrelated elements—namely, the *evidence*, the *individual*, and the *prospect*. The evidence is formalized by a set of explicit statements relating past and present market conditions to the prospect through an information vector. The individual transforms the evidence into a prospect. The role of the individual as the link between evidence and prospect raises a number of interesting questions that have not excited the interest of economic and financial theorists. For example, the perception, sorting, and interpretation of evidence is sidestepped in the economic disciplines.

In the same vein, the transformation of the original evidence in an action-oriented prospect is normally couched in probabilistic weights, such that, based on statistical inference, hypothesis is either accepted or rejected. The investment decisions of the firm are reported on the basis of a transformation that has reduced the evidence into a prospect, which is typically given in terms of one or more summary statistics. Financial theory is only incidentally concerned with the behavioral dynamics which govern the process of reduction of the original expectational discrepancies to an equilibrium solution. Neither is the theory concerned with the *heuristics* and *adaptation* that seem to characterize decision processes.[22]

The prospect is a specific view of the future, to which we assign a particular weight. Since the number of outcomes that can be considered by the individual is limited both by the type of expectation and his capacity to sort and manipulate probabilities of occurrence, the transformation results in a few outcomes. A simple extension of this operation results in the construction of a sure-prospect that reduces the evidence to a single outcome, with full weight attached to it.[23] However, the realized outcomes may depend on the behavior of the world, the behavior of the individual, or the interaction of both.

Normally, we refer to the process and environmental conditions that determine a possible state as a *mechanism*. Moreover, given the interdependence of economic organisms, our actual behavior generally depends on a set of expectations—each referring to different subjects. For example, in an investment decision, the entrepreneur estimates both the benefits and costs in terms of their effects upon the market valuation of the firm, thus linking his decision to three types of expectations.

Expectations lead to plans and decisions in the face of uncertainty, and as such they are embedded in time. The time dimension introduces another taxonomic consideration—namely, the sequential classification of expectations into *primary, secondary,* and *intermediate.* In primary expectations the evidence and the prospect are linked directly without the formation of intermediate expectations.[24] For example, a speculator employing a martingale system in the stock market bases his decisions on primary expectations. In a way, we can say that the so-called weak-form and semi-strong form tests of the random walk hypothesis[25] imply investment decisions based on primary expectations. Similarly, the various safety levels and financial ratios utilized in the management of working capital, are also based on primary expectational mechanisms.

Secondary expectations refer to situations where the final prospect is reached by stages, during which the original expectations adjust to new evidence by *clarification* or *revision.*[26] Investment decisions that are based on adaptive or heuristic search procedures allow the formation and evaluation of secondary expectations.[27] Finally, intermediate expectations provide the transition from primary to secondary.[28]

The formal transformation of evidence (premise) into a prospect (conclusion) is achieved by means of a logical relation. This logical link between premise and conclusion does not ordinarily contain any information about the disposition and attitudes of the individual. That is, assuming the existence of unambiguous evidence and the logical relation, the formalization of probability weights is completely objective. Indeed, the individual is assigned the role of a near-perfect mechanism that processes the information content of the various environmental stimuli. However, the clarity of logical relations is confounded by the uncertainty that is implicit in the time dimension of expectations. Since the financial decisions of household and firms are action-bound, we must proceed on the assumption that uncertainty can be reduced to measurable and insurable risk through some form of numerical probability.[29] In this vein, on the assumption that there obtains a deductive relation between the evidence and the prospect, we describe the ability of a hypothesis to withstand severe empirical tests as the degree of confirmation.[30]

Reduction of Evidence to a Certainty Equivalent

Prospects derived from evidence through some method of transformation cannot be sure-prospects, due to the inferential nature of our conclusions about the real world. However, for analytical purposes in finance-investment theory we assume that households and firms behave as if the computed prospects are indeed sure-prospect equivalents. There is a plethora of hypotheses regarding the way investors arrive at sure-prospects. For example, if the expected payoffs to which the decision makers adjust their market positions are monetary, sure-prospects can be derived by means of a formula. In such cases, the sure-prospect can be derived either from a single-valued datum, as with the elasticity of price expectations, or from the mean value of a multi-outcome prospect.

Typical examples of such behavior can be found in the use of crude investment criteria, e.g., payout and plowback, by corporate executives. As an extension, the risk adjusted versions of the standard investment criteria also fall in the same category. That is, to the extent that decision makers reduce the uncertainty of future flows to some mean value, e.g., expected net present value, or expected mean-return, they are assumed to operate as if the mean value were a sure-prospect. Another use of the formula reduction method allows the individual to introduce his subjective attitudes and adjust for the risk content of his decisions. In such cases, some measure of dispersion is explicitly employed,[31] such that even unsophisticated criteria, like expected payout, yield some useful information. On the other hand, when the payoffs to which decision makers adjust their positions are expressed in utilities, the prospects are derived by using the concept of *moral expectations*. Such prospects are, in effect, mean values of expected utility payoffs.[32]

However, the problem of verification of expectational transformation into a mean value prospect again confounds the researcher, since in business decisions, we cannot rely on *introspection* or *gambling experiments*. Thus, we are back at the original question. "How do businessmen transform the evidence into a prospect?" One avenue of investigation is offered by Gestalt psychology, where it is argued that human expectations approximate sure prospects. That is, what attracts the attention of the individual is either the totality of the evidence, or some strong individual characteristic of it, which he uses as his approximate sure prospect. For example, an investor in the stock market might try to predict either the level of some index (or security) or the rate of change in the index (or security), depending on whether the index was stable or highly volatile.[33]

A simple extension of the mean value hypothesis leads to the reduction of multi-outcome prospects in a two-stage sequence. *First*, the individual reduces the evidence to two summary statistical measures for central tendency and dispersion. *Second*, through the operation of indifference, he reduces the evidence to a certainty equivalent. An early example of such work has been provided by J. Marschak,[34] who utilized the terms "lucrativity" and "risk" to describe the summary measures that might be employed in the valuation of assets; the former refers to expected gain and the latter to expected deviation from some measure of expected gain. In subsequent developments, various methods of central tendency and dispersion have been employed.[35] And, although the specific summary measures are chosen on their ability to capture the complexity of composite returns, the literature seems to favor the mean-variance approach.[36]

The certainty equivalence technique for reducing the comprehensive evidence into a final choice had not attracted wide attention among investment theorists, until its reformulation by Markowitz to explain meaningful diversification.[37] A number of reasons have been proposed for the reluctance to accept this measure. *First* the measurement of risk aversion of the individual involves implicitly subjective considerations. *Second* there seems to be a number of internally consistent methods of deriving certainty equivalence functions, and a lack of objective criteria for the final choice. *Third* the simplicity of the technique does not capture the complexity of human actions in the process of transforming some external evidence to a prospect.

Subjective Factors in Expectations

Economic disciplines have traditionally viewed all kinds of psychologism with suspicion, whether it deals with the consumption or investment behavior of the individual. On this score, the theory of finance-investment has made no overt efforts to become the exception. However, a number of empirical studies have uncovered fresh evidence that corporate executives do behave as if they are seriously constrained by subjective and institutional factors in making financial decisions. The very popularity of such techniques as payout indicates a serious effort to replace the motivational assumption of market value maximization with a less taxing corporate goal.

Indeed, the quest for stabilization and reduction of uncertainty has been offered as a justification for the plowback method of financing. As Donaldson has reported, some financial executives are reluctant to resort to short-term borrowing for working capital needs, and instead go to extremes to avoid being caught in a liquidity-squeeze.[38] Similarly, as reported by Lintner, corporations seem to have established a target payout rate for dividends, as well as an adjustment horizon.[39] Such behavior as related above indicates the manifest role of personal and social factors in the financial decisions of economic units. In both cases the perception of the evidence was rationalized by management in terms of some stability in earnings that was preferred by stockholders.[40]

However, the perception and interpretation of the evidence are not the only elements in expectations that create problems.[41] A more serious problem is encountered in the transformation of the evidence into a prospect. To wit, psychologists have seriously questioned the ability of the human mind to sort, compute, and rank a large number of numerical probabilities.[42] In response to this question, it has been suggested that distinctions should be made in expectations by the terms of the behavior that a given external stimulus elicits. Psychologists distinguish between *habitual* and *nonhabitual* behavior.[43] Habitual behavior is determined by expectations that do not require a reorganization of the form into which the evidence and the prospect are combined; or the reorganization follows a familiar pattern and is performed routinely. Nonhabitual behavior is determined by expectations that require reorganization, and typically yields a new entity (whole). For example, Katona[44] reports that decisions on inventories, liquidity, and capacity considerations are considered by businessmen as habitual (routine). On the other hand, large-scale decisions regarding the acquisition of a new plant, or the merger with another firm elicit genuine (nonhabitual) behavior.

An alternative, and highly controversial, method of assigning weights to transformed outcomes has been proposed by Shackle.[45] Arguing that we cannot assign probability weights to outcomes through introspection, Shackle suggests a modified gambling experiment, which measures indirectly our surprise when something unexpected occurs. Thus, belief in the future occurrence of an event varies inversely with our surprise when the outcome does occur.[46] Of the many outcomes in a prospect, one or more are assigned to an *inner range* of the prospect with zero degree of potential surprise. Depending on how optimistic or pessimistic the individual is in his expectations, the inner range may be neutral or it may contain small gains and losses.

In Shackle's formulation there are only two outcomes on which the decision-maker focuses his attention: (1) There is a combination of profits and potential surprise, called the *primary focus gain*. (2) There is a combination of losses and potential surprise, called the *primary focus loss*. Shackle has attempted to apply his reduction technique to the problem of allocating the firm's funds between immediate and deferred investment, for liquidity management.[47] An extension of Shackle's *gambler indifference map* has been made by Angell,[48] who developed a *satisfaction function* per dollar invested. This function is related to the present value of the *most likely* gross gain from an investment. Further manipulation introduces the probable *dissatisfaction* (risk of loss), such that a new function, the *net satisfaction function* per dollar invested, emerges as a criterion for investment decisions.

In perspective, it seems that Shackle's framework is more appropriate for the explanation of expectational formation, and the learning through the element of surprise, than for the explanation of financial decisions. Moreover, its usefulness is restricted to rare nonhabitual decisions, whose odds are impossible to compute a priori. In the same vein its concentration on the extreme outcomes of *standardized focus gain and standardized focus loss* limits its wider applicability.[49]

The last method of reduction to be presented in this section deals with expectations that are basically asymmetric. In such cases, the decision maker sets a lower limit of monetary payoffs and adjusts his strategies accordingly. The original formulation of what is known as safety margins is attributed to Fellner, who attempted to explain the pricing policies of firms between the two world wars.[50] In the simplest form, *safety margins* are maximized by choosing a strategy that offers non-negtive payoffs from the most distant state of the world. The hypothesis stresses the importance of cash reserves as safety margins. A direct application of this concept has been made by Donaldson, who reported that businesssmen simulate ranges of future cash flows from −5 percent to +35 percent, and adjust their liquidity policies accordingly.[51] However, in Fellner, the outcomes of the different states are not arranged according to their probability weights. Rather, a best-guess state is chosen, and the desirability of the remaining outcomes is determined by their distance from this zero point.

A variant of the safety margins technique has been presented by Roy,[52] who utilized the mean value and standard error of payoffs to explain the behavior of investors concerned with survival. Roy's method has been successfully applied to diversification, but Markowitz's[53] formulation achieved the same results with fewer restrictions. Extensions of this technique have been applied to portfolio selection by Baumol,[54] and to capital budgeting by Hannsman[55] and Mao.[56]

Organizational Expectations, Adaptation, and Search Procedures

In the previous section we examined a number of hypotheses that combined the following characteristics: (1) The evidence was reduced to one or more summary statistical measures; (2) the summary measures were adjusted by the decision maker in accordance to his goal orientation, and reduced to a certainty-equivalence function. The subjective nature of expectations notwithstanding, the psychologism implied in the previous section was also meant to stress the limitations of the human mind as a receiver, processor, and transmitter of information. Evidence about such limitations, and the practice of selectively reducing the number of alternatives in a decision, has been reported primarily in terms of group interaction and organizational conflict.[57] However, this evidence is not restricted to financial decisions proper, but rather to generalized decision making in the face of uncertainty.

The expectational framework that will be briefly presented in this section is applied to formal organizations, whose members function and survive under conflict and stress. Subsequently, the emphasis is on role-playing and organizational adjustment. Such a new approach to expectations has been justified in terms of the following shortcomings in the existing theory:[58] (1) The assumption of continuous competition among the members of the organization is not consistent with the existing evidence regarding organizational adaptation, and emphasis on problem solving rather than planning. (2) The assumption of continuous search for information is not consistent with observed behavior. Organizational participants seem to be motivated by failure, and place emphasis on a few obvious alternatives. (3) Traditional theory places undue emphasis on the computational ability and precision of decision makers.[59] (4) Expectations are treated as exogenous independent variables that overlook the interaction between desire and expectations, as well as the acquisition and processing of information by organizations.

Expectations are again classified, in accordance with the type of behavior they elicit, into *programed* and *unprogramed*.[60] Unprogramed behavior involves search processes that are unsystematic, nonexhaustive, and involve changes from one frame of reference to another. It is further suggested that most investment decisions involve programed behavior, albeit very sophisticated. However, even programed decisions are subjected to the stabilizing influences of institutions and other environmental social systems. In this sense, rational decisions are made with the expectation that the other members of society will abide by the same rules of behavior. The key to the stability of organizational expectations lies in the feedback between individual and institutional expectations.

The empirical record of the organizational school of thought has contained some interesting studies. For example, Williamson[61] developed and tested a utility maximization model where the variable *discretionary investment* plays an important role in explaining short-run deviations from optimum resource allocation. Similarly, Clarkson[62] developed a *heuristic* model to simulate the investment decisions of a trust investment officer, while Crecine[63] utilized a similar framework to simulate municipal budgeting actions. In perspective, the introduction of heuristics and adaptation into the study of expectational perception and formation has expanded our knowledge about business decision-making practices.

Notes

1. See E. Solomon, *The Theory of Financial Management* (New York: Columbia University Press, 1963).

2. Compare F. Modigliani and K.J. Cohen, "The Role of Anticipations and Plans in Economic Behavior and their Use in Economic Analysis and Forecasting," *Studies in Business Expectations and Planning*, No. 4 (Urbana: University of Illinois, Bureau of Economic and Business Research, 1961).

3. The various concepts and theories of the firm are reviewed in J.W. McGuire, *Theories of Business Behavior* (Englewood Cliffs, N.J.: Prentice-Hall, 1964).

4. See S.A. Ozga, *Expectations in Economic Theory* (Chicago: Aldine Publishing Company, 1965).

5. Compare R.M. Cyert and J.G. March, *A Behavioral Theory of the Firm* (Englewood Cliffs, N.J.: Prentice-Hall, 1963).

6. For a recent methodological survey of the state of the art in finance-investment theory, see the following: M. Keenan, "The State of the Finance Field Methodology, Models of Equity Valuation: The Great Serm Bubble," *Journal of Finance, Proceedings* (May, 1970). Also in the same issue, E.F. Fama, "Efficient Capital Markets: A Review of Theory and Empirical Work."

7. The term "programed decisions" is used by Simon to refer to search behavior that is systematic and exhaustive, and made within a consistent frame of reference. See H.A. Simon, "The Role of Expectations in an Adaptive or Behavioristic Model," in M.J. Bowman, *Expectations, Uncertainty, and Business Behavior* (New York: Social Science Research Council, 1958). See also G. Katona, *Psychological Analysis of Economic Behavior* (New York: McGraw-Hill Book Co., 1951); where the terms "habitual" and "critical" are employed to denote "programed" and "unprogramed" decisions.

8. By legitimate literature, we mean the research that appears in such publications as the *Journal of Finance*, the *Journal of Business*, the *Industrial Management Review*, the *Journal of Financial and Quantitative Analysis*. Also included are, of course, researches that have appeared in other economic and management science journals, which have excited the interest of finance theorists.

9. This approach is congruent with the stress in the finance-investment literature where the institutional legitimation of expectations, through various forms of organizations and market structures, has received minimal attention.

10. For an elaboration of these views see G. Katona, "Business Expectations in the Framework of Psychological Economics (Toward a Theory of Expecta-

tions)," in M.J. Bowman (ed.) *Expectations, Uncertainty, and Business Behavior* (New York: Social Science Research Council, 1958), pp. 59-73. Also compare his *Psychological Analysis of Economic Behavior* (New York: McGraw-Hill, 1951).

11. Compare, for example, the following statement: "Expectations more nearly derive from the objective conditions than produce them." V.L. Bassie, National Bureau of Economic Research, *Studies in Income and Wealth* Vol. 17. (Princeton, N.J.: Princeton University Press, 1955), p. 11.

12. This is generally the position taken in the economic disciplines regarding the importance of expectations. However, traditionalists would argue that the mechanism of transforming evidence into prospect can be ascertained either by introspection or by laboratory experiments with gambling operations; on the other hand, behaviorists would stress the importance of observation and field experimentation in delineating the formation and adaptation of expectations, as well as the heuristics employed in reaching economic decisions.

13. One can argue that all inventory-type of models, characterized by normal and minimum levels, set in advance by management, are casual in the sense of reacting to a change in the dependent variable without examining the expectations which caused a change in the independent variable. Similarly, the various ratios favored by firms are reactive in nature in that the reaction of management to a change in the ratio is more or less predetermined.

14. Compare W.H. Locke Anderson, *Corporation Finance and Fixed Investment* (Boston: Harvard School of Business, Division of Research, 1959), pp. 124-25. See also J.R. Meyer and R.R. Glauber, *Investment Decisions, Economic Forecasting and Public Policy* (Boston: Harvard School of Business, Division of Research, 1964).

15. Compare, for example, the treatment of corporate dividend policy as an economic ruin game in M. Shubik, *Competition, Oligopoly, and the Theory of Games* (New York: John Wiley & Sons, 1957).

16. See the presentation of some of these theories in J.W. McGuire, *Theories of Business Behavior* (Englewood Cliffs, N.J.: Prentice-Hall, Inc., 1964), pp. 101-107.

17. Compare R.D. Edwards and J. Magee, *Technical Analysis and Stock Trends*, 5th Edition (Springfield, Mass.: John Magee, 1966).

18. See S.S. Alexander, "Price Movements in Speculative Markets: Trends or Random Walks, I," *Industrial Management Review*, (May, 1961). cf. also Fama, op. cit.

19. Compare, for example, the following statement by Georgescu-Roegen: "The controversy over the structure of expectations is in many ways similar to that of Pythagoras' time over the structure of length." "The Nature of Expectations and Uncertainty," in Bowman, op. cit.

20. Compare, for example, the following statement by Ruth Mack: "Proposition 2: The psychology of an expectation is immaterial in dealing with how

expectation-based actions of businessmen change." "Business Expectations and the Buying of Materials," in Bowman, loc. cit., p. 106.

21. It should be noted that the arguments over *introspection* and *gambling* experiments refer to *expectations proper*, rather than forecasts and plans, which, by their explicit formulation and definite form, allow verification by direct observation. Compare Modigliani and Cohen, op. cit., and Ozga, op. cit. Also, for an evaluation of investment surveys, see I. Friend, "Critical Evaluation of Surveys of Expectations, Plans, and Investment Behavior," in Bowman, op. cit., pp. 189-198.

22. Compare H. Simon, "A Formal Theory of Interaction in Social Groups," in H. Simon, *Models of Man: Social and Rational* (New York: John Wiley & Sons, 1957), pp. 99-114. See also H. Simon and H. Guetzkow, "Mechanisms Involved in Pressures Toward Uniformity in Groups," in Simon, op. cit., pp. 115-31, and J. Marschak, "Towards an Economic Theory of Organization and Information," in R.M. Thrall, C.H. Coombs, and R.L. Davis, *Decision Processes* (New York: John Wiley & Sons, 1956), pp. 197-220.

23. See K.J. Arrow, "Alternative Approaches to the Theory of Choice in Risk-Taking Situations," *Econometrica*, (October, 1951).

24. A well-known measure of the sensitivity of the prospect to changes in the primary expectations is provided by the elasticity of price expectations. Compare for example J.R. Hicks, *Value and Capital*, Second Edition (London: Oxford University Press, 1953). See also O. Lange, *Price Flexibility and Employment* (San Antonio, Texas: The Principia Press of Trinity University, 1945).

25. Compare Fama, op. cit.

26. A clarification of expectations occurs when a change in the original evidence yields a hitherto unknown answer. A revision, on the other hand, occurs when a change in the evidence yields new answers to the original questions. Compare Ozga, op. cit., pp. 32-37.

27. See G.P.E. Clarkson, *Portfolio Section: A Simulation of Trust Investment* (Englewood Cliffs, N.J.: Prentice-Hall, Inc., 1962). Compare also S.K. Gupta and J. Rosenhead, "Robustness in Sequential Investment Decisions," *Management Science*, (October, 1968), and R.C. Salazar and S.K. Sen, "A Simulation Model of Capital Budgeting Under Uncertainty," *Management Science* (October, 1968).

28. Expectations are themselves subject to expectations, and are called *conditional*. Thus we have conditional evidence, conditional propsects, conditional weights, and conditional outcomes. Such conditional expectations yield specific relations between the evidence, individual, and prospect, and normally result to clarification or revision.

29. The arguments of the classical and frequency schools of probability notwithstanding, the thorny problems of *comparability* and *ordinal measurability* of expectations remain very much with us, as a challenge to basic research. Cf. Georgescu-Roegen, op. cit., and Ozga, op. cit.

30. The term "degree of confirmation" is used by J.M. Keynes, *A Treatise on Probability* (London: MacMillan, 1921), pp. 29f. A more neutral term, "the degree of corroboration" has been suggested by K.R. Popper, *The Logic of Scientific Discovery* (New York: Science Editions, Inc., 1961), p. 251.

31. This seems to be standard practice in investment decisions. More sophisticated versions allow for the possible covariation between future flows, as in F. Millier, "Derivation of Probabilistic Information for the Evaluation of Risky Investments," *Management Science*, (April, 1963). Or they allow for the covariation of returns between projects, as in H. Markowitz, "Portfolio Selection," *Journal of Finance*, (March, 1952). A survey of adjustments for project interdependence is also provided in M.H. Weingartner, *Management Science*, (March, 1966).

32. The term "moral expectation" is attributed to D. Bernoulli, "Exposition of a New Theory on the Measurement of Risk," *Econometrica*, (January, 1954), translated by L. Sommer. Bernoulli attempted to improve upon the mean value of monetary payoffs as a decision prospect. Later developments have been made by J. Von Neumann and O. Morgenstern. Compare, for example, Arrow, op. cit., and Ozga, op. cit.

33. Compare Katona, op. cit., p. 31, and p. 40f. A more sophisticated version of the sure-prospect is offered by F. R. Knight, *Risk, Uncertainty and Profits* (Boston, Mass.: Houghton Mifflin Company, 1921). Professor Knight has argued that people try to reduce uncertainty by adjusting their strategies to expectations based on frequency distributions of outcomes. This can be done either by *consolidation* of payoffs through insurance, or *specialization* through restriction of activities.

34. See his "Money and the Theory of Assets," *Econometrica*, (October, 1938), and H. Makower and J. Marschak, "Asset Prices and Monetary Theory," *Economica*, (August, 1938). For later developments also see J. Tobin, "Liquidity Preference as Behavior Toward Risk," *Review of Economic Studies*, (February, 1958). Also see R.C.O. Mathews, "Expenditures, Plans and the Uncertainty Motive for Holding Money," *Journal of Political Economy*, (June, 1963).

35. For example, O. Lange has insisted that the modal return and range of probable outcomes are better descriptors of investment behavior by households and firms. See his *Price Flexibility and Employment*, op. cit., pp. 29-30. See also H. Markowitz, *Portfolio Selection*, (New York: John Wiley & Sons, 1959), pp. 53-55, for the equivalence of some measures where the probability distribution of returns can be described by one of the standard shaped curves.

36. The literature on portfolio selection has used these two measures consistently, whether it employs the full covariance model or some simplified index model. Compare, for example, W.F. Sharpe, *Portfolio Theory and Capital Markets* (New York: McGraw-Hill Company, 1970). Other measures of risk have included a lower confidence limit and the semivariance, where expectations are allowed some degree of asymmetry.

37. See Markowitz, op. cit., and D.E. Farrar, *The Investment Decision Under Uncertainty* (Englewood Cliffs, N.J.: Prentice-Hall, Inc., 1962).

38. Compare G. Donaldson, *Corporate Debt Capacity* (Boston: Harvard School of Business, Division of Research, 1961). See also Anderson, op. cit., and J.R. Meyer and E. Kuh, *The Investment Decision: An Empirical Study* (Cambridge, Mass.: Harvard University Press, 1957).

39. Compare J. Lintner, "Distribution of Incomes of Corporations Among Dividends, Retained Earnings, and Taxes," *The American Economic Review*, (May, 1956); see also his, "Dividends, Earnings, Leverage, Stock Prices and the Supply of Capital to Corporations," *The Review of Economics and Statistics* (August, 1962). Lintner's findings were also substantiated by two other studies: *Journal of Political Economy* (June, 1957); and J. Brittain, *Corporate Dividend Policy* (Washington, D.C.: The Brookings Institute, 1966).

40. For a different view on the perception of evidence regarding short-run managerial actions and the reaction of shareholders, compare O.E. Williamson, *The Economics of Discretionary Behavior: Managerial Objectives in a Theory of the Firm* (Englewood Cliffs, N.J.: Prentice-Hall, Inc., 1964).

41. Gestalt psychology has been invoked in explaining how the same evidence is perceived and interpreted differently by individuals. One of the reasons suggests that elements of the evidence are viewed as belonging to different sets. Thus, in transforming the evidence, the market participants reach different conclusions, since their prospects may not be altered in response to changes in the evidence, or they may change disproportionately.

42. Compare Meredith, in Bowman, op. cit., p. 80, See also his "Uncertainty, Expectation and Decision in Business Affiars," in G.F. Carter, G.P. Meredith, and G.L.S. Shackle, (eds.), *Uncertainty and Business Decisions* (Liverpool: University Press, 1954).

43. Compare Katona, op. cit., pp. 50-52.

44. Ibid., pp. 229-38.

45. See his, *Expectations in Economics* 2nd Edition (London: Cambridge University Press, 1952).

46. This formulation of surprise bears similarity to the "information content of a definite message" which is a decreasing function of the probability associated with an event. Compare H. Theil, *Economics and Information Theory* (Chicago, Ill.: Rand McNally and Co., 1967).

47. Compare his "Expectation and Liquidity," in Bowman, op. cit., pp. 30-44. Earlier attempts of Shackle have not satisfied the *principle of spreading the risks*. See, for example, R.A.D. Egerton, "Investment, Uncertainty and Expectations," *Review of Economic Studies*, (1954-55).

48. J.W. Angell, "Uncertainty, Likelihoods and Investment Decisions," *Quarterly Journal of Economics*, (February, 1960).

49. There are, of course, other theories of expectations that are based on extreme outcomes. Compare, for example, of *minimum subjective loss* in L.J.

Savage, "The Theory of Statistical Decisions," *Journal of the American Statistical Association*, (1951). Cf. also Hurwicz's *index of optimism-pessimism*, in R.D. Luce and H. Raiffa, *Games and Decisions* (New York: John Wiley & Sons, 1957), pp. 282-84.

50. Compare W. Fellner, "Average Cost Pricing and the Theory of Uncertainty," *Journal of Political Economy*, (June, 1948).

51. Donaldson, op. cit.

52. See A.D. Roy, "Safety First and the Holding of Assets," *Econometrica*, (July, 1952). See also T.G. Telser, "Safety First and Hedging," *Review of Economic Studies*, (1955) and J. Steindl, "On Risk," *Oxford Economic Papers*, (June, 1951).

53. Markowitz, op. cit.

54. W.J. Baumol, "An Expected Gain-Confidence Limit Criterion for Portfolio Selection," *Management Science*, (October, 1963). See also B.D. Nevins, "Leverage, Risk of Ruin and the Cost of Capital," *Journal of Finance*, (September, 1967).

55. Compare F. Hanssman, "Probability of Survival as an Investment Criterion," *Management Science*, (September, 1968).

56. See J.C.T. Mao, "Models of Capital Budgeting, E-V Vs. E-S," *Journal of Financial and Quantitative Analysis*, (December, 1970).

57. See R.M. Cyert and J.G. March, *A Behavioral Theory of the Firm* (Englewood Cliffs, N.J.: Prentice-Hall, Inc., 1963), pp. 44-83. See also the analytical effort by J. Marschak, op. cit.

58. Ibid., pp. 46-47.

59. The point has also been emphasized by Meredith, op. cit., and Shackle, op. cit.

60. Compare H.A. Simon, "The Role of Expectations in an Adaptive or Behavioristic Model," in Bowman, op. cit. pp. 49-58. This classification is similar to Katona's dichotomy of habitual and nonhabitual behavior, and is standard in the psychological literature.

61. Williamson, op. cit.

62. Clarkson, op. cit.

63. See J.P. Crecine, *Government Problem-Solving: A Computer Simulation of Municipal Budgeting* (Chicago: Rand McNally & Co., 1969).

Part IV:
Lifetime Utility Strategies

Sequential Investment-Consumption Strategies for Individuals and Endowment Funds with Lexicographic Preferences

Nils H. Hakansson

I. Introduction

As far as I have been able to discover, there was not a single formal model of the consumer-investor in the economics literature ten years ago which incorporated two of the more fundamental aspects of life: the fact that decisions are taken sequentially and the fact that they are made under uncertainty. In contrast, the last ten years, and in particular the last five, have seen a virtual explosion in the construction of sequential stochastic models of the consumer and quasi-consumer. Before examining the methodological foundations which made this progress possible, a very brief summary of the main papers to date dealing with the consumer-investor's recurring decision problem under risk may be appropriate.

The earliest papers appear to be due to Phelps [31] and to Yaari [40]. Phelps studied an individual with a certain income stream and a single risky investment opportunity, while Yaari examined a model of a consumer with an uncertain lifetime, but facing riskless investment returns.

The Phelps' investment-consumption model (with income stream) was generalized to the case of one riskless and several risky assets by Hakansson [14, 17] and by Leland [25], and, without income stream, by Levhari and Srinivasan [26], Samuelson [34], Merton [28], Hahn [13], and Pye [33]. Hakansson later extended his model to reflect an uncertain lifetime and the possibility of life insurance [15] and finally (without income stream), to incorporate a Markovian investment environment and state-dependent time preferences [19]. The properties of the induced utility of wealth of stochastic sequential models of the consumer-investor have been examined by Fama [11], Hakansson [16], and Neave [30]; their implications with respect to the demand for liquid assets have been studied by Dixit and Goldman [9]. Finally, Yaari [41] has tackled a sequential model in which the consumer faces an uncertain income stream.

In Section II, I shall review briefly the methodological foundations which have made possible the recent advances in the consumption-investment area. Section III then introduces certain lexicographic preference structures for the

This research was partially supported by a grant from the Dean Witter Foundation administered by the Institute of Business and Economic Research. The author is grateful to Fischer Black, Harry Markowitz, and Karlene Roberts for helpful comments.

175

purpose of representing various behavioral phenomena. The implications of such preferences are examined in Sections V-VIII in the context of some examples. In particular, the effects of lexicographic orderings concerning total consumption, subsistence level consumption, bequests, moonlighting, the maintenance of educational quality on the part of universities, and perpetual giving by foundations, especially on optimal risk taking, are examined and related to the properties of "conventional" models.

II. The Methodological Foundations

Since the focus of this conference is on methodology, I shall review, very briefly, the tools used in the development of the models referred to in the preceding section. The methodology itself warrants few comments since it relies almost exclusively on postulation, deduction, and induction, and (formal) empirical investigation has so far not accompanied any of the studies.

Whether one is concerned with prescriptive models or with descriptive representations of the consumer-investor, there seem to me to be five ingredients which are crucial to success. Four of these fall in the analytical area; the fifth I shall loosely refer to as empirical relevance. Since empirical relevance must ultimately determine the applicable analytical tools in any of the empirical sciences, I shall begin with this component.

While mathematicians and logicians may be interested in deductive systems per se, the empirical scientist generally does not build deductive systems for their own sake. His systems are usually intended to be representations of real world phenomena about which he wishes to inquire. The interface between model and reality, or between conception and perception, is now readily seen to be crucial. This is where the concept of empirical relevance becomes important.

Since no model can be a perfect replica of reality, a natural measure of the empirical scientist's skill in his choice of model is the extent to which the essence of (the) reality (modeled) is captured in the postulates. No objective measure of this skill is possible, since the phenomena which give rise to this skill, percention and the translation of perceived ideas into concepts, are highly subjective. However, the importance of this skill is brought out by the fact that the theorems of a model have empirical content only if the postulates do. No theory can be more secure than its foundations.

It was noted earlier that elementary consideration of empirical relevance demand that models of the consumer-investor recognize that economic decisions are made sequentially and under uncertainty. The first of these facts means that once a sequential model is constructed, the derivation of theorems requires skill in what is known as sequential decision theory, dynamic programing, and control theory. A certain familiarity with the analytical tool known as sequential decision theory is therefore indispensible to the researcher interested in models of the consumer-investor.

The recognition of uncertainty in a model is generally accomplished via probabilities. The presence of this ingredient in a sequential model clearly demands considerable knowledge of probability theory and stochastic processes on the part of the scientist who is searching for (new) theorems.

A third crucial element of a model of the consumer-investor is the preference structure. Its representation, as well as the subsequent search for model implications, demands a thorough knowledge of utility theory. Since empirically relevant cardinal utility functions are almost always nonlinear, skills in nonlinear programing are also necessary in extracting conclusions from a sequential, stochastic model of the investor-consumer.

In sum, the primary analytical tools which form the methodological foundation for studies of the consumer-investor are sequential decision theory, probability theory, utility theory, and nonlinear programing. In addition, success in this area of study also requires an ability to build empirical relevance into the model used. At the present time, most researchers in the consumption-investment field possess strength in three or four of the above areas. Those with pronounced skills in all five areas are few indeed.

As we look to the future, the most likely addition to the model building kit will be Bayesian processing of empirical observations in the form of econometric information (see Drèze[10]). The effect of this will be to add econometrics to the bag of skills which will be needed by the researcher in the consumption-investment area.

III. Lexicographic Preferences

Existing models of the consumer-investor are based on the Fisherian concept that consumption is the spring of all ultimate utility, although some also couple this with a Marshallian bequest motive. The point I want to stress is that the assumed preference structures obey Archimedes' axiom that everything has its price except, in some models, zero consumption, which is then avoided at all cost. But when this exception occurs, it does so by default since it appears only if the utility function is unbounded and a utility function which is consistent with the von Neumann-Morgenstern postulates [39] is always bounded [2]. In other words, present utility theory is founded on the notion that no part of an *economic* position is immune to an *economic* bribe. As long as my consumption level in some period is positive, the theory claims, I am always willing to give up some of this consumption for a *chance* at a higher consumption level in the same (or a different) period. Specifically, if consumption level x is preferred to level y, which in turn is preferred to level z ($x > y > z$), the von Neumann-Morgenstern theory asserts that there exist a number p, $0 < p < 1$, such that I'm indifferent between receiving y for sure and receiving x with probability p or z with probability $1 - p$. Thus, if $x > y > z > 0$ and y is the subsistence level, that theory suggests that, for a price ($x - y$ with probability $p < 1$), we are willing, upon consulting our preferences, to bring our consumption level in some years to zero, or at least arbitrarily close to zero, with positive probability. But is that really the case? If there is such a thing as a subsistence level, and the empirical evidence is pretty persuasive on this point, there is probably no amount of additional consumption in the present period or in future periods that would induce one to risk going below the subsistence level (presumably survival at less than the subsistence level is impossible in any period; remember also that we are speaking about preferences, or indifference curves, apart from opportunities).

The preceding suggests that preferences for consumption above the subsistence level are of a lower order (infinity) than for subsistence level consumption. Perhaps tradeoffs between periods exist only if the subsistence level is equaled or exceeded in each period. In other words, preferences may be lexicographic: every (stochastic) consumption program which insures subsistence in every period is preferred to every program that risks providing less than the subsistence level in some period(s). This, of course, does not rule out preferences among subsubsistence consumption programs. They, in turn, may be lexicographic: possibly every program which insures subsistence in the first n periods ($n < N$, the total (maximum) life-time in periods) is preferred to every program which does not insure subsistence in one or more of the first n periods.

Other examples of lexicographic orderings suggest themselves. A person may so prefer a way of living (consumption program) that he will gladly work hard enough to afford it; furthermore, given this pattern, he may gladly bequeath any fortune he might have, no matter how large, rather than spend anything more on himself or his family. Private universities seem unwilling to reduce internal endowment growth in the short run in order to get by with less fund-raising efforts for a given expenditure level. And charitable endowment funds appear to regard a perpetual life of substantial giving as ranking higher than anything else. We shall examine each of these situations in some detail in the latter part of the paper.

Before proceeding to the analysis proper, it is of interest to note that a lexicographic preference structure is implicitly assumed in a class of investment-consumption models that have been studied by mathematicians. These studies have focused attention on finding the investment strategies which minimize the probability of ruin when the individual must pay a cost of living charge each period (Truelove [37, 38], Ferguson [12]). The notion that human preferences are hierarchial in nature also has wide acceptance in the behavioral sciences. In a classic paper, Maslow, for example, wrote [27: 394-95]:

There are at least five sets of goals which we may call basic needs. . . . These basic goals are related to one another, being arranged in a hierarchy of prepotency. This means that the most prepotent goal will monopolize consciousness and will tend of itself to organize the recruitment of the various capacities of the organism. The less prepotent needs are minimized, even forgotten or denied. But when a need is fairly well satisfied, the next prepotent ("higher") need emerges, in turn to dominate the conscious life and to serve as the center of organization of behavior, since gratified needs are not active motivators.

The problem of representing lexicographic preferences under uncertainty by means of utilities has been intensively studied by Thrall and Dalkey [36], Hausner [23], Thrall [35], and Chipman [7]. Their central result, which also applies to the certainty case (Debreu [8]), is that an ordered vector space is required for representing non-Archemedan preferences.

As noted, ordinary utility theory rules out lexicographic preferences; hierarchial preference structures are specifically excluded by the continuity postulate. This suggests a possible methodological shortcoming facing the theory of the consumer-investor if we accept the existence of lexicographic preferences. However, the present framework is still of use in that it enables the determination of *conditionally* optimal investment and spending strategies "within layers"; the derivation of such policies will be the focal point of the following sections. In other words, even if von Neumann-Morgenstern utility theory is inappropriate for preference representation at the *global* level, it still serves well locally, that is, *within* each hierarchial layer. Clearly, it now becomes necessary to first determine which hierarchial "preference layer" applies in a given environmental situation.

IV. Preliminaries

In each case we assume that opportunities for decision occur at equally spaced points in time. The period of time between decision points j and $j + 1$ will be denoted period j.

The following basic notation will be adopted:

x_j = amount of equity capital at decision point j (the beginning of the jth period)

M_j = the number of investment opportunities available in period j

r_j-1 = rate of interest in period j, where $r_j > 1$

β_{ij} = proceeds per unit of capital invested in opportunity i, where $i = 2, \ldots, M_j$, in the jth period (random variable)

$F_j(y_2, y_3, \ldots, y_{M_j}) \equiv \Pr \left\{ \beta_{2j} \leqslant y_2, \beta_{3j} \leqslant y_3, \ldots, \beta_{M_j j} \leqslant y_{M_j} \right\}$.

z_{1j} = amount lent in period j (negative z_{1j} indicate borrowing) (decision variable)

$z^*_j(x_j)$ = an optimal lending (borrowing) policy in period j

z_{ij} = amount invested in opportunity i, $i = 2, \ldots, M_j$ at the beginning of the jth period (decision variable)

$\bar{z}_j \equiv (z_{2j}, \ldots, z_{M_j j})$

$z_j^*(x_j)$ = an optimal investment policy in period j

c_j = total amount consumed or expended on operations in period j (allocated at beginning of period)

$c_j^*(x_j)$ = an optimal consumption or spending policy in period j

y_j = non-capital income or gifts received at end of period j

$Y_j \equiv \dfrac{y_j}{r_j} + \ldots + \dfrac{y_N}{r_j \ldots r_N}$

$f_j(x_j)$ = the (induced) utility of wealth at decision point j under an optimal policy

We assume that the distribution functions F_j satisfy the boundedness conditions

$$\Pr\left\{ 0 \leqslant \beta_{ij} \leqslant B_i \right\} = 1 \qquad i = 2, \ldots, M_j, \text{ all } j, \tag{1}$$

$$E[\beta_{ij}] \geqslant r_j + \eta \qquad\qquad \eta > 0, \text{ some } i, \text{ all } j, \tag{2}$$

and the "no-easy-money condition"

$$\Pr\left\{ \sum_{i=2}^{M_j} (\beta_{ij} - r_j)\theta_i < \delta \right\} > 0 \qquad \text{for all } j \text{ and all } \theta_i \text{ such that} \tag{3}$$

$$\sum_{i=2}^{M_j} \theta_i = 1 \text{ and } \theta_i \geqslant 0,$$

where $\delta < 0$.

Conditions (1) reflect the fact that one can at most lose one's investment in a long position and that a finite investment will always bring a finite return over a finite time period. The "no-easy-money condition" (3) states that no combination of investments is available which guarantees a return at least equal to the rate of interest. (3) appears to be the weakest condition that the distribution functions F_j must satisfy when the prices of the various capital assets are in equilibrium in the absence of artificial margin requirements.

To keep the technical details at a minimum, we also assume in this paper that there exists a number $p > 0$ such that for all values $y_2, y_3, \ldots, y_{M_j}$ jointly assumed by $\beta_{2j}, \beta_{3j}, \ldots, \beta_{M_j j}$

$$\Pr\left\{ \beta_{2j} = y_2, \beta_{3j} = y_3, \ldots, \beta_{M_j j} = y_{M_j} \right\} \geqslant p \qquad j = 1, 2, \ldots \tag{4}$$

We also assume that there are no limits on borrowing, but that all debts must be fully secured. The latter requirement is necessary to achieve consistency with the standard assumption of a risk-free lending (see [22]) and to cope with the requirements of a multiperiod model of the reinvestment type.

V. The Unworldly Professor

We first consider an individual, A (the unworldly professor) whose preferences exhibit the following properties:

A1. A very strong liking of a particular life-style. This life-style requires consumption expenditures of c_j (>0) at the beginning of each of the remaining periods $j = 1, \ldots, N$ and brings an income stream of $y_j \geq 0$ at the end of each period $j = 1, \ldots, N$.

A2. If initial wealth x_1 and the income stream $y_1, \ldots, y_N$ should be insufficient to support the expenditure pattern $c_1, \ldots, c_N$ with probability 1, the individual would prefer (1) bringing his income up to the level necessary to afford $c_1, \ldots, c_N$ for sure by extra work (moonlighting) to (2) compromising in any way on $c_1, \ldots, c_N$.

A3. If initial wealth x_1 and the income stream $y_1, \ldots, y_N$ should be sufficient to support the expenditure pattern $c_1, \ldots, c_N$ with probability 1, the individual would prefer (1) bequeathing any accumulated wealth at the end of period N, x_{N+1}, to (2) increasing his consumption above $c_1, \ldots, c_N$. The utility of a bequest $x_{N+1} \geq 0$ is $b(x_{N+1})$, where b is monotone increasing and strictly concave.

A4. The avoidance of any extra work, no matter how small the probability of its necessity, is always preferred to any bequest x_{N+1}.

Let us first find the conditions under which the resources x_1 and $y_1, \ldots, y_N$ are sufficient for implementing $c_1, \ldots, c_N$ without extra work with probability 1. As noted, we have assumed that each of these elements are known with certainty at decision point 1.

At decision point N, A can borrow a maximum of y_N/r_N against income y_N to be received at the end of period N without risk of default. Thus, x_N and y_N will be sufficient to support c_N (with probability 1) if and only if

$$x_N + y_N/r_N \geq c_N$$

or, equivalently,

$$x_N \geq c_N - \frac{y_N}{r_N}$$

since if $x_N < c_N - y_N/r_N$, additional borrowed funds cannot be fully secured (by the "no-easy-money condition" (3)) and would therefore be unavailable. Moving backwards in time, we obtain by the same reasoning

$$x_j \geqslant C_j - Y_j \qquad j = 1, \ldots, N, \qquad (5)$$

and specifically,

$$x_1 \geqslant C_1 - Y_1, \qquad (6)$$

where

$$C_j \equiv c_j + \frac{c_{j+1}}{r_j} + \ldots + \frac{c_N}{r_j \ldots r_{N-1}},$$

as a necessary and sufficient condition for A to be able to avoid extra work with probability 1. The sufficiency of (6) follows from the observation that when (6) holds, the strategy

$$z_{1j}(x_j) = x_j - c_j$$
$$z_{ij}(x_j) = 0 \qquad i = 2, \ldots, M_j \qquad (7)$$

for $j = 1, \ldots, N$ always yields (5). The necessity of (6) can be seen from the observation that (7) and

$$x_1 > C_1 - Y_1 \qquad (8)$$

imply

$$x_j < C_j - Y_j \qquad j = 2, \ldots, N ; \qquad (9)$$

furthermore, (8) and any policy differing from (7) in some period implies, in view of (3),

$$\Pr \left\{ x_j < C_j - Y_j \right\} > 0 \quad j = 2, \ldots, N \qquad (10)$$

In other words, (10) states that A *may* have to do extra work if the present value of his income stream plus his wealth is less than the present value of his idealized consumption pattern. We shall not consider here the nontrivial problem of how he might distribute the extra work between the periods and/or how he might attempt to alleviate it altogether by risky investments when (8) holds.[1] Instead, we shall focus our attention on the case when

$$x_1 \geqslant C_1 - Y_1. \tag{6}$$

However, it is clear that (6) is the dividing line which in effect determines where in his preference hierarchy A finds himself and which "prepotent goals will monopolize consciousness" at the beginning of period 1. If (8) holds, the desire to achieve $c_1, \ldots, c_N$ "will tend of itself to organize the recruitment of the various capacities of the organism" (see A2). If (6) holds or (5) results in some period $j > 1$ (at least with strict inequality), "the next prepotent need" (the bequest motive) emerges "to serve as the center of organization of behavior" (see A3) and the need to moonlight can be "forgotten" (just how it can be "forgotten," in view of A4, will be shown later).

Suppose first that equality holds in (6) and consider any decision point j. If $x_j - c_j \leqslant 0$, there is nothing to invest in period j and no lender in sight to borrow beyond $c_j - x_j$ from since 100 percent collateral cannot be offered by (3). If $x_j - c_j > 0$, $x_j - c_j$ would be invested at the safe return $r_j - 1$; this avoids any need for extra work, as shown earlier, whereas if some portion of $x_j - c_j$ were placed in risky assets, (3) gives

$$\Pr \left\{ x_n < C_n - Y_n \right\} > 0 \quad n = j + 1, \ldots, N \tag{11}$$

and

$$\Pr \left\{ x_{N+1} > 0 \right\} > 0 \tag{12}$$

Thus, there would be some chance of extra work and some chance for a bequest. But by A4, no bequest, no matter how large, combined with an amount of extra work, no matter how small the probability of its necessity, is preferred to no work plus no bequest. Consequently, when (6) holds with equality, A would engage only in lending and borrowing (financial opportunities). Thus, holdings of risky assets are non-optimal whenever

$$x_1 = C_1 - Y_1. \tag{13}$$

In this case, extra work can and will be avoided, and no bequest will be made. The policy (7) is optimal.

Consider now the case when (6) holds with strict inequality. This means that A will consume amounts $c_1, \ldots, c_N$ and avoid all extra work; furthermore, he can begin to think about the possibility of making a positive bequest x_{N+1}. The necessity of 100 percent collateral implies that the constraint

$$\Pr \left\{ x_{N+1} \geqslant 0 \right\} = 1 \tag{14}$$

must be observed. (14), in turn, induces the constraints

$$\Pr \left\{ x_j \geqslant C_j - Y_j \right\} = 1 \quad j = 2, \ldots, N \tag{15}$$

in view of the "no-easy-money condition" (3). Note that *the constraints* (15) *are also implied by* A4 *since they are necessary to avoid extra work with probability* 1. By the principle of optimality [4: 83], we now obtain

$$f_j(x_j) = \underset{\bar{z}_j}{\text{Max}} \; E[f_{j+1}(x_{j+1})] \qquad j = 1, \ldots, N, \tag{16}$$

where

$$f_{N+1}(x_{N+1}) \equiv b(x_{N+1}), \tag{17}$$

subject to

$$\Pr\left\{ x_{j+1} \geq C_{j+1} - Y_{j+1} \right\} = 1 \; j = 1, \ldots, N \tag{18}$$

(where clearly $C_{N+1} - Y_{N+1} = 0$). Since expenditures must equal available funds at each decision point j and available funds at each following decision point are made up of the investment proceeds at that point, we have

$$\sum_{i=1}^{M_j} z_{ij} + c_j = x_j \qquad j = 1, \ldots, N \tag{19}$$

and

$$x_{j+1} = r_j z_{1j} + \sum_{i=2}^{M_j} \beta_{ij} z_{ij} + y_j \qquad j = 1, \ldots, N \tag{20}$$

Combining (19) and (20), we obtain

$$x_{j+1} = \sum_{i=2}^{M_j} (\beta_{ij} - r_j) z_{ij} + r_j(x_j - c_j) + y_j \tag{21}$$
$$j = 1, \ldots, N,$$

(16) and (17) now give

$$f_N(x_N) = \underset{z_N}{\text{Max}} \; E\left[b\left(\sum_{i=2}^{M_j} (\beta_{iN} - r_N) z_{iN} + r_N(x_N - c_N) + y_N\right) \right] \tag{22}$$

subject to

$$\Pr\left\{ \sum_{i=2}^{M_j} (\beta_{iN} - r_N) z_{iN} + r_N(x_N - C_N + Y_N) \geq 0 \right\} = 1 \tag{23}$$

But in view of (3), (23) can only be satisfied if

$$x_N - C_N + Y_N \geq 0 \tag{24}$$

Thus, $f_N(x_N)$ exists for $x_n \geq C_N - Y_N$; furthermore, it is monotone increasing and strictly concave (see Fama [11]). Since (24) coincides with constraint (18) for $j = N - 1$, we obtain by induction that $f_j(x_j)$ exist for $x_j \geq C_j - Y_j$, $j = 1, \ldots, N$, and is monotone increasing and strictly concave since we get, for any $j < N$,

$$f_j(x_j) = \text{Max } E \left[f_{j+1} (\sum_{i=2}^{M_j} (\beta_{ij} - r_j) z_{ij} + r_j (x_j - c_j) + y_j) \right] \tag{25}$$

subject to

$$\Pr \left\{ x_{j+1} \geq C_{j+1} - Y_{j+1} \right\} = 1 \,,$$

which gives the indicated result.

When (2) holds, the monotonicity and strict concavity of $f_1(x_1)$ implies that $z_{i_1}^* > 0$ for some $i \geq 2$ whenever

$$x_1 > C_1 - Y_1 \tag{26}$$

(see Hakansson [21]). Thus, when (6) holds with strict *in*equality, risky investments are always optimal. This in turn, in view of the "no-easy-money" condition (3), implies that a (positive) bequest will be left with positive probability when (26) holds.

If, and only if,

$$b(x_{N+1}) = \begin{cases} -x_{N+1}^{\gamma} & \gamma < 0 \\[2mm] \log x_{N+1} & \gamma = 0 \\[2mm] x_{N+1}^{\gamma} & 0 < \gamma < 1 \,, \end{cases} \tag{27}$$

$f_j(x_j)$ has the form

$$f_j(x_j) = a_j b(x_j - C_j + Y_j) + k_j \qquad j = 1, \ldots, N, \tag{28}$$

where a_j and k_j are constants, and the optimal investment strategy satisfies the separation property [29]. Thus, the optimal investment policy in period j has the form

$$z_{ij}^*(x_j) = v_{ij}^*(x_j - C_j + Y_j) \qquad i = 2, \ldots, M_j \tag{29}$$

$$z_{1j}^*(x_j) = x_j - c_j - \sum_{i=2}^{M_j} z_{ij}^*(x_j) \tag{30}$$

For each j, the v_{ij}^* are constants which depend *only on* the return distribution F_j, on the interest rate $r_j - 1$, and on (27); that is, the optimal policy is myopic (see [29, 20]). Thus, the important property of myopia remains *conditionally optimal* in the particular case of lexicographic preferences we have considered.

The larger the ideal consumption stream $c_1, \ldots, c_N$, or, more precisely, the larger its present value C_j, the more conservative the optimal investment policy $\bar{z}_j^*$ would be (see (29)). That is, the optimal amount invested in opportunity i is smaller the larger the consumption "demand" C_j is, or the smaller income Y_j is, *ceteris paribus*. However, this statement cannot be made in general; when $b(x_{N+1})$ is increasingly risk-averse in the Pratt-Arrow sense [32, 3], as it would be if b were quadratic, for example, the opposite is true, at least in some periods. But one thing that can safely be said is that the "investment base exposable to risk," $x_j - C_j + Y_j$, is always decreasing in C_j and increasing in Y_j.

Significant complications arise if one or more of the consumption stream $c_1, \ldots, c_N$, the interest rates $r_1, \ldots, r_N$, and the noncapital income stream $y_1, \ldots, y_N$ are viewed as stochastic. The same is ture if the individual's lifetime is considered to be random, with one exception. If A believes or acts as if his horizon is N but any lender attaches a positive probability to his death in each period j, the solvency constraints

$$\Pr\left\{ x_{j+1} \geqslant 0 \right\} = 1 \qquad\qquad j = 1, \ldots, N-1 \qquad (31)$$

must be added to (18). Note that when

$$-C_j + Y_j \leqslant 0 \qquad\qquad j = 2, \ldots, N \qquad (32)$$

holds,

$$x_{j+1} - C_{j+1} + Y_{j+1} \geqslant 0 \text{ implies } x_{j+1} \geqslant 0, \ j = 1, \ldots, N-1$$

Thus, (31) is never effective whenever (32) holds and can be ignored in that case; A would leave an estate (possibly zero) even if he dies "pre-maturely."

VI. The Burdened Family Man

We now turn our attention to individual B, who, unlike A, does not mind spending immodest sums on himself and on his family should the opportunity arise. However, while less charitable than A, B will not permit his consumption level to drop below a certain floor, which we shall call the subsistence level. We will not concern ourselves here with whether the "subsistence level" is physiologically or psychologically based, only with its existence. The following additional notation will be needed:

s_j = amount of subsistence level consumption in period j

$$S_j \equiv s_j + \ldots + \frac{s_N}{r_j \ldots r_{N-1}}$$

$$e_j \equiv c_j - s_j$$

Given that the subsistence level can be assured, we assume that B's preferences for excess consumption (consumption above the subsistence level) and his bequest x_{N+1} are representable by the functions

$$U_j(e_j, e_{j+1}, \ldots, e_N, x_{N+1}) \tag{33}$$

$$= u(e_j) + \alpha_j u(e_{j+1}) + \ldots + \alpha_j \ldots \alpha_{N-1} u(e_N)$$

$$+ \alpha_j \ldots \alpha_n b(x_{N+1}) \qquad j = 1, \ldots, N$$

Again, we must first find the conditions under which the preferences (33) will be "pre-dominant" (applicable).

The difference equations (21) now become

$$x_{j+1} = \sum_{i=2}^{M_j} (\beta_{ij} - r_j) z_{ij} + r_j(x_j - e_j - s_j) + y_j, \quad j = 1, \ldots, N \tag{34}$$

By the reasoning in Section V, three situations must be distinguished:

$$x_1 < S_1 - Y_1 \tag{35}$$

$$x_1 = S_1 - Y_1 \tag{36}$$

$$x_1 > S_1 - Y_1 \tag{37}$$

If (35) holds, B cannot achieve the subsistence level with probability 1. If his preferences in this situation are similar to A's (see A2), then he may choose to moonlight in order to reach it. The particular strategy to be used would depend on his disutility over time for extra work and the chances of gains from investments. The applicable model would be rather complex and will not be developed here (see note 1). However, if B's preferences are indeed lexicographic, then the utility functions (33) are only latent and therefore not applicable as long as

$$x_j < S_j - Y_j \tag{38}$$

for the decision point in question, j .

In analogy with (13), (36) rules out risky investment for all time, in view of (3), if B does not wish to risk having his resources fall below the subsistence level with positive probability in order to be able to exceed it with positive probability (see A4). In fact, this aspect of B's preferences induces the constraints

$$\Pr \left\{ x_j \geqslant S_j - Y_j \right\} = 1 \qquad j = 1, \ldots, N, \qquad (39)$$

while the solvency requirement implies the constraint

$$\Pr \left\{ x_{N+1} \geqslant 0 \right\} = 1 \qquad (14)$$

It should be noted, in analogy with Section V, that (14) also implies (39). B.s optimal strategy then becomes when (36) holds, for $j = 1, \ldots, N$:

$$c_j^*(x_j) = s_j \qquad (40)$$

$$z_{ij}^*(x_j) = 0 \qquad i = 2, \ldots, M_j, \qquad (41)$$

$$z_{1j}^*(x_j) = x_j - s_j \qquad (42)$$

Finally, when (37) holds, the utility function (33) is truly dominant and will remain so in view of (14) and (39) (unless x_j declines to $S_j - Y_j$ in some period, in which case (40)-(42) apply from that point on).

When the conditional utility functions (33) apply at some decision point n, B's decision problem may be stated, by the principle of optimality, as Problem B:

$$f_j(x_j) = \text{Max} \left\{ u(e_j) + \alpha_j E[f_{j+1}(x_{j+1})] \right\}, \qquad j = n, \ldots, N, \qquad (43)$$

where

$$f_{N+1}(x_{N+1}) \equiv b(x_{N+1}), \qquad (17)$$

subject to

$$\Pr \left\{ x_{N+1} \geqslant 0 \right\} = 1 \qquad (14)$$

and (hence)

$$\Pr \left\{ x_j \geqslant S_j - Y_j \right\} = 1 \qquad j = n, \ldots, N \qquad (39)$$

As noted, a solution to Problem B exists whenever

$$x_n \geqslant S_n - Y_n \qquad (44)$$

When $b(\cdot) = u(\cdot)$ and

$$u(e_j) = \begin{cases} -e_j{}^\gamma & \gamma < 0 \\ \log e_j & \gamma = 0 \\ e_j{}^\gamma & 0 < \gamma < 1, \end{cases} \tag{45}$$

the optimal strategies are analogous to those in [17] and it is readily verified that the solution has the form, for $j = n, \ldots, N$,

$$f_j(x_j) = A_j u(x_j - S_j + Y_j) + D_j \tag{46}$$

$$c_j^*(x_j) = B_j(x_j - S_j + Y_j) + s_j \tag{47}$$

$$z_{ij}^*(x_j) = (1-B_j)v_{ij}^*(x_j - S_j + Y_j) \quad i = 2, \ldots, M_j \tag{48}$$

$$z_{1j}^*(x_j) = x_j - c_j^*(x_j) - \sum_{i=2}^{M_j} z_{ij}^*(x_j) \tag{49}$$

where A_j, B_j and D_j are constants. As in [17] and [15], $0 < B_j < 1$ for all j and the constants v_{ij}^* depend only on u, F_j, and r_j. On the whole, the properties of the optimal strategies (47)-(49) differ from those in [17] and [15] in only one essential respect (the presence of s_j and S_j). This difference will now be examined more closely.

From (47), we see that $c_j(x_j) \geqslant s_j$ in each period (not surprising in view of our model). But when a subsistence level is *not* present (as in previous models), the optimal consumption level *may* drop down at least arbitrarily close to zero if the investments should turn out badly under the optimal policy. This appears intrinsically unreasonable *even though* for such a drop to be possible under the optimal policy, of course, the chances for a lavish consumption level in the future would have to be substantial.

The net impact of the subsistence level is to inhibit risk-taking. In the model we have examined, B would use the same investment mix (mutual fund) of risky assets as his neighbor for whom $S_1 = 0$. But B would expose to risk only fraction

$$\frac{x_j - S_j + Y_j}{x_j + Y_j}$$

of what his neighbor would if he had resources x_j and Y_j. As a result, B will experience a smoother consumption pattern.

In reviewing the papers which have combined the additive utility function form (33) with the iso-elastic functions (45), Pye [33] noted that the resulting utility of wealth functions $f_j(x_j)$ display stationary risk aversion over time (at least in the absence of a non-capital income stream). This led him to investigate the multiplicative form in conjunction with the class (45). His results showed that $f_j(x_j)$ now either displays increasing or decreasing risk aversion over time. Empirical observation and folklore both suggest that investment behavior becomes more conservative as the typical individual advances from middle to old age. For individuals whose earning power is greatest in their middle years and who retire at the normal time with or without a pension, $Y_j - S_j$ will typically decrease in j. Whenever this is the case, it is easily verified (see (45) and (46)) that $f_{j+1}(x)$ is more risk averse than $f_j(x)$ for all x and j in the present model. However, if wealth is defined as $x_j + Y_j$, a more reasonable definition in the present model since $y_j, \ldots, y_N$ can be exchanged for Y_j, then risk aversion at any given wealth level decreases with age whenever S_j decreases in j.

VII. The Embattled University

Consider a (private) university which has "arrived" in the sense that it already has the physical plant, the faculty, and the students required to offer a "quality" education. The "building" period having been completed, one might expect that the goals which were predominant during the development phase would fade into the background and be replaced by a new predominant set of goals, that of maintaining the quality of the university for an indefinite future "at all cost." Let us consider the higher-order specific preferences which might reasonably be expected to emerge in relation to this goal.

Assume that the current spending level is c_1 and that an average compound long-run growth rate, g, of that level is visualized as necessary if the university is to be able to continue to offer a quality education.[2] While the growth rate in total spending may depart from g in any given year, wide fluctuations cannot be tolerated if quality is to be maintained—assume therefore that proportion p of c_1, which we denote s_1, is required to grow at rate g *without* fluctuation. Denoting the endowment and other spendable funds at the beginning of period j by x_j and "income" from outside sources in period j by y_j (tuition, grants, gifts, etc.), we obtain the following difference equation in analogy with (34) (assuming for simplicity stationary investment returns and opportunities, we can drop subscript j on β_{ij}, M_j, and r_j):

$$x_{j+1} = \sum_{i=2}^{M} (\beta_i - r) z_{ij} + r(x_j - e_j - s_j) + y_j \quad j = 1, 2, \ldots \quad (50)$$

Again, it is clear that for the university to be able to maintain quality under rising costs, its resources x_1 and its "income" $y_1, y_2, \ldots$ must in some sense be sufficient. Typically, of course, these resources are not adequate without considerable activity in the fund-raising area (one of the "components" of y_j). But it is also clear that a shrewd investment policy can help to offset the need for gifts. Since investment decisions generally require less sweat and are more pleasurable to conduct than fund-raising activities (at least from the point of view of university people), a basic preference for "minimizing" the necessary fund-raising by "maximizing" investment results would appear to be held quite naturally among university administrators. Lexicography in this area, and at this level, seems self-evident: would anyone prefer more fund-raising, with some positive probability, to an avoidable "sub-optimal return" on invested funds (no matter how small the probability)?

Operationally, of course, there is no way the preferences just mentioned can be implemented in a single period since investment returns are random (how do you "maximize" a random variable?). In a multi-period context, however, the average return generally begins to obey the law of large numbers, at least in a compound sense. But if we consider several periods, the disutilities of fund-raising in different periods must be related to each other; this relationship is usually referred to as the time-preference aspect. Suppose, for purposes of exposition, that the university administration wishes to keep the differences d_j given by[3]

$$d_j \equiv y_j - rs_j \qquad\qquad j = 1, 2, \ldots \qquad\qquad (51)$$

constant. Since s_j grows (exponentially) at rate g, the assumption that

$$d_j = d \qquad\qquad j = 1, 2, \ldots \qquad\qquad (52)$$

implies that the level of fund-raising activities in various years, or at least total "income" y_j, be closely related to the spending pattern in those years. While assumption (52) simplifies our analysis (and does not seem unreasonable), it is not critical for the main result to be derived.

Let

$$D \equiv \frac{d}{r-1}, \qquad\qquad\qquad\qquad (53)$$

$$P_j \equiv \frac{e_j}{x_j + D} \qquad\qquad j = 1, 2, \ldots, \qquad\qquad (54)$$

and

$$R_j(\bar{z}_j) \equiv \sum_{i=2}^{M} (\beta_i - r) \frac{z_{ij}}{(x_j + D)(1 - p_j)} + r \quad j = 1, 2, \ldots \tag{55}$$

Clearly, D is the present value of the stream $d_1, d_2, \ldots = d, d, \ldots$ discounted at $r - 1$. It corresponds to $Y_j - C_j$ in Section V and to $Y_j - S_j$ in Section VI; in the present model this difference is the same in each period. Thus, the university can achieve the "bare-bones" spending levels $s_1, s_2, \ldots$ with probability 1 if and only if

$$x_j \geqslant -D \qquad\qquad j = 1, 2, \ldots \tag{56}$$

so that, in analogy with our previous models,

$$\Pr \left\{ x_{j+1} \geqslant -D \right\} = 1 \qquad j = 1, 2, \ldots \tag{57}$$

becomes an investment constraint in each period j. It is also clear that minimizing D also minimizes the necessary fund-raising in each period: the smaller D is the smaller d is (see (53) and the smaller d is the smaller the stream $y_1, y_2, \ldots$, which includes gifts, is (see (51)). p_j, a decision variable (except for $j = 1$ since $e_1 = c_1 - s_1$ is fixed), is simply the proportion of the "free" funds $x_j + D \, (\geqslant 0)$ spent on operations in period j in excess of the "subsistence" level s_j while $R_j(\bar{z}_j)$, a random variable, is $1 +$ the return of the "free" funds actually invested in period j, $(1 - p_j)(x_j + D)$. Note that the constraint (57) is equivalent to the constraint

$$\Pr \left\{ R_j(\bar{z}_j) \geqslant 0 \right\} = 1 \qquad j = 1, 2, \ldots \tag{58}$$

The difference equation (50) now becomes, using (51), (54), and (55),

$$x_{j+1} = (1 - p_j)(x_j + D)(R_j - r) + r \left(x_j - p_j(x_j + D) + \frac{d}{r} \right) \tag{59}$$

$$= (1 - p_j)(x_j + D)R_j - D$$

Thus, we obtain, in view of (58),

$$x_{j+1} + D = (x_j + D)(1 - p_j)R_j \tag{60}$$

$$= (x_j + D)(1 - p_j) \exp(\log R_j(\bar{z}_j)),$$

which in turn gives

$$x_{j+1} + D = (x_1 + D) K_j^{\,j} \tag{61}$$

where K_j , a random variable, is given by

$$K_j \equiv \prod_{n=1}^{j} (1-p_n)^{\frac{1}{j}} \exp\left[\frac{1}{j} \sum_{n=1}^{j} \log R_n(\bar{z}_n) \right] \tag{62}$$

But for investment policies such that $\log R_1, \log R_2, \ldots$ obey the law of large numbers, we obtain for all $\epsilon > 0$

$$\Pr\left\{ |K_j - E[K_j]| > \epsilon \right\} \to 0 \quad \text{as } j \to \infty \tag{63}$$

But c_j can only grow at an average compound rate g in the long run if its two components s_j and e_j do. Since s_j grows at rate g in each period by assumption, it follows that e_j must grow at rate g also, but only in a long-run sense. Since p_j is constrained by $p_j < 1$ (otherwise e_n cannot exceed 0 for $n = j+1, j+2, \ldots$; see (57) and (60) and recall the implications of (36)), this is only possible if $x_1 + D$ grows at an average compound long-run growth rate of at least g (see (54) and (61)). Thus, we must have, in view of (61) and (63),

$$E[K_j] \geqslant 1 + g \qquad\qquad j \text{ large} \tag{64}$$

for the university to be able to satisfy its educational goals. (61), (62) and (63) now imply that the larger $p_1, p_2, \ldots$, are, the larger $E[\log R_1]$, $E[\log R_2], \ldots$ must be for g to be achieved. But the larger $p_1, p_2, \ldots$ are, the smaller D can be (see (54)). Thus, to minimize D and hence the necessary fund-raising, the university should invest in such a way as to[4]

$$\text{Maximize } E\left[\log R_j(\bar{z}_j)\right] \qquad\qquad \text{each } j \tag{65}$$

with respect to $\bar{z}_j$. The investment policy which maximizes (65), known as the growth-optimal policy, is unique, myopic, does not risk ruin, is consistent with the von Neumann-Morgenstern postulates,[5] and calls for substantial, but not excessive, risk aversion which is *decreasing* in the level of assets x_j (see Hakansson [21] for a more complete discussion; also Breiman [5] and Latané [24]). All of these properties are highly desirable and/or valuable; the only drawback of the growth-optimal policy resides in its computational complexity.

The preceding result is of some interest in relation to the central conclusion of the Ford Foundation's Advisory Committee on Endowment Management [1: 45]:

In our opinion, the most important present responsibility of the trustees of these institutions with respect to endowment is to shift their objective to maximizing the long-term total return. We believe the total return can be increased sufficiently to permit both a larger annual contribution to operations and greater long-term growth.

Strictly speaking, of course, this statement is, as we have noted, nonoperational since long-run return is a random variable and random variables cannot be maximized. But, as (63) shows, the average *compound* return in the long run tends to its expected value[6] for most policies by the law of large numbers and this expectation certainly can be maximized. Since this maximization implies the investment rule (65) and the resulting policy yields compliance with the law of large numbers [21], this rule is not only "consistent" with the Advisory Committee's conclusion but provides the specificity needed for its implementation.

The logarithmic utility function of *wealth* implied by (65) [21] automatically finds "the best reward-to-risk potentials" (see [1: 34]). Note that (65) does *not* imply "maximum uncertainty with respect to short-term fluctuations in the value of portfolios" [1: 53]. This is because (65) does *not* choose the riskiest portfolio in each period: the consequences of such choices are often disastrous in the long run (see Hakansson [18] [22]). In other words, maximization of expected average compound return over the long run does *not* imply maximization of expected return in each period. The first lesson to be learned from (65) is that to be successful in the long run, *one must be risk averse*. But this is not sufficient. Poor performance in the long run can be due to *too little* risk taking as well as to *too much* exposure of one's capital to potential gains and losses. The beauty of investment rule (65), besides its simplicity, is that it subjects the endowment to just the right amount of risk in each period in terms of maximal *long-run* investment results.

An Example

As an illustration of the rather dramatic savings in fund-raising and tuition which are made possible by even modest departures from the optimal management of the endowment, let us consider a simple example:

g (the required long-run growth rate in operating expenditures to maintain educational quality[7])   6.5%

c_1 (current operating budget) $88 million

s_1 ("subsistence" level which must grow at rate g (75% of c_1)) $66 million

x_1 (initial (present) endowment) $600 million

  r (1+ return on bonds)   1.05   (5%)

  β_2 (1+ return on stocks) $\begin{cases} .70 \text{ with probability } .5 & (-30\%) \\ \\ 1.75 \text{ with probability } .5 & (75\%) \end{cases}$ (66)

For simplicity, we assume there is only one stock ($M=2$) available for investment and that stationary p_j are desired. [8] Maximizing (65), we obtain

$$z_{2j}^* (x_j) = .75 (x_j + D)(1 - p) \quad j = 1, 2, \ldots \tag{67}$$

i.e., that three-quarters of the funds available for investment should be put into stocks each period. This results in a long-run compound growth rate of investable ("free") capital almost certainly equal to 11.4 percent since

$$\exp \left\{ E \left[\log R_j (\bar{z}_j^*) \right] \right\} = 1.114$$

(see note 6). We now obtain from (62)-(64)

$$(1 - p) 1.114 = 1 + g = 1.065 \tag{68}$$

or $p = .044$. But by (54),

$$p_1 = \frac{88 - 66}{600 + D} = .044 = p$$

which gives $D = -100$ and $d = -5$ (see (53)). Thus, (51) gives

$$y_1 = d + rs_1 = -5 + 1.05 \cdot 66 = 64.3$$

which means that tuition, grants, and gifts must total $64.3 million in the first year. In the jth year, they would have to be

$$y_j^* = -5 + 1.05 \cdot 66 \cdot 1.065^{j-1} \quad j = 1, 2, \ldots \tag{69}$$

Suppose now that a sub-optimal investment policy z_2' is used which yields a long-run average compound growth rate on investible ("free") capital of only 8.9 percent[9] rather than the optimal 11.4 percent. The preceding calculations now yield $p' = .022$ and $d' = 20$ so that we obtain

$$y'_j = 20 + 1.05 \cdot 66 \cdot 1.065^{j-1} \qquad j = 1, 2, \ldots$$

Since $y'_j - y^*_j = \$25$ million for each j, the sub-optimal investment policy implies that the university must raise *$25 million every single year from tuition, grants and gifts* than would be necessary under an optimal investment policy.

Under the optimal policy, the university would allocate its $600 million in initial resources as follows for the first year:

To operations	$ 88 million
To investments in stocks (see (67))	358.5 million
To investment in bonds	153.5 million
Total	$600 million

Furthermore, total operating expenditures would *almost certainly* grow from $88 million for c_1 at an average compound rate, over many periods, of 6.5 percent would satisfy

$$c_j \geqslant 66 \cdot 1.065^{j-1} \qquad j = 1, 2, \ldots$$

i.e., they would be supported by a substantial growing floor even in the worst circumstances of "bad luck" in the investment area.

It should be emphasized that the investment policy (65) is optimal with respect to the minimization of fund-raising activities under much more general conditions than those assumed here. Stationarity in any form or aspect is not crucial. In particular, the time-pattern for fund-raising given by (52) can be relaxed without effecting the optimal investment policy.

VIII. The Perpetual Foundation

As the reader might infer, the investment policy which is optimal for the university described in Section VII is also virtuous from the point of view of charitable endowment funds. Assume that the first-order goal of such funds is to be able to continue a program of substantial[10] giving eternally. Clearly, a sufficient condition for this to be possible is that

$$r_j \geqslant \epsilon \qquad\qquad j = 1, 2, \ldots \qquad\qquad (70)$$

for some $\epsilon > 1$, i.e., that the interest rate does not converge to zero. Either (2) or (70) turns out to be a necessary condition for the first-order goal to be feasible if no additional infusion of capital is made, i.e., $y_j = 0, j = 1, 2, \ldots$ In practice, the fund's management may prefer, above all else, that the assets of the fund actually grow at some average rate to compensate for the effects of inflation. Given this primary goal, sensible secondary goal would appear to be giving of as "much as possible each year."

Let x_1 denote the present net worth of the fund or the bequest establishing it and assume for simplicity that no further capital infusions are expected ($y_1 = y_2 = \ldots = 0$). Under stationary investment returns, we then obtain (see (50))

$$
\begin{aligned}
x_{j+1} &= \sum_{i=2}^{M} (\beta_i - r) z_{ij} + r(x_j - c_j) \quad j = 1, 2, \ldots \\
&= x_1 L_j{}^j,
\end{aligned}
$$

(71)

where

$$
L_j \equiv \prod_{n=1}^{j} (1 - q_n)^{\frac{1}{j}} \exp \left[\frac{1}{j} \sum_{n=1}^{j} \log R_n(\bar{z}_n) \right]
$$

(72)

$$
q_j \equiv \frac{c_j}{x_j}
$$

(73)

i.e., q_j is the annual donation in period j as a proportion of x_j and, as before, $Rj(v_j) \equiv x_{j+1}/(x_j - c_j)$, is $1+$ plus the return on investable capital. If the time-preference for giving is "stationary" with respect to assets, i.e., if it is desired that

$$
q_j = q \qquad\qquad \text{all } j,
$$

then we can indeed "maximize the donation in each period" (q) while achieving an average compound long-run growth rate of the fund's net assets of g since we can, as before, obtain for all $\epsilon > 0$

$$
\Pr \left\{ |L_j - 1 - g| > \epsilon \rightarrow 0 \right\} \text{ as } j \rightarrow \infty
$$

(74)

with appropriate choices of q and investment policies $\bar{z}_1, \bar{z}_2, \ldots$ In analogy with Section VII, we obtain from (72) and (74) that

$$
q^* = 1 - \frac{1 + g}{\exp \ E[\log R_j(\bar{z}_j^*)]} \text{ and } j
$$

where $z_j^-{}^*$ is the solution to (65). Thus, if the available investment opportunities are given by (66) and the fund's average compound long-run growth rate g is desired to be 1/4 percent per annum, then the fund could give away 10 percent of its net worth each year by employing a growth-optimal investment policy. Under any other (substantially different) policy, it would have to be content with giving away less than 10 percent of net assets.

IX. Concluding Note

The notion of lexicographic preferences has close ties to Maslow's theory of human behavior. While the von Neumann-Morgenstern postulates are not consistent with such preferences at the global level, no conflict arises *within* the various levels of the preference hierarchy, i.e., the postulates are valid for "local" outcomes. Operationally, the effect of this is that the expected utility function to be maximized at each level (except the lowest) becomes coupled to one or more constraints which must hold with probability 1.

The employment of lexicographic preference structures in economic models generally enables one to obtain more realistic implications than in the absence of such preferences under uncertainty. For example, they are apparently necessary to prevent choices which *may* reduce the "optimal" consumption level below the subsistence line. The assumption of lexicographic preferences also uncomplicates the decision analysis in that the total decision problem is broken down into sub-problems, only one of which is applicable at any point in time, in line with Maslow's theory.

Notes

1. The applicable preferences appear difficult to capture. At one extreme, optimal behavior may call for going to work immediately so as to minimize the value of j for which (5) can be satisfied with probability 1. The optimal strategy for other individuals may be to postpone moonlighting as long as possible, investing in the meantime so as to minimize the probability of having no moonlight at all.

2. Growth in operating costs, of course, does not imply that the student body and/or the faculty must grow. These may conceivably be reduced although there would appear to be a minimum physical size associated with the depth and breadth that is necessary to provide a "quality" education.

3. The factor r (1 plus the interest rate) appears because operating funds were assumed to be set aside at the beginning of the year while inflows were assumed to be available at the end of the year.

4. When (1) and (3) hold, a bounded optimal policy always exists; when (4) holds, the solvency constraint (58) is never binding.

5. Except that the logarithmic function is unbounded.

6. Under *stationary returns and policies*, $E[K_j-1]$ decreases in j and becomes in the limit, whenever (63) holds,

$$(1-p_j)\exp(E[\log R_j(\overline{z}_j)]) - 1 \qquad \text{any } j$$

where $R_j(\overline{z}_j)-1$ is the periodic distribution of return on capital available for investment, $(1-p_j)(x_j+D)$ [22].

7. This figure is the estimate arrived at by Cheit [6: 138-139].

8. This would essentially agree with the conclusion of the Ford study group [1: 46].

9. In our example, this rate would be achieved by investing either

$$z_{2j}(x_j) = 1.22(x_j+D)(1-p)$$

or

$$z_{2j}(x_j) + .28(x_j+D)(1-p)$$

in each period, i.e., by investing 122 percent (this would require margin purchases) or 28 percent of "free" capital in stocks.

10. In relation to *present* assets.

Bibliography

1. Advisory Committee on Endowment Management. *Managing Educational Endowments*. New York: The Ford Foundation, 1969.
2. Arrow, Kenneth. *Aspects of the Theory of Risk-bearing*. Yrjö Jahnssonin Säätiö, Helsinki, 1965.
3. ———. "Comment on Duesenberry's 'The Portfolio Approach to the Demand for Money and Other Assets.'" *Review of Economics and Statistics*. Supplement, February 1963.
4. Bellman, Richard. *Dynamic Programming*. Princeton, New Jersey: Princeton University Press, 1957.
5. Breiman, Leo. "Investment Policies for Expanding Business Optimal in a Long-run Sense." *Naval Research Logistics Quarterly*. December 1960.
6. Cheit, Earl. *The New Depression in Higher Education*. New York: McGraw-Hill, 1971.
7. Chipman, John. "The Foundations of Utility." *Econometrica*. April 1960.
8. Debreu, Gerard. "Representation of a Preference Ordering by a Numerical Function." *Decision Process*. Edited by R.M. Thrall, C.H. Coombs, and R.L. Davis. New York: John Wiley, 1954.
9. Dixit, Avinash, and Goldman, Steven. "Uncertainty and the Demand for Liquid Assets." *Journal of Economic Theory*. December 1970.
10. Drèze, Jacques. "Econometrics and Decision Theory." CORE Discussion Paper No. 7040. Heverlee, Belgium: Université Catholique de Louvain, October 1970.
11. Fama, Eugene. "Multi-period Investment Consumption Decisions." *American Economic Review*. March 1970.
12. Ferguson, Thomas. "Betting Systems Which Minimize the Probability of Ruin." *Journal of the Society of Industrial and Applied Mathematics*. September 1965.
13. Hahn, Frank. "Savings and Uncertainty." *The Review of Economic Studies*. January 1970.
14. Hakansson, Nils. "Optimal Investment and Consumption Strategies for a Class of Utility Functions," Ph.D. dissertation. University of California at Los Angeles, 1966.
15. ———. "Optimal Investment and Consumption Strategies under Risk, an Uncertain Lifetime, and Insurance." *International Economic Review*. October 1969.
16. ———. "Friedman-Savage Utility Functions Consistent with Risk Aversion." *The Quarterly Journal of Economics*. August 1970.
17. ———. "Optimal Investment and Consumption Strategies under Risk for a Class of Utility Functions." *Econometrica*. September 1970.
18. "Capital Growth and the Mean-variance Approach to Portfolio Selection." *Journal of Financial and Quantitative Analysis*. January 1971.

202

19. ___. "Optimal Entrepreneurial Decisions in a Completely Stochastic Environment." *Management Science: Theory*. March 1971.

20. ___. "On Optimal Myopic Portfolio Policies, with and without Serial Correlation of Yields." *Journal of Business*. July 1971.

21. ___. "Multi-period Mean-variance Analysis: Toward a General Theory of Portfolio Choice." *Journal of Finance*. September 1971.

22. ___. "Mean-Variance Analysis of Average Compound Returns." *Capital Market Theory*. Edited by Myron Scholes. Praeger (forthcoming).

23. Hausner, Melvin. "Multidimensional Utilities." *Decision Processes*. Edited by R.M. Thrall, C.H. Coombs, and R.L. Davis. New York: John Wiley, 1954.

24. Latané, Henry. "Criteria for Choice among Risky Ventures." *Journal of Political Economy*. April 1959.

25. Leland, Hayne. *Dynamic Portfolio Theory*. Ph.D. dissertation, Harvard University, May 1968.

26. Levhari, David, and Srinivasan, T.N. "Optimal Savings under Uncertainty." *Review of Economic Studies*. April 1969.

27. Maslow, A.H. "A Theory of Human Motivation." *Psychological Review*. July 1943.

28. Merton, Robert. "Lifetime Portfolio Selection Under Uncertainty: The Continuous-time Case." *The Review of Economics and Statistics*. August 1969.

29. Mossin, Jan. "Optimal Multiperiod Portfolio Policies." *Journal of Business*. April 1968.

30. Neave, Edward. "Multiperiod Consumption Investment Decisions and Risk Preference." *Journal of Economic Theory*. March 1971.

31. Phelps, Edmund. "The Accumulation of Risky Capital: A Sequential Utility Analysis." *Econometrica*. October 1962.

32. Pratt, John. "Risk Aversion in the Small and in the Large." *Econometrica*. January-April 1964.

33. Pye, Gordon. "Lifetime Portfolio Selection with Age Dependent Risk Aversion." Working Paper IP-167. University of California, Berkeley: Institute of Business and Economic Research, May 1971.

34. Samuelson, Paul. "Lifetime Portfolio Selection by Dynamic Stochastic Programming." *Review of Economics and Statistics*. August 1969.

35. Thrall, Robert. "Applications of Multidimensional Utility Theory." *Decision Processes*. Edited by R.M. Thrall, C.H. Coombs, and R.L. Davis. New York: John Wiley, 1954.

36. Thrall, Robert, and Dalkey, Norman. "A Generalization of Numerical Utilities." RM-724. Santa Monica, California: The Rand Corporation, November 1951.

37. Truelove, Alan. "A Multi-stage Investment Process." RM-4025. Santa Monica, California: The Rand Corporation, March 1964.

38. ———. "Betting Systems in Favorable Games." *Annals of Mathematical Statistics*. April 1970.

39. von Neumann, John, and Morgenstern, Oskar. *Theory of Games and Economic Behavior*. Princeton University Press, 1947.

40. Yaari, Menahem. "Uncertain Lifetime, Life Insurance, and the Theory of the Consumer." *Review of Economic Studies*. April 1965.

41. ———. "A Law of Large Numbers in the Theory of Consumer's Choice Under Uncertainty." Working Paper No. CP-330. University of California, Berkeley: Center for Research in Management Science, March 1971.

Part V:
Testing Portfolio Strategies and Investing Timing Rules

10 Multi-Period Portfolio Strategies

Frank C. Jen

The strategy of buy and hold has been suggested as the best strategy to invest in one security by many random-walk theorists. The strategy of buy and hold a portfolio has also been regarded as a benchmark to evaluate other strategies. The paper shows that rebalancing to even proportion strategy can be superior to buy and hold under certain conditions. After discussing the problem in the introduction, Section II illustrates the crux of the problem by simple games. Section III demonstrates analytically that buy and hold has the same mean but higher variance than rebalancing for securities having common but independent means and variances. Using the analytical result and the assumption that wealth is log-normally distributed, we derive in Section IV the probability distribution of difference in wealth between one draw from each of the two wealth distributions. Simulation is then used to demonstrate that the theoretical results hold in practice. Section V studies the economics of rebalancing and buy and hold strategies using dynamic portfolio models and explores the role of utility function in portfolio decision making. Section VI concludes the study by summarizing the results and suggests areas for further research.

Introduction

Given that there is no inside information, the strategy of buy and hold has been suggested as the best strategy to invest in one security by many random-walk theorists [e.g., 6]. Though buy and hold a *portfolio* of securities has never been formally suggested as the best strategy to invest in a portfolio, studies by writers such as Levy [12] and Jensen [10] have used *buy an equal amount* of various securities *and hold them* (hereafter BH) as a standard to evaluate the performance of other trading strategies. Fisher and Lorie [8] have further tabulated extensively the performance of buy and hold an equal amount of all securities listed in the New York Stock Exchange for different holding periods. Use of

The author acknowledges helpful discussions with members of Workshop in Finance particularly Professor Andrew Chen, whose comments on my draft were very helpful. My research assistant Arthur Hierl wrote and ran the necessary programs for simulations in this paper within a very short period of time in order to enable me to present my results at this symposium. His assistance is gratefully acknowledged.

Fisher-Lorie's result as a benchmark to evaluate the performance of other strategies has been suggested by many writers [e.g., 6].

Recently, however, periodic rebalancing to an even proportion of wealth among all securities (hereafter RBEP) is proposed by many writers, [4], [5], [11], as an alternative to buy and hold an equal amount of all securities initially. The strategy calls for an investor to distribute his initial wealth evenly among M securities and redistribute his wealth periodically to maintain an even proportion among the same M securities. These writers demonstrated through simulation that an investor following the RBEP strategy can on the average outperform BH strategy if transaction costs are assumed to be zero.[1]

Though these writers have in general not demonstrated that RBEP will outperform BH when transaction costs are taken into consideration, Cheng and Deets [4] show analytically that if random-walk hypothesis holds and if transaction cost is ignored, the expected value of a portfolio following BH is greater than that of a portfolio following RBEP. They further show analytically that the more frequent the portfolio is rebalanced to allow an equal distribution of assets among M securities, the greater BH will outperform RBEP. They then observe through a simulation of price of 30 stocks in the Dow Jones Industrials for the past 30 years that RBEP consistently outperform BH. The observation is inconsistent with their analytical result that the expected value of BH is higher than RBEP. They suggest therefore that random-walk hypotehsis is invalid.

While it is possible that their conclusion is valid, the evidences presented fail to consider the shape of the probability distribution of future wealth. Even if the expected value of BH is higher than that of RBEP, it does not mean that for a sample of one observation, the outcome will necessarily follow the ordering in terms of expected values. Indeed, if the probability distributions of portfolios under both BH and RBEP are highly positively skewed, it is quite possible that for a sample of one, the value of the sample representing ending wealth will not follow the same order as the expected values. The reason is that for highly positively skewed distributions, expected value is not necessarily the best estimate of *one and only one* draw from the distribution. The argument will first be demonstrated by considering a market consisting of 1, 2, and M games with exactly the same payoff characteristics. The case of a market consisting of 1, 2, and M securities with exactly the same return characteristics will then be explored and some analytical results derived using an assumption that the sum of different log-normal distributions can be approximated by a log-normal distribution. Simulation is then used to see whether RBEP can on the average actually outperform BH for a market of securities with common mean and variances. Other security combinations are also used in the simulation in order to see whether RBEP can always outperform BH. The paper finally discusses factors affecting the forms of utility function and their relationship with probability distributions of wealth.

II. The Probable Outcome of
Playing Some Simple Games

We will consider the portfolio strategy problem by introducing a single game. Cases of 1, 2, and M games will be considered.

One Game Case

Consider a game AA that has the following two time-invariant states of nature as to its payoff period (R_1 and R_2)

$$P(R_1 = 1.20) = 0.90 \qquad (1)$$

$$P(R_2 = 0) = 0.10$$

The expected payoff ($\overline{R}$) of the game AA is 1.08 and its geometric mean (G) is $0.$ [2]

Assuming now an investor has an initial wealth W_0 of \$1. Assume further that game AA is the only one available and that the investor can only hold the wealth by playing the game. The probability distribution of his wealth n periods hence (W_n) is:

$$P_1 (W_n = 1.20^n) = 0.90^n \qquad (2)$$

$$P_1 (W_n = 0) = 1 - 0.90^n$$

From (2), the expected value and variance of investor's wealth at period n can be easily derived. They are:

$$E_1 (W_n) = [0.90^n \times 1.20^n + 0 \times (1 - 0.90^n)] = 1.08^n \qquad (3)$$

$$V_1 (W_n) = 1.20^{2n} \times 0.90^n - 1.08^{2n}$$

Where the subscripts to P, E and V refer to playing one game only. It is easy to see from (3) that both $E_1(W_n)$ and $V_1(W_n)$ are increasing functions of n. However, as n gets longer, the probability distribution of wealth in (2) becomes more positively skewed, because $P(W_n = 0)$ increases exponentially while $P[W_n = W_0(1.20)^n]$ decreases exponentially.[3] Since an investor is only entitled to *one* outcome from the game at a point in time, it is clear that as n increases, the probability he will be ruined increases despite the fact that the $E_1 (W_n)$ is an increasing function of time. Hence, expected value is not a good measure of probable future wealth in this case.

Two and M *Games Case*

Assume however that there is an additional game BB that has exactly the same payoff distributions as AA. Further, the payoff on both games are independently distributed and an investor is allowed to hold his assets in both games at a proportion he chooses. Presumably, an investor wants to minimize variances of his future wealth for given expected values. He will then divide his initial dollar evenly between AA and BB. The probability distribution of his wealth one period hence is:

$$P_2 [W_1 = 1.20] = 0.90^2$$

$$P_2 [W_1 = \frac{1}{2}(1.20)] = 2(0.90)(0.10) \tag{4}$$

$$P_2 [W_1 = 0] = 0.10^2$$

And further:

$$E_2 (W_1) = 1.08, \quad V_2 (W_1) = \frac{1}{2}(1.20^2)(0.90)(0.10)$$

After the first play, one of the strategies an investor has is to freeze his winnings in the game he won. The strategy is of course equivalent to buy and hold in the securities case. The probability distribution of future wealth under this strategy is:

$$P_2 [W_n = 1.20^n] = 0.90^{2n} \tag{5}$$

$$P_2 [W_n = \frac{1}{2}(1.20^n)] = 2 \times 0.90^n \times \sum_{k=0}^{n-1} \binom{n}{k}(0.90)^k (0.10)^{n-k}$$
$$= 2(0.90^n)(1 - 0.90^n)$$
$$P_2 [W_n = 0] = (1 - 0.90^n)^2$$

The expected value of the game is still 1.08^n, but the variance of the game is:

$$V_2 (W_n) = \frac{1}{2}(1.20^{2n})(0.90^n)(1 - 0.90^n) \tag{6}$$

As in the one game case, the expected value of playing two games is an increasing function of n. Further, $P_2 (W_n=0)$ also approaches one as n approaches infinity. However, $P_2 (W_n=0) < P_1 (W_n=0)$ for all n's. The wealth distribution for play two games is further less skewed than that for one game as a comparison of Equations (4) and (5) will reveal.

Another play strategy at period 1 is to redistribute his total wealth each period evenly among the two games. The strategy is of course equivalent to RBEP in securities case. To enable us to find the wealth distribution n periods hence systematically, we need to rewrite the definitions as:

$$
\begin{aligned}
P_{11\,t} &= P(R_{11} \cdot \quad = 1.20) = 0.90 \\
P_{12\,t} &= P(R_{12} \cdot \quad = 0) \quad = 0.10 \\
P_{21\,t} &= P(R_{21} \cdot \quad = 1.20) = 0.90 \\
P_{22\,t} &= P(R_{22} \cdot \quad = 0) \quad = 0.10
\end{aligned}
\tag{7}
$$

The probability distribution of wealth n periods hence is:

$$
P_2 \left[W_n = \prod_{t=1}^{n} \frac{1}{2}(R_{1jt} + R_{2kt}) \right] = \prod_{t=1}^{n} P_{1jt} \times P_{2kt}
\tag{8}
$$

for all possible combinations of j and k over time

$$
j = 1,2 \quad \text{and} \quad k = 1,2 .
$$

Equation (8) is very cumbersome to use to derive mean and variance analytically. We will therefore only use it to compute the mean and variance for $n=3$. The wealth distribution at period 3 is:

$$
\begin{aligned}
P_2 \left[W_3 = 1.20^3 \right] &= 0.90^6 \\
P_2 \left[W_3 = 1.20^2 \times 0.60 \right] &= 0.90^4 (2 \times 0.90 \times 0.10)3 = 3(0.90^5)(0.10)(2) \\
P_2 \left[W_3 = 1.20 \times 0.60^2 \right] &= 0.90^2 (2 \times 0.90 \times 0.10)^2 3 = 3(0.90^4)(0.10^2)(2^2) \\
P_2 \left[W_3 = 0.60^3 \right] &= (2 \times 0.90 \times 0.10)^3 = 2^3 (0.9^3)(0.1^3) \\
P_2 \left[W_3 = 0 \right] &= 1 - 0.90^6 - 6(0.90)^5(0.10) - 12(0.90^4)(0.10^2) - 8(0.9^3) \\
&\qquad (0.1^3) = .029701
\end{aligned}
\tag{9}
$$

The expected value of W_3 is still 1.08^3. The variance is:

$$
V_2{}^{RBEP}(W_3) = \frac{1}{2}(1.20^6)(0.90^3)(0.2565)
\tag{10}
$$

While the variance for BH for $n=3$ from Equation (6) is:

$$
V_2^{BH}(W_3) = \frac{1}{2}(1.20^6)(0.90^3)(1 - 0.90^3)
$$

$V_2^{RBEP}(W_3)$ is therefore smaller than $V_2^{BH}(W_3)$. Further, $P_2^{RBEP}(W_3=0)$ is smaller than $P^{BH}(W_3=0)$. Thus, the risk of ruin is also smaller for rebalancing strategy. Further, wealth distribution for RBEP will be less positively skewed than that for BH.[4]

The generalization to the case of M games is straight forward. As M gets larger, the distribution will become less skewed. Indeed, as M approaches infinity, variance of the final outcome using RBEP is reduced to zero. In that case, the geometric mean for the portfolio will approach the arithmetic mean, in spite of the fact that the geometric mean of individual assets is zero. The reason for this phenomenon is that the risk of an individual asset approximated by $\frac{1}{2}\sigma^2$ implicit in the computation of geometric mean is diversified away. Hence, if geometric mean of a portfolio is used as a criterion in decision making, Sharpe's market model should be used as an approximation to decompose returns into the systematic part which is non-diversifiable from the unsystematic part which is diversifiable.

III. The Probable Outcome of Investing in Securities

We will now consider the problem of determining whether RBEP or BH is superior using securities as the investment media.

One Security Case

In a real world, investors use securities instead of games to invest their wealth. Assume that there is only one security paying no dividend, its price for period $t+1$ is log-normally distributed with mean of $\mu+\ln P_t$ and variance of σ^2.[5] Further assume an investor starts also with \$1. An investor investing all his dollar in the security will have the probability distribution of his future wealth a log-normal one with the parameters:

$$W_n \sim \Lambda(n\mu + \ln W_0, \ n\sigma^2)$$ (10)

However, the arithmetic mean, variance, and median of W_n (a_n, β_n^2 and Md_n) are [1, p. 8]:

$$a_n = \exp\left\{n\mu + \frac{n\sigma^2}{2}\right\}$$

$$\beta_n^2 = \exp\left\{2n\mu + n\sigma^2\right\}[\exp[n\sigma^2] - 1]$$ (11)

$$Md_n = \exp \left\{ n\mu + 1nP_0 \right\}$$

More importantly, for all log-normal distributions, the probability that the final portfolio value represented by one observation from the distribution has a value greater than arithmetic mean a_n is inversely related to the size of variance.[6] Since $\sigma^2 > 0$, $n\sigma^2$ increases as the period of investment gets longer. Hence, as n increases, the skewness of the distribution increases and thus, the probability that investor's wealth at the end of the period will exceed mean decreases.

Incidentally, the geometric mean of wealth is the median of the distribution and is itself distributed $\Lambda(\mu, \frac{\sigma^2}{n})$ [1, p. 11] when the wealth is distributed log-normally as in this one security case. Hence maximizing geometric mean alone in a log-normal framework is equivalent to maximizing the median of the distribution while ignoring variance of the median. If a one-parameter (mean or median) utility function has to be used, median is clearly superior to mean as the decision parameter because the value of one observation from a highly skewed distribution representing final wealth is probably closer to median than mean. If however, an investor is using more than one parameter as his decision criterion, he can clearly choose a utility function having a form that will yield better results than that of maximizing the geometric mean. The *form* of the utility function will however depend on the shape of the wealth distribution under consideration.[7]

Two and M Securities Case

Let us assume that there are two securities having exactly the same probability distribution as to their return characteristics. Their returns are log-normally distributed and can be represented as:

$$\frac{P_{it}}{P_{i,\,t-1}} = \exp \quad \mu \quad \exp \quad V_i \quad \equiv \theta \times \epsilon_i \text{ for all } t \qquad (12)$$

Where i refers to the ith security

$\theta \equiv \exp \quad \mu$ is the mean return including return of principal

$V_i \sim N(0, \sigma^2)$ and $\epsilon_i \sim \Lambda(0, \sigma^2)$

Further, we assume that: (1) for each stock, errors are intertemporally independently distributed and (2) between stocks, errors are independently distributed. That is:

$$f(\epsilon_{it}, \epsilon_{i,t+1}) = f(\epsilon_{it})f(\epsilon_{i,t+1}) \tag{13}$$

$$g(\epsilon_{it}, \epsilon_{jt}) = g(\epsilon_{it})g(\epsilon_{jt})$$

To minimize variance, an investor will divide his dollar evenly between these two securities. If he follows BH, the probability distribution of his wealth at period n is:

$$W_n^{BH} = \sum_{i=1}^{2} \frac{1}{2} \prod_{t=1}^{n} \theta \epsilon_{it} = \theta^n \frac{1}{2} (\prod_{t=1}^{n} \epsilon_{1t} + \prod_{t=1}^{n} \epsilon_{2t}) \tag{14}$$

Equation (14) indicates the probability distribution of wealth is an average of two log-normal distributions though the exact shape of the distribution is unknown. Its expected value is:

$$E(W_n^{BH}) = \exp\left\{ n\mu + \frac{1}{2}n\sigma^2 \right\} \tag{15}$$

Proof

$$\text{given } \epsilon\cdot \sim \Lambda(0, \sigma^2), \qquad\qquad \theta \equiv \exp\left\{ \mu \right\}$$

By property of log-normal distribution:

$$\prod_{t=1}^{n} \epsilon\cdot_t \sim \Lambda(0, n\sigma^2)$$

$$E(\prod_{t=1}^{n} \epsilon\cdot_t) = \exp\left\{ \frac{1}{2} n\sigma^2 \right\}$$

Hence: $E(W_n^{BH}) = \theta^n \exp\left\{ \frac{1}{2} n\sigma^2 \right\} = \exp\left\{ n\mu + \frac{1}{2}n\sigma^2 \right\}$ Q.E.D.

Its variance is:

$$V(W_n^{BH}) = \frac{1}{2}\exp\left\{ 2n\mu + n\sigma^2 \right\} [\exp\left\{ n\sigma^2 \right\} - 1] \tag{16}$$

Proof given:

$$V(\prod_{t=1}^{n} \epsilon_{1t}) = V(\prod_{t=1}^{n} \epsilon_{2t}) = V(\prod_{t=1}^{n} \epsilon\cdot_t), \text{Cov}(\epsilon_{1t}, \epsilon_{2t}) = 0$$

By (11):
$$V(\prod_{t=1}^{n} \epsilon\cdot_t) = \exp\left\{n\sigma^2\right\}[\exp\left\{n\sigma^2\right\} - 1]$$

Hence:
$$V(W_n^{BH}) = \frac{\theta^{2n}}{4} V(\prod_{t=1}^{n} \epsilon_{1t} + \prod_{t=1}^{n} \epsilon_{2t}^2)$$

$$= \frac{1}{2}\exp\left\{2n\mu + n\sigma^2\right\}[\exp\left\{n\sigma^2\right\} - 1] \quad Q.E.D.$$

If an investor follows *RBEP*, the probability distribution of his wealth is:

$$W_n^{RBEP} = \prod_{t=1}^{n} \frac{1}{2} \sum_{i=1}^{2} \theta\epsilon_{it} = \theta^n \prod_{t=1}^{n} (\frac{\epsilon_{1t} + \epsilon_{2t}}{2})$$

(17)

$$= \frac{\theta^n}{2^n} \sum_{\substack{j,k \\ j\neq k}} \prod_{\substack{j=1 \\ j\neq k}}^{n} \epsilon_{1j} \prod_{\substack{k=1 \\ k\neq j}}^{n} \epsilon_{2k}$$

Equation (17) indicates the probability distribution of wealth is also a weighted sum of different log-normal distributions.

Its expected value is:

$$E(W_n^{RBEP}) = \exp\left\{n\mu + \frac{1}{2}n\sigma^2\right\}$$

(18)

Proof
$$\prod_{\substack{j=1 \\ j\neq k}}^{n} \epsilon_{1j} \prod_{\substack{k=1 \\ j\neq k}}^{n} \epsilon_{2k} \sim \Lambda(0, n\sigma^2)$$

There are 2^n terms in
$$\sum_{\substack{j,k \\ j\neq k}} \prod_{\substack{j=1 \\ j\neq k}}^{n} \epsilon_{1j} \prod_{\substack{k=1 \\ k\neq j}}^{n} \epsilon_{2k}$$

$$\therefore E(W_n^{RBEP}) = \frac{\theta^n}{2^n} \times 2^n \times \exp\left\{\frac{1}{2}n\sigma^2\right\} = \exp\left\{n\mu + \frac{1}{2}n\sigma^2\right\}$$

Its variance is:

$$V(W_n^{RBEP}) = \exp\left\{2n\mu + n\sigma^2\right\}\left[\left(\frac{\exp\left\{\sigma^2\right\}+1}{2}\right)^n - 1\right] \quad (19)$$

Proof given: $f(\bar{\epsilon}_t, \bar{\epsilon}_{t+1}) = f(\bar{\epsilon}_t)f(\bar{\epsilon}_{t+1})$

where: $\bar{\epsilon}_t = (\epsilon_{1t} + \epsilon_{2t})/2 = \bar{\epsilon}\cdot$

$$E(\bar{\epsilon}_t) = E(\bar{\epsilon}\cdot) = \exp\left\{\frac{1}{2}\sigma^2\right\}$$

$$V(\bar{\epsilon}_t) = V(\bar{\epsilon}\cdot) = \frac{1}{2}V(\epsilon\cdot)$$

$$G(\bar{\epsilon}\cdot) = \frac{V(\bar{\epsilon})}{[E(\bar{\epsilon})]^2} = \frac{\exp\left\{\sigma^2\right\}[\exp\left\{\sigma^2\right\}-1]}{2\exp\left\{\sigma^2\right\}} = \frac{\exp\left\{\sigma^2\right\}-1}{2}$$

By Goodman's equation [9, p. 11]:

$$V(\prod_{t=1}^{n}\bar{\epsilon}_t) = [E(\prod_{t=1}^{n}\bar{\epsilon}_t)]^2[\binom{n}{1}G(\bar{\epsilon}) + \binom{n}{2}(G(\bar{\epsilon}))^2 + \binom{n}{3}(G(\bar{\epsilon}))^3$$

$$+\ldots+\binom{n}{n}(G(\bar{\epsilon}))^n] = [E(\prod_{t=1}^{n}E\bar{\epsilon}_t)]^2[(G(\bar{\epsilon}) + 1)^n - 1]$$

where

$$G(\bar{\epsilon}) = \frac{V(\bar{\epsilon})}{[E(\bar{\epsilon})]^2}$$

Hence:

$$V(W_n^{RBEP}) = V(\theta^n\prod_{t=1}^{n}\bar{\epsilon} = \theta^{2n}[E(\prod_{t=1}^{n}\bar{\epsilon}_t)]^2[(G(\bar{\epsilon})+1)^n - 1]$$

$$= \exp\left\{2n\mu + n\sigma^2\right\}[(\frac{\exp\left\{\sigma^2\right\}+1}{2})^n - 1] \qquad Q.E.D.$$

Comparing (15) with (18), we derive the result that the expected values of the two strategies are the same, that is:

$$E(W_n^{BH}) = E(W_n^{RBEP}) \tag{20}$$

Therefore, *in the long run*, the two strategies are expected to yield the same result. Variance of BH from (16) is however greater than that of variance of RBEP from (19), that is:

$$V(W_n^{BH}) > E(W_n^{RBEP}) \tag{21}$$

Proof   To prove (21), we need to prove:

$$\frac{1}{2}[\exp\{n\sigma^2\} - 1] > (\frac{\exp\{\sigma^2\} + 1}{2})^n - 1$$

or

$$\theta(n) = \frac{1}{2}\exp\{n\sigma^2\} - (\frac{\exp\{\sigma^2\} + 1}{2})^n + \frac{1}{2} > 0$$

Now given:

$$\sigma^2 > 0, \exp\{\sigma^2\} > 1 \text{ or } \exp\{\sigma^2\} > (\exp\{\sigma^2\} + 1)/2$$

By mathematical induction :

$$\phi(0) = \phi(1) = 0$$

$$\phi(2) = \frac{1}{2}\exp\{2\sigma^2\} - (\frac{\exp\{\sigma^2\} + 1}{2})^2 + \frac{1}{2}$$

$$= \frac{1}{4}(\exp\{\sigma^2\} - 1)^2 > 0 = \phi(1) = \phi(0)$$

$$\phi(n+1) = \frac{1}{2}\exp\{(n+1)\sigma^2\} - (\frac{\exp\{\sigma^2\} + 1}{2})^{n+1} + \frac{1}{2}$$

$$= \frac{1}{2}\exp\{n\sigma^2\}\exp\{\sigma^2\} - (\frac{\exp\{\sigma^2\} + 1}{2})^n (\frac{\exp\{\sigma^2\} + 1}{2}) + \frac{1}{2}$$

$$> \frac{1}{2} \exp\left\{n\sigma^2\right\} \quad - \left(\frac{\exp\left\{\sigma^2\right\} + 1}{2}\right)^n + \frac{1}{2} = \phi(n)$$

Since: Let $\exp\left\{\sigma^2\right\} = A$, $(\exp\left\{\sigma^2\right\} + 1)/2 = B$:

$$AA^n - BB^n + C = B\left(\frac{AA^n}{B} - B^n\right) + C > A^n - B^n + C$$

When $A > B > 1$

Hence: $\phi(2) > \phi(1) = \phi(0)$, $\phi(n+1) > \phi(n)$

or: $V(W_n^{BH}) > V(W_n^{RBEP})$ $Q.E.D.$

The results contained in equations (14) to (21) can be generalized to a world with M securities having exactly the same and independent return distributions by replacing the 2 in the denominator in both (14) and (17) and adjust other results accordingly. However, the higher the M, the less will be the difference between $V(W_n^{BH})$ and $V(W_n^{RBEP})$ and actually, the difference vanishes as $M \to \infty$. Further, the longer the period under consideration, the more will be the difference in the variances of the two strategies.[8] Moreover, the greater $V(\epsilon)$ itself is, the more the variances of the two strategies differ.

Although (20) and (21) hold in general, we need to know the shape of the probability distribution of wealth before we can deduce the characteristic of the value of one draw from the distribution. If both W_n^{BH} and W_n^{RBEP} are normally distributed, W_n^{RBEP} will be preferred by an investor because of its lower variance as Tobin [15] has pointed out. If however, the shapes of the wealth distributions are not normal, additional important implications may be derived from (20) and (21) as we shall demonstrate in the next section.

IV. Characteristics of One Draw from the Wealth Distributions

In a portfolio framework, an investor is only entitled to one draw from the wealth distributions at a point in time. Hence, we need to know the shape of the wealth distributions.

Distribution of the Ratio of W_n^{RBEP} *to* W_n^{BH}

Equations (14) and (17) indicate that wealth distributions are weighted sum of log-normal distributions. Although the sum of log-normal distribution is not a log-normal distribution when the number of securities is finite, an investor can in the long run at most lose his original investment, but can multiply his investment without limit. The fact thus suggests that wealth distribution is highly positively skewed and may even be approximatable by a log-normal distribution. We assume therefore both W_n^{BH} and W_n^{RBEP} can be approximated by a log-normal distribution with their parameters $E(W)$ and $V(W)$ as valued in (15), (16), (18) and (19). Using this assumption, we can use the convolution operation to derive the probability distribution of the *ratio* between W_n^{RBEP} and W_n^{BH} representing the characteristc of the ratio between the value of one draw from each of the two distributions. The probability distribution of the ratio is:

$$\frac{W_n^{RBEP}}{W_n^{BH}} \quad \Lambda(\mu_{RB} - \mu_{BH}, \ \sigma_{RB}^2 + \sigma_{BH}^2 - 2\sigma_{RB,BH}) \quad (22)$$

Where μ and σ^2 denote mean and variance of log W, the subscript refers to the stragegy followed and $\sigma_{RB,BH}$ refers to covariance between wealth of the two strategies. We will now prove this theorem:

THEOREM Assume wealth at the nth period is log-normally distributed regardless of the strategy used, the mean of the logarithm of wealth using the rebalancing strategy is greater than that using the buy and hold.

Proof we want to prove $\mu_{RB} > \mu_{BH}$.

Let: $\mu_{RB} - \mu_{BH} = \delta$ \qquad\qquad (i)

From (20) and (11):

$$E(W_n^{BH}) = E(W_n^{RBEP}) = \exp\left\{ n\mu_{BH} + \frac{n\sigma_{BH}^2}{2} \right\} = \exp\left\{ n\mu_{RB} + \frac{n\sigma_{RB}^2}{2} \right\}$$

Hence: $\sigma_{RB}^2 - \sigma_{BH}^2 = 2\delta$ \qquad\qquad (ii)

From (21) and (11):

$$V(W_n^{BH}) = \exp\left\{ 2n\mu_{BH} + n\sigma_{BH}^2 \right\} [\exp\left\{ n\sigma_{BH}^2 \right\} - 1]$$
$$> V(W_n^{RBEP}) = \exp\left\{ 2n\mu_{RB} + n\sigma_{RB} \right\} [\exp\left\{ n\sigma_{RB}^2 \right\} - 1] \quad (iii)$$

By (i) and (ii):

$$\exp\left\{ 2n\mu_{BH} + n\sigma_{BH}^2 \right\} = \exp\left\{ 2n\mu_{RB} + n\sigma_{RB}^2 \right\}$$

Hence (iii) implies:

$$\exp\left\{n\sigma_{BH}^2\right\} - 1 > \exp\left\{n\sigma_{RB}^2\right\} - 1$$

or $\qquad \sigma_{BH}^2 > \sigma_{RB}^2$ $\qquad\qquad\qquad\qquad\qquad$ (iv)

Substituting (ii) into (iv), we have:

$$\delta > 0 \qquad\qquad\qquad\qquad\qquad\qquad\qquad (v)$$

By (i):

$$\mu_{RB} > \mu_{BH} \qquad\qquad\qquad\qquad\qquad Q.E.D.$$

Since the ratio of wealth is distributed symmetrically in logarithm, and further the theorem proven indicates that the mean of the log-normal is positive, the probability that W_n^{RBEP} ex post represented by one observation from the distribution of W_n^{RBEP} is greater than W_n^{BH} ex post [denoted by $P(W_n^{RBEP} > W_n^{BH})$] will be greater than 0.50, that is:

$$P(W_n^{RBEP} > W_n^{BH}) > 0.50 \qquad\qquad\qquad (23)$$

and further:

$$P(W_n^{RBEP} > W_n^{BH}) = f[M, n, V(\epsilon)] \qquad\qquad (24)$$

$$\frac{\partial P}{\partial M} < 0, \quad \frac{\partial P}{\partial n} > 0, \quad \frac{\partial P}{\partial V(\epsilon)} > 0$$

The result in (23) holds because of the assumption that W_n^{RBEP} and W_n^{BH} are both log-normally distributed. Indeed, it is easy to see that if both W's are normally distributed, the arithmatic difference of one draw from each of the two distributions will be normally distributed with a mean of zero. In that case, $P(W_n^{BH} > W_n^{RBEP}) = 0.50$ and thus superiority of RBEP over BH can only be justified on the ground that RBEP has smaller variance. The assumption that wealth is distributed log-normally leads however to the strong result stated in (23) and (24). The assumption clearly needs some testing before the theoretical result can be accepted as a general one. Simulation is therefore run to give some insights to this question.

Before presenting the simulation results, we note that conditions (23) and (24) hold in *addition* to the fact that $E(W_n^{BH}) = E(W_n^{RBEP})$ and $V(W_n^{BH}) > V(W_n^{RBEP})$. The conditions hold however *only* when all assets have common mean and variance and are independently distributed.[9] When all assets do not have common mean and variance, it is is quite possible that:

$$P(W_n^{RBEP} > W_n^{BH}) > 0.50$$

$$E(W_n^{BH}) > E(W_n^{RBEP}) \tag{25}$$

$$V(W_n^{BH}) > V(W_n^{RBEP})$$

Under these conditions, whether RBEP or BH is a better strategy must depend on other criteria to be specified by the investor.[10]

Simulation Results

To test whether (23) holds in practice, simulations were conducted to see whether RBEP can outperform BH most of the time for a portfolio started with $1 evenly divided between five (or fifteen) stocks with common means and variances but independently distributed Data used in each simulation consists of the means and standard deviations of weekly changes of stock prices in logarithms for Pittsburgh Steel (high variance) and General Motors (low variance) for the period 1956-60 estimated by Cootner [2, p. 236]. In order to allow us to derive results for a long period, we multiply Cootner's means and standard deviations for weekly changes by four and two respectively thus making the parameters measuring changes between four-week intervals. We further let each portfolio run for 240 periods (approximately twenty years) with each period's price change for each stock independently determined by a random draw from the log-normal distribution of returns using the appropriate parameters. Wealth positions for both strategies for each of the 240 periods are then computed from which 240 wealth relatives in logarithm (hereafter wealth relatives) are derived. The mean and variance of these wealth relatives for both BH and RBEP are then calculated. The run is repeated for 50 times and the grand mean and mean of variance of wealth relatives for each strategy are computed.[11] In addition, the number of times $W_{240}^{RBEP} > W_{240}^{BH}$ is counted.

The result of the simulation (Table 10-1) indicates that for all four cases, the null hypothesis that $P(W_n^{RBEP}) = P(W_n^{BH}) = 0.50$ has to be rejected at least at the 5 percent level. The result thus confirms the prediction in equation (23) that a portfolio using RBEP will have a probability of greater than 50 percent of attaining a larger final wealth position than a portfolio using BH given that the investment media consists of a number of independent stocks having common means and variances. The difference in grand mean is however insignificant as predicted by equation (20). Further, RBEP outperforms BH more often when the variance of the stocks in the portfolio is higher. The number of stocks in the portfolio has however only a mild effect on $P(W_n^{RB} > W_n^{BH})$; the latter does decline slightly as M is increased from 5 to 15.

The question remains is whether RBEP is still superior to BH as a strategy in a

Table 10-1

Simulation Results: Various Performance Measures of Final Wealth for BH and RBEP for 240 Periods

	High Variance Stock ($\mu = -.0010$, $\sigma = .1330$, n=240)		Low Variance Stock ($\mu = .0016$ $\sigma = .0416$ n=240)	
	BH	RBEP	BH	RBEP
For Five Stocks (50 runs):				
Grand Mean of logrithm of wealth relatives	−.003950	−.002123	−.002524	.002552
Mean of variance of logrithm of wealth relatives	.006695	.003520	.000389	.000343
Number of portfolios superior to the other strategy	13	37	18	32
For Fifteen Stocks (50 runs):				
Grand Mean	−.003561	−.002348	.002393	.002434
Mean of variance	.003764	.001191	.000138	.000115
Number of portfolios superior to the other strategy	15	35	19	31

world of securities with unequal means and variances. Analytical results are not presented here, but we run a simulation of five stocks with four of them having GM (Pittsburgh Steel) parameters and the other one having same variance but mean of 0.0. Results indicate that RBEP still outperforms BH more than 50 percent of the time. However, for the low variance case, the grand mean of BH is numerically though not significantly higher even though RBEP portfolios outperform BH portfolios 29 out of 50 times. For the high variance case, the grand mean of RBEP is still higher and RBEP outperforms BH 32 out of 50 times.

In addition, simulations were run for 5, 15, and 30 stocks having non-common means and variances.[12] BH outperforms RBEP nearly 100 percent of the time. The observation is consistent with Cheng and Deets' analytical results, though not consistent with their simulation results. The difference in results could be due to the fact that our stocks are more dissimilar than Cheng and Deets' stocks. It is of course also possible that Cheng and Deets' conclusion that market prices do not follow a random-walk is correct.

Taking all the simulation results together, the evidence supports very strongly our theoretical prediction in (23) and (24) that RBEP can outperform BH more than 50 percent of the time when the stocks have common means and variances. Further, the higher the variance of the stocks that are included in the portfolio, the more often RBEP outperforms BH, even if the expected value of the portfolio may be the same, because wealth distributions are generally positively skewed.

V. The Economics of Rebalancing

We have compared RBEP with BH for a portfolio with stocks of common means and variances and found BH wanting. A question can be raised however as to whether RBEP is itself an optimal strategy, that is, is there another strategy superior to RBEP?

Chen, Jen, and Zionts [3] have used the dynamic programing approach to formulate a dynamic portfolio revision model from which an investor can derive the proportion he should allocate his initial wealth to different securities. The model will be used here to find the conditions under which RBEP is an optimal strategy. Following Chen et al.'s formulation, we will let an investor maximize the utility of his wealth at period n by investing $\gamma_i W_0$ in earning asset i:

$$\text{Max } U(W_n) = \text{Max } U_0 \left[(\gamma_{10} + \gamma_{20} + \ldots + \gamma_{m0}) W_0 \right] \qquad (25)$$
$$\gamma_{i0}$$

Where γ_{i0} are proportion of W_0 to be invested in asset i, $i = 1, \ldots, m$ U_0 is the derived utility function which transforms the utility of wealth at period n to that at period 0.

If all assets have the same mean and variance, for many forms of ability functions, the optimal proportion at period 0 will be

$$\gamma_{10} = \ldots = \gamma_{m0} = k \qquad (26)$$

Further, if the distributions of returns of all assets are stationary over time, and that the time period n is sufficiently large:

$$\gamma_{ij} = k \qquad \text{for} \qquad i = 1, \ldots m \qquad (27)$$
$$j = 1, \ldots t$$

That is, for all time periods up to t, an investor should rebalance his investment each period to maintain his original equal proportion in each security. Under such conditions, RBEP becomes an optimal strategy to be followed by an investor in a dynamic setting.

In general, however, assets will not have the same mean and variance at a point in time, nor will the distributions of their returns be stationary. Hence, rebalance to equal proportion at all times cannot be an optimal strategy and may even be a strategy inferior to buy and hold an equal proportion of assets because RBEP will force an investor to be perpetually on a non-optimal time path.

However, given the distributions of asset returns are stationary and that n is large, rebalancing to the proportion originally chosen will be an optimal policy when there is no transaction costs.[13]

To buy and hold an equal proportion of different assets, however, is seldom an optimal strategy either because the assumptions required to make BH an optimal strategy over time are even more stringent than those for RBEP—specifically, even in a world of transaction costs, unless the variance of assets are all very small, thus forcing the *ex post* returns on all assets to deviate only slightly from the *ex ante* expectations, and further that the return distributions of all assets are approximately stationary. BH cannot be optimal because investors can find situations where he can benefit by changing the composition of his portfolios.

In the final analysis, therefore, one should expect investors to rebalance his portfolio by changing the composition frequently if not every period. Such rebalancing can be achieved by investing the new cash inflow from dividends or other sources in a proportion different from that in the current portfolio if the *ex post* returns do not deviate substantially from the *ex ante* means. If however, *ex post* returns do frequently deviate significantly from *ex ante* means because the variances of returns of many assets in the portfolio are large, rebalancing should not only be a frequent phenomenon, but also may involve selling a part of existing holidays. Indeed, we should not be too surprised at the phenomenon that performance funds have higher turnover ratios than ordinary common stock funds because the former has many securities of high variances in their portfolios.

Finally, we would like to comment briefly on the problem of selecting a proper form of utility function—a problem that has attracted much attention recently since Feldstein [7] pointed out that an investor's indifference curve can be non-convex.

Given that an investor maximizes U_n is only entitled to one observation from a distribution at a point in time, one way to handle the problem is for an investor to specify the properties he desires on the one observation he deserves. Given an investor's specifications and a thorough analysis of various shapes of probability distributions of future wealth through an analysis of return distributions and investment strategies, a suitable form of utility function may be derived from which an investor can find the optimal way of allocating his wealth.

An alternative way to find a suitable form of utility function is to use convolution to derive the distribution of difference of one sample from two possible probability distributions of wealth and decide the one that is superior, as we have done in equation (22). The method needs much further refinement before it can be made operational, however, because there are too many probability distributions to consider. Note the method is in many respects similar to the concept of stochastic dominance.

Conclusion

We have shown analytically that the strategy of rebalancing to equal proportion into different assets with common means and variables can increase the probability of having a higher final portfolio value. The reason is that the rebalancing strategy can reduce the variance of a portfolio. Such a reduction in variance will increase the probability of having a higher final portfolio value because the probability distribution of wealth is highly skewed. The analytical results are further confirmed by simulation.

We have also discussed the economics of rebalancing and demonstrated that in general rebalancing should be the rule and not the exception. The traditional notion of optimality of buy and hold is thus seriously contradicted. We further suggest that in selecting a proper form of utility function, more attention should be paid to the property of one observation from the wealth distribution.

Finally, it still remains to be seen whether rebalancing is superior to buy and hold in real life where securities have correlated and unequal means. It also remains to be seen on how rebalancing as an optimal strategy will affect the price of these assets in an overall capital assets pricing framework.

Notes

1. There are of course many other strategies (e.g., filter rules of Alexander, Levy's relative strength strategy) that have been shown to have outperformed buy and hold if transaction costs are neglected. After transaction costs are taken into account, however, these strategies will no longer outperform BH.

2. $G = (1.20)^{.90}(0)^{.10}) = 0$.

3. Readers may attribute positive skewness to the numerical values used. This is not the case. Future wealth is generally distributed with positive skewness due to the fact that an investor, without borrowing, can at most lose his original investment, but can multiply his investment without limit when the period is long.

4. Although only the case for W_3 is worked out, the result is believed to hold true for all n's.

5. This assumption is of course consistent with that of random-walk theorists though some may claim that stock prices have stable-Paretian distribution. Note further that the distribution is assumed to be time-invariant, an assumption that enabled many writers to estimate the variance of securities by using successive price ratios over time.

6. For a log-normal distribution having a variance of $n\sigma^2$ the proportion of area greater than mean is distributed $\eta\,(\,\frac{\sigma\sqrt{n}}{2}\,|\,0,1\,)$. For example, when $n\sigma^2 = 1$, $P(\,X > a\,) = 0.3085$. See [1, p. 154].

7. By this logic, investors will seldom have *one* utility function that is applicable to all possible wealth distributions.

8. This can be proved by demonstrating $\frac{\partial}{\partial n} \frac{1}{2} [\exp\{n\sigma^2\} -1)]$ $1 >$ $\frac{\partial}{\partial n}(\frac{\exp\{\sigma^2\}+1}{2})^n$ using the fact that $\sigma^2 > 1n(\frac{\exp\{\sigma^2\}+1}{2})$ when $\exp\{\sigma^2\} > 1$.

9. The result still holds if all assets have common covariances.

10. I would like to thank Professor Paul Samuelson whose comment on my earlier draft leads to the addition of this paragraph. All remaining errors are of course mine.

11. Mathematically, mean and variance of wealth relatives per period for the jth run for both BH and RBEP are computed by:

$$\overline{X}_j = \frac{\overset{240}{\underset{t=1}{}}(1n\ W_{jt}-1n\ W_{j,t-1})}{240}$$

$$\sigma_j^2 = \underset{i}{}(X_{ij}-\overline{X}_j)^2 / 239$$

For all runs, these statistics are also computed:

$$\overline{\overline{X}} = \sum_{j=1}^{50} \overline{X}_j / 50 \qquad \overline{\sigma^2} = \sum_{j=1}^{50} \sigma_j / 50$$

12. Parameters estimated by Cootner [2, p. 236] are used.

13. Transaction cost reduces the frequency of rebalancing by increasing the threshold of rebalancing. Hence, even in a world of transaction cost, rebalancing will not be eliminated as a viable strategy.

Bibliography

1. Aitchinson J., and Brown, J.A.C. *The Lognormal Distribution.*. Cambridge, 1963.
2. Cootner, Paul H. "Stock Prices: Random vs. Systematic Changes." *Industrial Management Review*, Spring 1962. Reprinted in Cootner, ed. *The Random Character of Stock Market Prices* Revised Edition pp. 231-52.
3. Chen, Andrew; Jen, Frank C.; and Zionts, Stanley. "The Optimal Portfolio Revision Policy." *Journal of Business*, January 1971, pp. 51-61.
4. Cheng, Pao Lun; Deets, M. King. "Portfolio Returns and the Random Walk Theory." *Journal of Finance*, March 1971, pp. 11-30.
5. Evans, John L. "An Analysis of Portfolio Maintenance Strategies." *Journal of Finance*, June 1970, pp. 561-71.
6. Fama, Eugene. "Random Walks in Stock Market Prices." *Financial Analyst Journal*, September-October 1965, pp. 55-59.
7. Feldstein, M.S. "Mean-Variance Analysis in the Theory of Liquidity Preference and Portfolio Selection." *Review of Economic Studies*, January 1969, pp. 5-12.
8. Fisher, L., & Lorie, J.H. "Rates of Return on Investments in Common Stocks." *Journal of Business*, January 1964, pp. 1-21.
9. Goodman, Leo A. "On the Exact Variance of Products." *Journal of the American Statistical Association*, December, 1960, pp. 708-13.
10. Jensen, Michael. "Risk, the Pricing of Capital Assets and the Evaluation of Investment Portfolios." *Journal of Business*, April 1969, pp. 167-247.
11. Latané, Henry A., and Young, William E. "Test of Portfolio Building Rules." *Journal of Finance*, September 1969, pp. 595-612.
12. Levy, Robert A. "Relative Strength as a Criterion for Investment Selection." *Journal of Finance*, December 1967, pp. 595-610.
13. Samuelson, Paul. "The Fundamental Approximation Theorem of Portfolio Analysis in Terms of Means, Variances and Higher Moments." *Review of Economic Studies*, January 1971, pp. 537-42.
14. Tobin, James. "Comment on Borch and Feldstein." *Review of Economic Studies*, January 1969, pp. 13-14.
15. ———. "The Theory of Portfolio Selection." in F.H. Hahn and F.P.R. Brechling (eds.), *The Theory of Interest Rates*. London, Macmillan, 1965.

11

A Cross-Sprectral Analysis of the Lead-Lag Structure of Money Supply-Stock Prices

James L. Bicksler

Purpose and Relevance

The purpose of this paper is to investigate the lead-lag structure of money supply and stock market changes as espoused by Beryl Sprinkel (hereafter the Sprinkel Forecasting Framework is termed SFF).

It is commonly recognized that the market factor is an important ingredient in the determination of yields and prices of financial securities. King's factor analytic investigation showed that the market explains a sizable magnitude of the variability of security returns.[1] This finding has also been confirmed by Blume, Fisher-Lorie, and Officer.[2] Finance theory a la the capital asset pricing model of Mossin-Sharpe-Fama-Treynor et al. also incorporates the market factor as a prime determinant of incremental yield over the risk free rate. Indeed, in an efficient capital market, non-market risk tends to be diversified away. Systematic or market risk is then the only risk in which the market pays a premium for bearing.[3] Thus one major suggestion for improving investment performance is increased accuracy in assessing market swings.

Despite the obvious usefulness of a valid framework for stock market forecasting, systematic and confirmed knowledge in this arena is extremely limited. A number of methods, such as the Dow-Jones theory, the sunspot theory, etc., appear to be completely discredited. SFF appears to have avoided many of the gross errors of other market forecasting "systems" and has a *seeming* a priori appeal of both (1) the theoretical framework of quantity theory-monetarism, and (2) National Bureau leading-lagging indicator empiricism.

Sprinkel's Forecasting Framework

SFF will be discussed via (1) its theory before empiricism rationale and (2) the empirical evidence that Sprinkel presented to test his framework. The rationale of the causal relationship between money stock changes and changes in levels of a market index is based upon the quantity theory of Hume, Fisher, and others and its modern derivative of Friedmanian monetarism. Essentially the argument is based upon the lessons of monetary history uncovered by Friedman-Schwartz.[4] These lessons are:

229

1. Changes in the stock of money are associated closely with changes in the level of economic activity, money income, and prices.
2. The interrelation between change in the monetary stock and economic activity has been highly stable.
3. The monetary stock has an independent origin and is not simply a response to changes in economic activity.[5]

While Sprinkel details a transmission mechanism linking monetary stock change and changes in the level of the market index, its specification is sufficiently general that it cannot be viewed as a key operational strand in his analysis. Indeed, its nondescript nature is probably due to our incomplete knowledge of the channels of monetary policy.[6] In this regard, note Friedman's comment that "the adjustment process of economic variables to changes in money stock are typically described in terms of a verbal statement of solution of an incompletely specified system of simultaneous equations. The precise adjustment path depends on how the missing elements of the system are specified and on the numerical values of the parameters."[7]

SFF is tested in the spirit of positivism and the following chain of empirical facts reflect his method of investigation.

1. Both changes in the stock of money and changes in the market index are leading indicators.
2. The lead time for changes in the monetary supply is "significantly" longer than the lead time for the market level indicator.[8]
3. It follows from (2) that the money stock can be used to predict changes in the level of the market index.[9]
4. The lead-lag relationships and estimates are derived by NBER cycle indicator methodology which, of course, is part and parcel of the business cycle peak and trough reference dating works of Burns-Mitchell.[10]

A Priori Assessment of SFF

The following a priori assessment is offered of the conceptual, structural, and predictive parameters of the SFF.

1. The utilized empirical approach a la the National Bureau has the limitations inherent in NBER methodology. For example, Koopmans brands Burns-Mitchell empiricism as "measurement without theory" and an investigation at the "Kepler stage" of economic investigation being that their lead-lag turning points statistics are selected on the basis of a pedestarian type of statistical tool.[11] Likewise, Milton Friedman views the Bureau's reference cycle dating scheme as "a fairly crude technique for

estimating timing relations . . . "[12] Consequently, "it must be remembered
that the determination of turning points (of cycles) for the economy as
well as for the stock market by the National Bureau of Economic Research
is made on an essentially qualitative, even strongly subjective, basis. Leads
and lags obtained for such series, though qualitatively expressed, do not
have the firm character of leads and lags that are the result of spectral
analysis into which no comparable subjective elements enter.[13] Stated in
the context of money-stock prices forecasting framework, Sprinkel's
inferences are based on an "eye-balling" of data and this technique is not
methodologically appealing.

2. A multitude of problems, Klein feels "dilute the use of NBER methods as
a predictive device."[14] Indeed, Evans concludes that "as a practical
method of forecasting, the leading indicators cannot be used very effectively or accurately."[15] With regard to stock prices as a leading indicator,
R.A. Gordon argues that "though stock prices do tend to lead business
activity, they are of only limited value as a forecasting device. The lead is
highly variable; on occasion it fails to appear; and in addition, stock prices
go through irregular fluctuations of their own that make it difficult to
determine when a significant business-cycle turn has actually occurred."[16]
Furthermore, John Gurley feels that when the money supply variable is
the Friedman "step function" then "the money peak or trough here come
after the peak or trough in general business in one third of the cases."[17]

3. The NBER statistical indicators does not include the monetary stock as a
leading indicator. According to Geoffrey Moore, one of the chief investigators in this domain, the money supply is too erratic and its non-station-
ary lead-lag structure with reference cycle turning points does not permit
it to be selected as one of NBER leading indicators.[18]

4. The semi-strong form of the efficient markets model indicates that no
publicly available informational parameter can be utilized to derive a
"profitable" trading rule. As Fama notes "the evidence in support of the
efficient markets model is extensive and (somewhat uniquely in economics) contradictory evidence is sparse."[19] The efficient (inefficient)
capital markets condition is the *sine qua non* for the non-existence
(existence) of a "profitable" trading rule derived from the SFF. The
quantity theory provides only a description of the causal links between
economic variables. Thus a "profitable" trading rule based on the empiricism of the SFF is not contingent on the quantity theory explanation of
the change in economic activity.[20] Indeed, Modigliani states that, "We still
cannot see any direct mechanism through which the rate of change of
money could affect market values except possibly because operators take
that variable as an indicator of things to come. But even this explanation is
hardly credible."[21]

5. While Sprinkel does not imply instantaneous or even short stationary

adjustment paths of market prices to changes in money supply and with due respect to his qualifications, there does emerge a view that the "empirical evidence strongly suggests that monetary changes will provide some useful guidance to future investment timing decisions."[22] Friedman's comment that "if the adjustment is slow, delayed, and sophisticated, then crude evidence may be misleading and a more subtle examination of the record may be needed to disentangle what is systematic from what is random and erratic" is pertinent.[23] Since these adjustment paths are postulated to be extraordinarily complicated, a more sophisticated tool of probabilistic inference is needed for verification of the SFF.[24]

6. While a quantity theory rationale is provided by Sprinkel, nothing is explicitly set forth stating conditions for equilibrium security prices within a portfolio context a la Sharpe-Lintner-Mossin. Hence, the theoretical underpinnings of Sprinkel's capital asset pricing framework under uncertainty are completely lacking.

The above a priori critique of SFF can be summarized as suggesting that (1) the NBER forecasting methodology is not theoretically satisfying, (2) it does not have "good" predictability, (3) that even if the NBER framework is "valid," the SFF espoused lead-lag relationship is not consistent with the NBER set of indicators, (4) quantity theory-monetarism when linked with the efficient markets hypothesis is not consistent with the SFF property of denying that capital market prices will be sub-martingales or a weaker variant such as the well-known Samuelson property that "properly anticipated prices fluctuate randomly,"[25] (5) the "detection" of adjustment paths invariably involves sophisticated econometric analysis, and (6) a security pricing framework a la the portfolio adjustment process of investors is not provided and hence the implied theory of stock price movements is unappealing.

Research Design

This paper investigates the lead-lag structure of changes in the monetary stock and changes in the level of the market index via the commonly used technique of cross-spectral analysis. Spectral analysis decomposes an information series into a large number of independent components each associated with a particular frequency. Measurement is made of each frequency's contribution to the variance of the given series and this gives insights into, for example, cycles of an economic variable. Cross-spectral analysis is a more relevant technique for prediction of the market factor. The essence of cross-spectral analysis is that the two economic series which are assumed to be jointly covariance stationary are decomposed into a number of uncorrelated components each belonging to a particular frequency. The estimates of the covariance between the two series at each frequency is measured by the squared coherency spectrum, which is commonly termed simply, coherence. Other prime interpretative instruments for cross-spectral analysis are provided by the measures of gain and phase.[26]

The cross-spectral for this investigation is of the stationary stochastic series representing money stock and the market index. The data utilized are the Board of Governors-Federal Reserve System money supply and the Standard and Poor's 425 market index. These are the identical sources that Sprinkel utilizes.[27,28] The time series is monthly data 1920 through 1970, which is 51 years of 612 data points. The coherence, phase, and gain statistics are computed for the relevant cross-spectral functions. Several lags (12, 20, 25, 35, and 50) were used to estimate the cross-spectra.

The detrending technique utilized to remove non-stationarity from the data series was the first differences of the logarithms. The a priori rationale for using the logarithm first differences was Friedman's view "that this device effectively eliminates trend."[29,30]

The estimated spectra are consistent with Granger's view of the "typical spectral shape of an economic variable" in that there was higher power at the lower frequencies and that the power declined as the frequency increased.[31] The coherence values for money supply and S&P index are "very low" with values being somewhat higher at the low frequencies.[32] The two highest values of the coherence were 0.30 and 0.18.[33] In general, there were higher coherencies at the low frequency levels. The relatively flat cross-spectra suggests a pure white noise process and thus is postulated that the two series are unrelated and hence, contrary to Sprinkel's conclusion, there appears to be no lead-lag structure between the two economic variables of money supply and stock prices.[34]

These results are consistent with Granger-Morgenstern's finding that "there are virtually no cycles of any ordinary duration in stock market prices, whether in individual stocks or in aggregate indexes,"[35] as well as our a priori knowledge derived from the semi-strong form of the efficient markets model.

Conclusions, Implications, and Suggestions for Further Research

The evidence from cross-spectral analysis indicates that there is no lead-lag relationship between money supply and stock prices. That is, expectations about future returns incorporate monetary policy anticipations a la the semi-strong form of Fama's efficient market hypothesis. Further, if Klein is correct in "that there is no point in trying to construct models that are purely of use in prediction and deny that such models have existence of their own apart from structural models: and that the best predictions will be made from best structural models," then there appears to be little a priori rationale for the SFF in a world of efficient capital markets.[36]

For financial economists intending to engage in further empirical investigations in this domain, a few suggestions may be of value. An incredibly large number of lead-lag structures could be postulated and there are numerous distributed lag techniques (Almon, Pascal, exponentially weighted, unrestricted, etc.) which could be utilized to test alternative hypotheses.[37] In order for the empiricism not to be simply a fishing for maximum R^2's expedition or some variant thereon, some rationale for lag structures would be useful.[38] At the present time, there is little prior knowledge of the theory of lags. Instead of cavalierly choosing lag structures in an ad hoc fashion, it would be advisable to examine (1) the correlogram for statistical properties in the structure of serial dependence and (2) the spectral density function, to fathom out second-order characteristics of the stationary stochastic process being analyzed. However, as Griliches comments, one should "not expect the data to give a clear-cut answer about the exact form of the lag. The world is not that benevolent."[39]

Also, as Zellner notes, "it is important to study a model's performance under extreme conditions (large changes in exogenous variables, for example). When the conditions of a simulation experiment are such as to strain a model, some of its weaknesses become apparent. Also, it is the case that extreme conditions be encountered in using the model in practice. Since periods of extreme conditions are often vitally important, establishing a model's operating characteristics under such conditions is vital."[40] Further, the use of Box-Jenkins techniques as applied to multiple time series may be useful in the search for a pattern of serial dependence. Such techniques are not competitive with traditional econometric analysis, but can be viewed in a complementary role.

To conclude, the question of timing or, as Keynes views it, investments as a game of Snap, Old Maid, or Musical Chairs, viewed in a modern day dynamic market factor context, still remains a viable problem. Two caveats are in order. First, a "profitable" mechanical rule for processing public information parameters about the monetary stock is incompatible with the efficient markets hypothesis. Second, inference of lead-lag relationships between economic variables is one of the most thorny problems facing economic scientists as it is plagued by numerous methodological and operational difficulties.

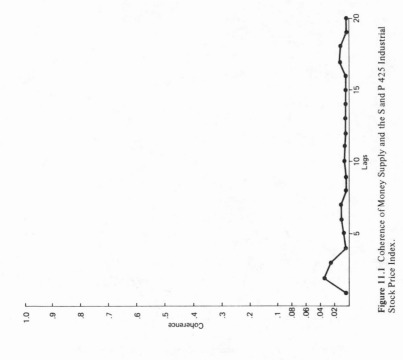

Figure 11.1 Coherence of Money Supply and the S and P 425 Industrial Stock Price Index.

Figure 11.2 Coherence of Money Supply and the S and P 425 Industrial Stock Price Index.

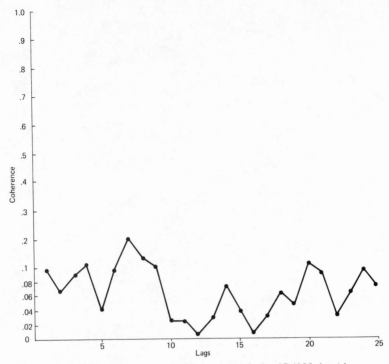

Figure 11.3 Coherence of Money Supply and the S and P 425 Industrial Stock Price Index.

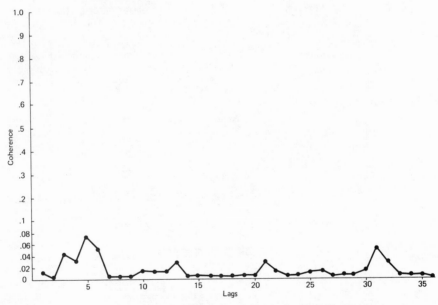

Figure 11.4 Coherence of Money Supply and the S and P 425 Industrial Stock Price Index.

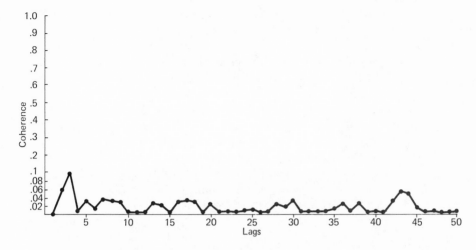

Figure 11.5 Coherence of Money Supply and the S and P 425 Industrial Stock Price Index.

Appendix I–Spectral Analysis

Spectral analysis investigates behavior in the frequency rather than the time domain.[41] It is postulated that we are dealing with a population characterized by a density function whose parameters are unknown. A basic assumption to spectral analysis is that the series is covariance stationary. Under certain conditions, the random variables constituting the stochastic process can be decomposed into a large number of sinusoids each having different nonstochastic frequencies.

Specifically, postulate a stochastic process by $\left\{ X_t, \ t \epsilon N \right\}$ and whose elements or random variables represent the sample time series, $\left\{ x_t, \ t = 1, 2, \ldots, n \right\}$. It can be shown that both the spectral density (e.g., power spectrum of the process) and the covariance kernal (e.g., covariance function) are Fourier transforms. Any covariance stationary process can be represented as

$$x(t) = \int_0^\infty \cos \lambda t \ du \ (\lambda) + \int_0^\infty \sin \lambda t \ dv \ (\lambda)$$

where $du \ (\lambda)$ and $dv \ (\lambda)$ are amplitudes described as random variables and the integrals are regarded as sums. This means that the time series, $x(t)$, is decomposed into different frequencies of sines and cosines having amplitudes described via $du \ (\lambda)$ and $dv \ (\lambda)$. Hence, the power spectrum gives the magnitude of the amplitude at different frequencies (the number of frequency bands is chosen a priori). Equivalently, the power spectrum measures the additive contribution to total variance from a particular interval. In sum, the spectral density conveys information about both the source of and the properties of the frequency domain of the particular stochastic process examined. Naturally, if a band is a source of a high proportion of the total variance, then it is deemed a more important frequency interval than a band whose power is small.

The examination in the frequency domain of two time series is termed cross-spectral analysis. It is postulated that both of the two stochastic processes, $\left\{ X_t, \ teN \right\}$ and $\left\{ Y_t, \ teN \right\}$ are jointly covariance. As in the univariate domain, there exists quasi-analogous relationships of Fourier transforms, the cross-covariance kernal of the bivariate stochastic processes, and cross-spectral densities. The cross-spectrum of the two time series is twice the Fourier transforms, $[dx(\lambda), dy(\lambda)]$, of the covariances and is denoted by:

$$dF_{xy}(\lambda) = E[dx(\lambda) \ dy(\lambda)]$$

A transformation of this cross-spectrum can be represented as:

$$dF_{xy}(\lambda) = dC_{xy}(\lambda) - jdQxy(\lambda)$$

This cross-spectrum can be viewed as a sum of two parts. The first is the co-spectrum between $x(t)$ and $y(t)$ while the latter: $dQ_{xy}(\lambda)$, called the quadrature spectrum, is the complex part of the function. Thus, the latter is the covariance of the amplitudes out of phase, while the former is the covariances of the amplitude in phase. With appropriate estimates of the spectrum of the input series and the cross-spectrum components of the input and output series then, the gain, $[G(\lambda)]$, and phase angle $[\phi(\lambda)]$, can be estimated.

$$\hat{G}(\lambda) = \frac{\sqrt{\hat{c}_{xy}(\lambda)^2 + \hat{q}_{xy}(\lambda)^2}}{f_{xx}(\lambda)}$$

$$\hat{\phi}(\lambda) = \arctan\left[\frac{-\hat{q}_{xy}(\lambda)}{c_{xy}(\lambda)}\right]$$

The gain statistic is a measure of the magnitude of the amplitude for each particular frequency and bears an analogous relation to the interpretation of a coefficient in regression analysis. The phase statistic measures the average lead or lag of one series with another series at each frequency. The lead-lag structure can be used for determination of, for example, cyclical relationships in the two variables and in turn for forecasting and prediction.[42] Both the gain and phase statistics are functions of the angular frequency measured in radians.

Coherency measures the degree of relatedness between the two series and is the square of the correlation between the amplitudes of the frequency bands of the two series.

Coherency can be represented as:

$$\frac{(d_{xy}(\lambda)^2)}{d_{xx}(\lambda) \, d_{yy}(\lambda)}$$

It thus makes use of the phase and quadrature components of the two series. It is equivalent to the coefficient of determination (R^2) statistic of regression analysis. If the coherency is low, the phase and gain statistics are not meaningful as there is no systematic relationship between the two series. Further, the phase statistic becomes extremely erratic when the coherency is low.

Notes

1. Benjamin R. King, "Market and Industry Factors in Stock Market Behavior," *Journal of Business*, January 1966, pp. 139-90.

2. Marshall E. Blume, "The Assessment of Portfolio Performance: An Application of Portfolio Theory," Ph.D. dissertation, University of Chicago, 1968; Lawrence Fisher and James Lorie, "Some Studies of Variability of Returns on Investments in Common Stocks," *Journal of Business*, April 1970; and Robert Officer, "An Examination of the Time Series Behavior of the Market Factor of the New York Stock Exchange," Ph.D. dissertation draft, July 1971.

As an aside, studies by Blume and Fisher-Lorie as well as King, argue that the variability of the market has declined for the post World War II period. However, Officer recently proposed that this artifact was simply a result of inclusion of the high level of variability of the market index in the 1930s and that post-World War II behavior should be viewed as a return to "normal" levels of market level variability.

3. Eugene F. Fama, "Efficient Capital Markets: A Review of Theory and Empirical Work," *Journal of Finance*, May 1970, pp. 383-417; and Michael C. Jensen, "The Foundations and Current State of Capital Market Theory," *Studies in Capital Market Theory* New York, N.Y.: Praeger Publisher, forthcoming.

4. This is admittedly a slight translation and extension of Sprinkel's argument which tends to be structured more in an episodic sense of the transmission process.

5. Milton Friedman and Anna Jacobson Schwartz, *A Monetary History of the United States 1867-1960* Princeton, New Jersey; National Bureau of Economic Research, Princeton University Press, 1963, p. 676.

6. A number of alternative explanatory descriptions of this transmission process have been postulated. For example, Ritter-Silber state that "the belief

that fluctuations in the money supply provide the key to movements in stock prices is based on the proposition that the money supply exercises a unique influence over virtually all economic activity, and that this influence can be pinpointed in terms of specific cause and effect.

"Its application to the stock market is straightforward. Increases in the money supply give the public additional liquidity, part of which spills over into the stock market. Since the supply of existing stocks is more or less fixed, this incremental demand raises their price. Some stocks will go up more than others and some will go down, depending on the prospects for particular companies, but overall the average of stock price will rise." See Lawrence S. Ritter and William S. Silber, *Money* New York, N.Y.: Basic Books, Inc., 1970, pp. 130-31.

Keran integrates within a monetarist econometric model of the U.S. economy a stock price equation which according to his analysis and evidence suggest that "changes in the nominal money stock have little direct impact on the stock price, but a major indirect influence on stock prices through their effect on inflation and corporate earnings expectations." See Michael W. Keran, "Expectations, Money and the Stock Market," Research Department, Federal Reserve Bank of St. Louis, Reprint Series Number 63, January 1971, p. 31.

The Keran paper has a number of limitations that vitiate any possible usefulness. Among these are the lack of a justification for the use of Almon lags, high serial correlation, ad hoc model specifications, and mixing of variables measured in levels and rates of changes. See Merton H. Miller, "Comment on Money and Stock Prices: The Channels of Influence," *Journal of Finance*, May 1972, preliminary version. A recent extension of Keran's work that still, unfortunately, contains many of the same basic flaws is Michael J. Hamburger and Levis A. Kochin, "Money and Stock Prices: The Channels of Influence," preliminary revision, December 1971.

Sprinkel seems to give more emphasis to direct effects via liquidity impacts, but then eludes to the possibility that the Keran view might be correct. Sprinkel, op. cit., p. 231. These postulated differences are not particularly crucial for Sprinkel, or perhaps relevent in view of our limited knowledge of the monetary transmission process.

7. Milton Friedman, *A Theoretical Framework for Monetary Analysis*, National Bureau of Economic Research, Occasional Paper Number 112, New York, N.Y.. 1971, p. 59. Note that this view represents a departure from a prior tentative sketch of the mechanism transmitting monetary changes developed in Milton Friedman and Anna Schwartz, "Money and Business Cycles," *Review of Economics and Statistics*, February 1963, Supplement, pp. 59-63.

8. This is based on a visual examination or "eye-balling" of the relevant time series. Sprinkel used both (1) rate of change and (2) changes in the level of money supply vis á vis stock prices in his analysis.

9. It is interesting to note that Friedman-Schwartz in their interpretation of the monetary history of the United States did not specify a lead-lag relationship between money supply and stock prices.

10. Sprinkel's empirical evidence does not utilize any new data sources nor does it employ any tools of statistical analysis beyond those employed by Burns-Mitchell. Indeed, it can be argued that Sprinkel does not in fact totally employ the validation techniques of Burns-Mitchell. For example, Sprinkel makes no use of the analysis of variance test that Burns-Mitchell applied to cycle durations, amplitudes and time lags. See Arthur F. Burns and Wesley C. Mitchell, *Measuring Business Cycles*, National Bureau of Economic Research Studies in Business Cycles, Number 2, New York, N.Y., 1946, p. 392.

11. Tjalling C. Koopmans, "Measurement Without Theory," *Review of Economic Statistics*, August 1947, pp. 186-203.

12. Milton Friedman, "The Lag in Effect of Monetary Policy," *Journal of Political Economy*, October 1961, p. 453.

13. Clive W. J. Granger and Oskar Morgenstern, *Predictability of Stock Market Price* Lexington, Mass.: Heath Lexington Books, 1970, pp. 141-43.

14. L.R. Klein, *An Essay on the Theory of Economic Predictions* Chicago, Illinois: Markham Publishing Company, 1971, p. 91.

15. Michael K. Evans, *Macroeconomic Activity Theory Forecasting and Control: An Econometric Approach* New York, N.Y.: Harper and Row Publisher, 1969, p. 460.

16. R.A. Gordon, *Business Cycles*, Second Edition New York, N.Y.: Harper and Row Publishers, 1961, p. 514.

17. John Gurley, "Book Review of Milton Friedman's Optimum Quantity of Money and Other Essays," *Journal of Economic Literature*, December 1969, p. 1190.

18. Based on communication with Geoffrey Moore, Commissioner of Labor Statistics, Department of Labor, Washington, D.C., August 1971. Besides not being 1 of the 8 leading indicators in the Moore Study, the money supply also is not one of the 30 leading indicators reported monthly in *Business Conditions Digest* (formerly *Business Cycle Developments*).

19. Eugene F. Fama, op. cit., pp. 383-417.

20. Friedman indeed argues that the important differences between economists are empirical not theoretical. See Friedman, *A Theoretical Framework of Money Supply*, p. 61.

21. Franco Modigliani, "Monetary Policy and Consumption," *Consumer Spending and Monetary Policy: The Linkages*, Federal Reserve Bank of Boston, Conference Series No. 5, June, 1971, p. 21.

22. Sprinkel, op. cit., p. 222.

23. Friedman, op. cit., p. 62.

24. Sharpe's comment that "the actual dynamic process through which disequilibrium is turned into equilibrium is likely to be very complex. Prices of other securities (and hence the location of the capital market line) are likely to change. The process may be smooth and rapid or slow and jerky," lends credence to this view. See William F. Sharpe, *Portfolio Theory and Capital Markets* New York, N.Y.: McGraw-Hill Book Company, 1970, p. 101.

25. Paul A. Samuelson, "Proof that Properly Anticipated Prices Fluctuate Randomly," *Industrial Management Review*, Spring, 1965, pp. 41-49.

26. The interested reader is recommended to several useful books on spectral analysis for economic series such as C.W.J. Granger and M. Hatanaka, *Spectral Analysis of Economic Time Series* Princeton, New Jersey: Princeton University Press, 1965; G.M. Jenkins and D.G. Watts, *Spectral Analysis and Its Applications* San Francisco, California: Holden Day, 1968; and G.S. Fishman, *Spectral Methods in Econometrics* Cambridge, Mass.: Harvard University Press, 1969.

27. The S&P high and low for the month was averaged to obtain a surrogate representing the observation for that period.

28. The six month average definition of money supply was not utilized. The rationale was the famous Slutsky theorem which demonstrated that cycles could be generated solely via use of smoothing procedures. Similarly, Adelman argued that the Kuznets long cycles were simply an artifact derived from the use of moving average smoothing techniques and Howrey's found that ten year cycles were misread as long cycles again because of bias introduced via smoothing. See Irma Adelman, "Long Swings-Fact or Artifact," *American Economic Review*, June 1965, p. 446; and E. Philip Howrey, "A Spectrum Analysis of the Long-Swing Hypothesis," *International Economic Review*, June 1968, pp. 228-52. It is well known that moving averages suppress information about changes, particularly, if the eye-ball technique is used.

29. Milton Friedman and Anna J. Schwartz, "Money and Business Cycles," in *Optimum Quantity of Money and Other Essays* Chicago, Illinois: Aldine Publishing Company, 1969, p. 193. Granger also argues that most economic time series have the spectrum of logarithms. See Clive G.W.Granger, "The Typical Spectral Shape of an Economic Variable," *Econometrica*, January 1966, pp. 150-61.

30. It should be noted that the use of data in the form of levels or growth rates while changing the look of the spectra do not affect the magnitudes of the coherence or phase angle.

31. Granger, op. cit., p. 151.

32. Granger-Morgenstern in interpreting the coherence diagrams specified the following qualitative interpretations to the coherence values: Very high: Many coherence values above 0.95. High: Some coherence values above 0.8; most above 0.5. Moderate: Most coherence values between 0.6 and 0.3. Low: Few coherence values above 0.4. Very Low: Majority of values below 0.25. See Clive W.J. Granger and Oskar Morgenstern, "Spectral Analysis of New York Stock Market Prices," *Kyklos*, 1963, p. 20.

33. Since the coherences are extremely low, the phase and gain spectra are not meaningful and hence are not provided. That is, the confidence intervals of the phase and gain statistics are unreliable when the coherence approaches zero as the variance and gain estimates tend towards infinity.

34. However, it is recognized that there are a number of subtleties (e.g., if it

is postulated that the relationship between the series is characterized by a complicated feedback mechanism) in cross-spectral analysis which makes inferences tentative and subject to furthering validation via more refined techniques.

35. Clive W.J. Granger and Oskar Morgenstern, *Predictability of Stock Prices* Lexington, Mass.: Heath Lexington Books, 1970, p. 41.

36. Klein, op. cit., p. 99.

37. Jorgenson empirically evaluates a myrid of distributed lag functions for the investment process and concludes that the choice of the weighting scheme is crucial for a satisfactory representation of its time structure. See Dale W. Jorgenson, "Econometric Studies of Investment Behavior: A Survey," *The Journal of Economic Literature*, December 1971, pp. 1134-38.

38. Indeed, SFF is an example of what Nerlove views as "the virtual lack of theoretical justification for the lag structures, superimposed on basically static models." See Marc Nerlove, "On Lags in Economic Behavior," *Econometrica*, May 1972, forthcoming.

39. Zvi Griliches, "Distributed Lags: A Survey," *Econometrica*, January 1967, p. 46. Griliches' article also contains a number of profound comments on the use of distributed lag structures in econometric analysis.

40. Arnold Zellner, "The Care and Feeding of Econometric Models," University of Chicago, Graduate School of Business, Selected Paper Number 35, p. 13.

41. Labys-Granger provide an intuitive analogy of the concept via a radio transmitter. See Walter C. Labys and Clive W.J. Granger, *Speculation, Hedging and Commodity Price Forecasts* Lexington, Mass.: D.C. Heath and Company, 1970, pp. 44-47.

42. Hause describes a number of the subtleties interpreting lead-lag relationships in spectral analysis. See John C. Hause, "Spectral Analysis and the Definition of Lead-Lag Relations, " *American Economic Review*, March 1971, pp. 213-17.

About the Editor

James L. Bicksler is Associate Professor at Rutgers University-Graduate School of Business. His degrees include a B.A. from Beloit College in 1959 and a Ph.D. in finance and economics from New York University-Graduate School of Business in 1967. Among his publications include contributions to the *Journal of Finance, Journal of Financial and Quantitative Analysis, Southern Economic Journal* and the *American Economic Review* (forthcoming).